Python
Training Guide

Python
Training Guide

Edited by

Mercury Learning and Information

BPB PUBLICATIONS
B-14, CONNAUGHT PLACE, NEW DELHI-110001

FIRST EDITION 2015

ISBN: 978-81-8333-541-6

Original English Language Edition Published and
Copyright © Mercury Learning and Information, USA.

Original ISBN: 978-1-938549-85-4

Distributors:

COMPUTER BOOK CENTRE
12, Shrungar Shopping Centre,
M.G.Road, BENGALURU –560001
Ph: 25587923/25584641

MICRO BOOKS
Shanti Niketan Building,
8, Camac Street, KOLKATA–700017
Ph: 22826518/22826519

MICRO MEDIA
Shop No.5, Mahendra Chambers,
150 DN Rd. Next to Capital Cinema,
V.T. (C.S.T.) Station, MUMBAI–400001
Ph: 22078296/22078297

DECCAN AGENCIES
4-3-329, Bank Street,
HYDERABAD–500195
Ph: 24756967/24756400

BPB PUBLICATIONS
B-14, Connaught Place,
NEW DELHI-110001
Ph: 23325760/43526249

BPB BOOK CENTRE
376 Old Lajpat Rai Market,
DELHI–110006
Ph: 23861747

INFOTECH
G-2, Sidhartha Building,
96 Nehru Place,
NEW DELHI–110019
Ph: 26438245

BPB PUBLICATIONS
20, Ansari Road, Darya Ganj,
NEW DELHI–110002
Ph: 23254990/23254991

Published by Manish Jain for BPB Publications, B-14, Connaught Place, New Delhi -110001 and Printed by him at Akash Press,

I'd like to dedicate this book to my parents –
may this bring joy and happiness into their lives.

TABLE OF CONTENTS

Chapter 6: Working with JSON and XML **127**

PREFACE

WHAT IS THE PRIMARY VALUE PROPOSITION FOR THIS BOOK?

This book endeavors to provide you with as much relevant information about Python 2.7 as possible that can be reasonably included in a book of this size.

THE TARGET AUDIENCE

This book is intended to reach an international audience of readers with highly diverse backgrounds in various age groups. While many readers know how to read English, their native spoken language is not English (which could be their second, third, or even fourth language). Consequently, this book uses standard English rather than colloquial expressions that might be confusing to those readers. As you know, many people learn by different types of imitation, which includes reading, writing, or hearing new material. This book takes these points into consideration to provide a comfortable and meaningful learning experience for the intended readers.

GETTING THE MOST FROM THIS BOOK

Some programmers learn well from prose, others learn well from sample code (and lots of it), which means that there's no single style that can be used for everyone. Moreover, some programmers want to run the code first, see what it does, and then return to the code to delve into the details (and others use the opposite approach). Consequently, there are various types of code samples in this book: Some are short, some are long, and others "build" from earlier code samples.

WHY ARE SOFTWARE INSTALLATION INSTRUCTIONS NOT INCLUDED?

There are useful Websites containing installation instructions for Python for various platforms, and this book contains links for those Websites. Instead of repeating instructions for each platform in this book, the space that would take up is used for Python material. In general, this book attempts to avoid "filler" content as well as easily accessible setup steps that are available online.

HOW WAS THE CODE FOR THIS BOOK TESTED?

The code samples in this book have been tested in Python version 2.7.5 on a MacBook Pro with OS X 10.8.5.

WHAT DO I NEED TO KNOW FOR THIS BOOK?

The most useful prerequisite is some familiarity with another scripting language, such as Perl or PHP. Knowledge of other programming languages, such as Java, can also be helpful, because it provides exposure to programming concepts and constructs. The less technical knowledge you have, the more diligence you will need to understand the various topics that are covered.

NOTE *If you want to be sure that you can grasp the material in this book, glance through some of the code samples to get an idea of how much is familiar to you and how much is new for you.*

WHY DOES THIS BOOK HAVE 200 PAGES INSTEAD OF 500 PAGES?

First, this book is part of a Pocket Primer series whose books are close to 200 pages. Second, the target audience consists of readers ranging from the beginner to the intermediate level in terms of their knowledge of programming languages. During the preparation of this book, every effort has been made to accommodate all of those readers so that they will be adequately prepared to explore more advanced features of Python during their self-study.

WHY ARE THERE SO MANY CODE SAMPLES IN THE CHAPTERS?

One of the primary rules of exposition of virtually any kind is "show, don't tell" While this rule is not taken literally in this book, it's the motivation for showing first and telling second. You can decide for yourself if show-first-then-tell is valid in this book by performing a simple experiment: When you see the code samples and the accompanying graphics effects in this book, determine if it's more effective to explain ("tell") the visual effects or to show them. In accordance with the adage "a picture is worth a thousand words," this book endeavors to provide both the pictures and the words.

DOESN'T THE CD OBVIATE THIS BOOK?

The CD that accompanies this book contains all the code samples to save you time and effort from the error-prone process of manually typing code into a text file. In addition, there are situations in which you might not have easy access to the CD. Furthermore, the code samples in the book are supplemented with explanations that are not available on the CD.

DOES THIS BOOK CONTAIN PRODUCTION-LEVEL CODE SAMPLES?

The primary purpose of the code samples in this book is to illustrate various features of the Python language. Clarity has higher priority than writing more compact code that is more difficult to understand (and possibly more prone to bugs). If you decide to use any of the code in this book in a production Website, you ought to subject that code to the same rigorous analysis as the other parts of your HTML Web pages.

WHY COVER PYTHON 2.X INSTEAD OF PYTHON 3.X?

The code samples in this book use version 2.7.5 because there is a large installed base of Python code that uses version 2.x, and there's a good chance that you will be writing code for Python 2.x and/or handling Python 2.x code that has been written by other people. After you have a solid grasp of Python 2.x you can proceed to Python 3.x, which will make it likelier that you will maintain a clear mental map of the differences in these two releases of Python.

BOOKS BY THE AUTHOR

1) *HTML5 Canvas and CSS3:*

http://www.amazon.com/HTML5-Canvas-CSS3-Graphics-Primer/ dp/1936420341

2) *jQuery, HTML5, and CSS3:*

http://www.amazon.com/jQuery-HTML5-Mobile-Desktop-Devices/ dp/1938549031

3) HTML5 Pocket Primer:

http://www.amazon.com/HTML5-Pocket-Primer-Oswald-Campesato/ dp/1938549104

4) *jQuery Pocket Primer:*

   http://www.amazon.com/dp/1938549147

5) *Google Glass Pocket Primer* (TBD)
6) *CSS3 Pocket Primer* (TBD)

O. Campesato
Freemont, CA
April, 2014

ABOUT THE TECHNICAL EDITOR

Simeon Franklin is a long-time Pythonista and Technical Instructor. He currently works for Twitter and has taught at many tech giants (Intel, Facebook, Cisco, Motorola). He can frequently be found helping to organize the Python community in the Bay Area.

## CHAPTER 1

INTRODUCTION TO PYTHON

This chapter contains an introduction to Python, with information about useful tools for installing Python modules, basic Python constructs, and ways to work with some data types in Python.

The first part of this chapter covers installation of Python, some Python environment variables, and use of the Python interpreter. You will see Python code samples and also learn how to save Python code in text files that you can launch from the command line. The second part of this chapter shows you how to work with simple data types, such as numbers, fractions, and strings. The final part of this chapter discusses exceptions and how to use them in Python scripts.

If you like to read documentation, one of the best third-party `stdlib` documentation is `pymotw` ("Python Module of the Week"), by Doug Hellman, and its homepage is here:

http://pymotw.com/2/

NOTE *The Python scripts in this book are for Python 2.7.5, and although most of them are probably compatible with Python 2.6, these scripts are not compatible with Python 3.*

TOOLS FOR PYTHON

The Anaconda Python distribution is available for Windows, Linux, and Mac, and it is downloadable here:

http://continuum.io/downloads

Anaconda is well suited for modules such as `numpy` and `scipy` (discussed in Chapter 7), and if you are a Windows user, Anaconda appears to be a better alternative.

easy_install and pip

Both easy_install and pip are very easy to use when you need to install Python modules.

Whenever you need to install a Python module (and there are many in this book), use either easy_install or pip with the following syntax:

```
easy_install <module-name>
pip install <module-name>
```

NOTE *Python-based modules are easier to install, whereas modules with code written in C are usually faster in terms of performance, but more difficult to install.*

virtualenv

The virtualenv tool enables you to create isolated Python environments, and its homepage is here:

http://virtualenv.org/en/latest/virtualenv.html

virtualenv addresses the problem of preserving the correct dependencies and versions (and, indirectly, permissions) for different applications. If you are a Python novice you might not need virtualenv right now, but keep this tool in mind if you find yourself working in complex environments.

IPython

Another very good tool is IPython (which won a Jolt award), and its homepage is here:

http://ipython.org/install.html

Two very nice features of IPython are tab expansion and "?", and an example of tab expansion is shown here:

```
python
Python 2.7.5 |Anaconda 1.6.1 (x86_64)| (default, Jun 28 2013,
22:20:13)
Type "copyright", "credits" or "license" for more information.

IPython 0.13.2 -- An enhanced Interactive Python.
?          -> Introduction and overview of IPython's features.
%quickref -> Quick reference.
help       -> Python's own help system.
object?   -> Details about 'object', use 'object??' for extra details.

In [1]: di
%dirs   dict    dir     divmod
```

In the preceding session, if you type the characters di, IPython responds with the following line, which contains all the functions that start with the letters di:

```
%dirs   dict    dir     divmod
```

If you enter a question mark ("?"), `IPython` provides textual assistance, the first part of which is here:

```
IPython -- An enhanced Interactive Python
==========================================

IPython offers a combination of convenient shell features, special
commands and a history mechanism for both input (command history)
and output (results caching, similar to Mathematica). It is
intended to be a fully compatible replacement for the standard
Python interpreter, while offering vastly improved functionality
and flexibility.
```

The next section shows you how to check whether or not Python is installed on your machine, and also where you can download Python.

PYTHON INSTALLATION

Before you download anything, check if you have Python already installed on your machine (which is likely if you have a Macbook or a Linux machine) by typing the following command in a command shell:

```
python -V
```

The output for the Macbook used in this book is here:

```
Python 2.7.5 :: Anaconda 1.6.1 (x86_64)
```

NOTE *Install Python 2.7.5 (or the closest version possible) on your machine so that you will have the same version of Python that was used to test the Python scripts in this book.*

If you need to install Python on your machine, navigate to the Python homepage and select the downloads link, or navigate directly to this Website:

http://python.org/download/

In addition, `PythonWin` is available for Windows, and its homepage is here:

http://cgl.ucsf.edu/Outreach/pc204/pythonwin.html

Use your preferred text editor, provided that it can create, edit, and save Python scripts (don't use Microsoft Word) and save them as plain text files.

After you have Python installed and configured on your machine, you will be ready to work with the Python scripts in this book.

SETTING THE PATH ENVIRONMENT VARIABLE (WINDOWS ONLY)

The PATH environment variable specifies a list of directories that are searched whenever you specify an executable program from the command line. A very good guide to setting up your environment so that the Python executable is always available in every command shell is here:

http://blog.pythonlibrary.org/2011/11/24/python-101-setting-up-python-on-windows/

LAUNCHING PYTHON ON YOUR MACHINE

There are three different ways to launch Python:

- Use the Python Interactive Interpreter
- Launch Python scripts from the command line
- Use an integrated development environment (IDE)

The next section shows you how to launch the Python interpreter from the command line, and later in this chapter you will learn how to launch Python scripts from the command line and also about Python IDEs.

NOTE *The emphasis in this book is on launching Python scripts from the command line or entering code in the Python interpreter.*

The Python Interactive Interpreter

Launch the Python interactive interpreter from the command line by opening a command shell and typing the following command:

```
python
```

You will see the following prompt (or something similar):

```
Python 2.7.5 |Anaconda 1.6.1 (x86_64)| (default, Jun 28 2013, 22:20:13)
[GCC 4.0.1 (Apple Inc. build 5493)] on darwin
Type "help", "copyright", "credits" or "license" for more information.
>>>
```

As a simple example, type the expression 2 + 7 at the prompt:

```
>>> 2 + 7
```

Python displays the following result:

```
9
>>>
```

Press ctrl-d to exit the Python shell.

You can launch any Python script from the command line by preceding it with the word python. For example, if you have a Python script myscript. py that contains Python commands, launch the script as follows:

```
python myscript.py
```

As a simple illustration, suppose that the Python script `myscript.py` contains the following Python code:

```
print 'Hello World from Python'
print '2 + 7 = ', 2+7
```

When you launch the preceding Python script, you will see the following output:

```
Hello World from Python
2 + 7 =  9
```

PYTHON IDENTIFIERS

A Python identifier is the name of a variable, function, class, module, or other Python object, and a valid identifier conforms to the following rules:

- Starts with a letter A to Z or a to z, or an underscore (_)
- Contains zero or more letters, underscores, and digits (0 to 9)

NOTE *Python identifiers cannot contain characters such as @, $, and %. Python is a case-sensitive language, so* Abc *and* abc *are different identifiers in Python.*

In addition, Python has the following naming conventions (Python classes are discussed in Chapter 8):

- Class names start with an uppercase letter and all other identifiers with a lowercase letter
- An initial underscore is used for private identifiers
- Two initial underscores is used for strongly private identifiers

A Python identifier with two initial and two trailing underscore characters indicates a language-defined special name.

LINES, INDENTATION, AND MULTI-LINES

Unlike other programming languages (such as Java or Objective-C), Python uses indentation instead of curly braces for code blocks. Indentation must be consistent in a code block, as shown here:

```
if True:
    print "ABC"
    print "DEF"
else:
    print "ABC"
    print "DEF"
```

Multi-line statements in Python can terminate with a new line or the back-slash ("\") character, as shown here:

```
total = x1 + \
        x2 + \
        x3
```

Obviously, you can place x1, x2, and x3 on the same line, so there is no reason to use three separate lines; however, this functionality is available in case you need to add a set of variables that do not fit on a single line.

You can specify multiple statements in one line by using a semicolon (";") to separate statements from each other, as shown here:

```
a=10; b=5; print a; print a+b
```

The output of the preceding code snippet is here:

```
10
15
```

> **NOTE** *The use of semicolons and the continuation character (for multi-line state-ments) is discouraged in Python.*

QUOTATIONS AND COMMENTS IN PYTHON

Python allows single (`'`), double (`"`) and triple (`'''` or `"""`) quotes for string literals, provided that they match at the beginning and the end of the string. You can use triple quotes for strings that span multiple lines. The following examples are legal Python strings:

```
word = 'word'
line = "This is a sentence."
para = """This is a paragraph. This paragraph contains
more than one sentence."""
```

A string literal that begins with the letter "r" (for "raw") treats everything as a literal character and "escapes" the meaning of meta characters (which are discussed in more detail in Chapter 4), as shown here:

```
a1 = r'\n'
a2 = r'\r'
a3 = r'\t'
print 'a1:',a1,'a2:',a2,'a3:',a3
```

The output of the preceding code block is here:

```
a1: \n a2: \r a3: \t
```

You can embed a single quote in a pair of double quotes (and vice versa) to display a single quote or a double quote. Another way to accomplish the same result is to precede a single or double quote with a backslash character and enclose both in a pair of double quotes. The following code block illustrates these techniques:

```
b1 = "'"
b2 = '"'
b3 = '\''
b4 = "\""
print'b1:',b1,'b2:',b2
print'b3:',b3,'b4:',b4
```

The output of the preceding code block is here:

```
b1: ' b2: "
b3: ' b4: "
```

A hash sign (#) that is not inside a string literal is the character that indicates the beginning of a comment. Moreover, all characters after the hash sign and up to the physical line ending are part of the comment (and ignored by the Python interpreter). Consider the following code block:

```
#!/usr/bin/python
# First comment
print "Hello, Python!";  # second comment
```

This will produce the following result:

```
Hello, Python!
```

A comment may come after a statement or expression on the same line:

```
name = "Tom Jones" # This is also a comment
```

You can place comments on multiple lines as follows:

```
# This is comment one
# This is comment two
# This is comment three
```

A blank line in Python is a line containing only white space, a comment, or both.

SAVING YOUR CODE IN A MODULE

Earlier you saw how to launch the Python interpreter from the command line and then enter Python commands. However, anything you type in the Python interpreter is valid only for the current session: if you exit the interpreter and then launch the interpreter again, your previous definitions are no longer valid. Fortunately, Python enables you to store code in a text file, as discussed in the next section.

A *module* in Python is a text file that contains Python statements. In the previous section, you saw how the Python interpreter enables you to test code snippets whose definitions are valid for the current session. If you want to retain the code snippets and other definitions, place them in a text file so that you can execute that code outside of the Python interpreter.

The outermost statements in a Python module are executed from top to bottom when the module is imported for the first time; this code execution sequence will set up its variables and functions.

A Python module can be run directly from the command line, as shown here:

```
python First.py
```

As an illustration, place the following two statements in a text file called `First.py`:

```
x = 3
print x
```

Now type the following command:

```
python First.py
```

The output from the preceding command is 3, which is the same result as executing the preceding code from the Python interpreter.

When a Python module is run directly, the special variable __name__ is set to __main__. You will often see the following type of code in a Python module:

```
if __name__ == '__main__':
    # do something here
    print 'Running directly'
```

The preceding code snippet enables Python to determine if a Python module was launched from the command line or imported into another Python module.

SOME STANDARD MODULES IN PYTHON

The Python Standard Library provides many modules that can simplify your own Python scripts. A list of the Standard Library modules is here:

http://python.org/doc/

Some of the most important Python modules are cgi, datetime, math, os, pickle, random, re, socket, sys, time, and urllib.

The code samples in this book use the modules math, os, random, re, socket, sys, time, and urllib. You need to import these modules to use them in your code. For example, the following code block shows you how to import four standard Python modules:

```
import datetime
import re
```

```
import sys
import time
```

The code samples in this book import one or more of the preceding modules, as well as other Python modules. In Chapter 8 you will learn how to write Python modules that import other user-defined Python modules.

THE HELP() AND DIR() FUNCTIONS

An Internet search for Python-related topics usually returns a number of links with useful information. Alternatively, you can check the official Python documentation site:

http://docs.python.org

In addition, Python provides the help() and dir() functions that are accessible from the Python interpreter. The help() function displays documentation strings, whereas the dir() function displays defined symbols.

For example, if you type help(sys) you will see documentation for the sys module, whereas dir(sys) displays a list of the defined symbols.

Type the following command in the Python interpreter to display the string-related methods in Python:

```
>>> dir(str)
```

The preceding command generates the following output:

```
['__add__', '__class__', '__contains__', '__delattr__', '__doc__',
'__eq__', '__format__', '__ge__', '__getattribute__', '__getitem__',
'__getnewargs__', '__getslice__', '__gt__', '__hash__', '__init__',
'__le__', '__len__', '__lt__', '__mod__', '__mul__', '__ne__',
'__new__', '__reduce__', '__reduce_ex__', '__repr__', '__rmod__',
'__rmul__', '__setattr__', '__sizeof__', '__str__', '__subclasshook__',
'_formatter_field_name_split', '_formatter_parser', 'capitalize',
'center', 'count', 'decode', 'encode', 'endswith', 'expandtabs',
'find', 'format', 'index', 'isalnum', 'isalpha', 'isdigit', 'islower',
'isspace', 'istitle', 'isupper', 'join', 'ljust', 'lower', 'lstrip',
'partition', 'replace', 'rfind', 'rindex', 'rjust', 'rpartition',
'rsplit', 'rstrip', 'split', 'splitlines', 'startswith', 'strip',
'swapcase', 'title', 'translate', 'upper', 'zfill']
```

The preceding list gives you a consolidated "dump" of built-in functions (including some that are discussed later in this chapter). Although the max() function obviously returns the maximum value of its arguments, the purpose of other functions such as filter() or map() is not immediately apparent (unless you have used them in other programming languages). In any case, the preceding list provides a starting point for finding out more about various Python built-in functions that are not discussed in this chapter.

Note that while dir() does not list the names of built-in functions and variables, you can obtain this information from the standard module __builtin__ that is automatically imported under the name __builtins__:

```
>>> dir(__builtins__)
```

The following command shows you how to get more information about a function:

```
help(str.lower)
```

The output from the preceding command is here:

```
Help on method_descriptor:

lower(...)
    S.lower() -> string

    Return a copy of the string S converted to lowercase.
(END)
```

Check the online documentation and also experiment with `help()` and `dir()` when you need additional information about a particular function or module.

COMPILE-TIME AND RUNTIME CODE CHECKING

Python performs some compile-time checking, but most checks (including type, name, and so forth) are *deferred* until code execution. Consequently, if your Python code references a user-defined function that that does not exist, the code will compile successfully. In fact, the code will fail with an exception *only* when the code execution path references the nonexistent function.

As a simple example, consider the following Python function `myFunc`, which references the nonexistent function called `DoesNotExist`:

```
def myFunc(x):
    if x == 3:
        print DoesNotExist(x)
    else:
        print 'x: ',x
```

The preceding code will fail only when the `myFunc` function is past the value 3, after which Python raises an error.

In Chapter 2, you will learn how to define and invoke user-defined functions, along with an explanation of the difference between local and global variables in Python.

Now that you understand some basic concepts (such as how to use the Python interpreter) and how to launch your custom Python modules, we will discuss primitive data types in Python in the next section.

SIMPLE DATA TYPES IN PYTHON

Python supports primitive data types, such as numbers (integers, floating-point numbers, and exponential numbers), strings, and dates. Python also supports more complex data types, such as lists (or arrays), tuples, and dictionaries, all of which are discussed in Chapter 3. The next several sections discuss some of the Python primitive data types, along with code snippets that show you how to perform various operations on those data types.

WORKING WITH NUMBERS

Python provides arithmetic operations for manipulating numbers in a straightforward manner that is similar to that used in other programming languages.

The following example assigns numbers to two variables and computes their product:

```
>>> x = 4
>>> y = 7
>>> x * y
28
```

The following examples demonstrate other arithmetic operations involving integers:

```
>>> 2+2
4
>>> 4/3
1
>>> 3-8
-5
```

Notice that division ("/") of two integers is actually a truncation in which only the integer portion of the result is retained. The following example converts a floating-point number into exponential form:

```
>>> fnum = 0.00012345689000007
>>> "%.14e"%fnum
'1.23456890000070e-04'
```

You can use the int() function and the float() function to convert strings to numbers:

```
word1 = "123"
word2 = "456.78"
var1 = int(word1)
var2 = float(word2)
print "var1: ",var1," var2: ",var2
```

The output from the preceding code block is here:

```
var1:  123  var2:  456.78
```

Alternatively, you can use the eval() function:

```
word1 = "123"
word2 = "456.78"
```

```
var1 = eval(word1)
var2 = eval(word2)
print "var1: ",var1," var2: ",var2
```

If you attempt to convert a string that is not a valid integer or a floating-point number, Python raises an exception, so it's advisable to place your code in a try/except block (discussed later in this chapter).

Working with Other Bases

Numbers in Python are in base 10 (the default), but you can easily convert numbers to other bases. For example, the following code block initializes the variable x with the value 1234 and then displays that number in bases 2, 8, and 16, respectively:

```
>>> x = 1234
>>> bin(x) '0b10011010010'
>>> oct(x) '0o2322'
>>> hex(x) '0x4d2' >>>
```

Use the format() function if you want to suppress the 0b, 0o, and 0x prefixes, as shown here:

```
>>> format(x, 'b') '10011010010'
>>> format(x, 'o') '2322'
>>> format(x, 'x') '4d2'
```

Negative integers are displayed with a negative sign:

```
>>> x = -1234
>>> format(x, 'b') '-10011010010'
>>> format(x, 'x') '-4d2'
```

The chr() Function

The Python chr() function takes a positive integer as a parameter and converts it to its corresponding alphabetic value (if one exists). The letters A through Z have the decimal representations 65 through 90 (which corresponds to hexadecimal 41 through 5a), and the lowercase letters a through z have the decimal representations 97 through 122 (hexadecimal 61 through 7a).

Here is an example of the use of the chr() function to print uppercase A:

```
>>> x=chr(65)
>>> x
'A'
```

The following code block prints the ASCII values for a range of integers:

```
result = ""
for x in range(65,90):
  print x, chr(x)
  result = result+chr(x)+' '
print "result: ",result
```

NOTE *Python 2 uses ASCII strings, whereas Python 3 uses UTF-8.*

You can represent a range of characters with the following line:

```
for x in range(65,90):
```

However, the following equivalent code snippet is more intuitive:

```
for x in range(ord('A'), ord('Z')):
```

If you want to display the result for lowercase letters, change the preceding range from (65,90) to either of the following statements:

```
for x in range(97,122):
for x in range(ord('a'), ord('z')):
```

The round() Function in Python

The Python round() function enables you to round decimal values to the nearest degree of precision (number of digits) that is specified by the number in the second position:

```
>>> round(1.23, 1)
1.2
>>> round(-3.42,1)
-3.4
```

Formatting Numbers in Python

Python allows you to specify the number of decimal places of precision to use when printing decimal numbers, as shown here:

```
>>> x = 1.23456
>>> format(x, '0.2f')
'1.23'
>>> format(x, '0.3f')
'1.235'
>>> 'value is {:0.3f}'.format(x) 'value is 1.235'
>>> from decimal import Decimal
>>> a = Decimal('4.2')
>>> b = Decimal('2.1')
>>> a + b
Decimal('6.3')
>>> print(a + b)
6.3
>>> (a + b) == Decimal('6.3')
True
>>> x = 1234.56789
>>> # Two decimal places of accuracy
>>> format(x, '0.2f')
'1234.57'
>>> # Right justified in 10 chars, one-digit accuracy
>>> format(x, '>10.1f')
' 1234.6'
>>> # Left justified
>>> format(x, '<10.1f') '1234.6 '
```

```
>>> # Centered
>>> format(x, '^10.1f') ' 1234.6 '
>>> # Inclusion of thousands separator
>>> format(x, ',')
'1,234.56789'
>>> format(x, '0,.1f')
'1,234.6'
```

WORKING WITH FRACTIONS

Python supports the `Fraction()` function (which is defined in the `fractions` module), which accepts two integers that represent the numerator and the denominator (which must be nonzero) of a fraction. Several examples of defining and manipulating fractions in Python are shown here:

```
>>> from fractions import Fraction
>>> a = Fraction(5, 4)
>>> b = Fraction(7, 16)
>>> print(a + b)
27/16
>>> print(a * b)
35/64
>>> # Getting numerator/denominator
>>> c = a * b
>>> c.numerator
35
>>> c.denominator 64
>>> # Converting to a float >>> float(c)
0.546875
>>> # Limiting the denominator of a value
>>> print(c.limit_denominator(8))
4
>>> # Converting a float to a fraction >>> x = 3.75
>>> y = Fraction(*x.as_integer_ratio())
>>> y
Fraction(15, 4)
```

Before we delve into Python code samples that work with strings, let's take a look at Unicode and UTF-8, both of which are character encodings.

UNICODE AND UTF-8

A Unicode string consists of a sequence of numbers that are between 0 and `0x10ffff`, where each number represents a group of bytes. An *encoding* is the manner in which a Unicode string is translated into a sequence of bytes. Among the various encodings, Unicode Transformation Format 8 (UTF-8) is perhaps the most common, and it's also the default encoding for many systems. The digit 8 in UTF-8 indicates that the encoding uses 8-bit numbers, whereas UTF-16 uses 16-bit numbers (but is less common).

The ASCII character set is a subset of UTF-8, so a valid ASCII string can be read as a UTF-8 string without any re-encoding required. In addition, a Unicode string can be converted into a UTF-8 string.

WORKING WITH UNICODE

Python supports Unicode, which means that you can render characters in different languages. Unicode data can be stored and manipulated in the same way as strings. Create a Unicode string by prepending the letter "u", as shown here:

```
>>> u'Hello from Python!'
u'Hello from Python!'
```

Special characters can be included in a string by specifying their Unicode values. For example, the following Unicode string embeds a space (which has the Unicode value 0x0020) in a string:

```
>>> u'Hello\u0020from Python!'
u'Hello from Python!'
```

Listing 1.1 displays the contents of Unicode1.py that illustrates how to display a string of characters in Japanese and another string of characters in Chinese (Mandarin).

LISTING 1.1 Unicode1.py

```
chinese1 = u'\u5c07\u63a2\u8a0e HTML5 \u53ca\u5176\u4ed6'
hiragana = u'D3 \u306F \u304B\u3063\u3053\u3043\u3043 \u3067\
u3059!'

print 'Chinese:',chinese1
print 'Hiragana:',hiragana
```

The output of Listing 1.1 is here:

```
Chinese: 將探討 HTML5 及其他
Hiragana: D3 は かっこいい です!
```

The next portion of this chapter shows additional operations (such as concatenation) that you can perform with strings in Python.

WORKING WITH STRINGS

A string in Python2 is a sequence of ASCII-encoded bytes. You can concatenate two strings using the "+" operator. The following example prints a string and then concatenates two single-letter strings:

```
>>> 'abc'
'abc'
>>> 'a' + 'b'
'ab'
```

You can use "+"or "*" to concatenate identical strings, as shown here:

```
>>> 'a' + 'a' + 'a'
'aaa'
>>> 'a' * 3
'aaa'
```

You can assign strings to variables and print them using the `print` command:

```
>>> print 'abc'
abc
>>> x = 'abc'
>>> print x
abc
>>> y = 'def'
>>> print x + y
abcdef
```

You can "unpack" the letters of a string and assign them to variables, as shown here:

```
>>> str = "World"
>>> x1,x2,x3,x4,x5 = str
>>> x1
'W'
>>> x2
'o'
>>> x3
'r'
>>> x4
'l'
>>> x5
'd'
```

The preceding code snippets show you how easy it is to extract the letters in a text string, and in Chapter 3 you will learn how to "unpack" other Python data structures.

You can extract substrings of a string, as shown in the following examples:

```
>>> x = "abcdef"
>>> x[0]
'a'
>>> x[-1]
'f'
>>> x[1:3]
'bc'
>>> x[0:2] + x[5:]
'abf'
```

However, you will cause an error if you attempt to "subtract" two strings, as you probably expect:

```
>>> 'a' - 'b'
Traceback (most recent call last):
  File "<stdin>", line 1, in <module>
TypeError: unsupported operand type(s) for -: 'str' and 'str'
```

The `try/except` construct in Python (discussed later in this chapter) enables you to handle the preceding type of exception more gracefully.

Comparing Strings

You can use the methods `lower()` and `upper()` to convert a string to lowercase and uppercase, respectively, as shown here:

```
>>> 'Python'.lower()
'python'
>>> 'Python'.upper()
'PYTHON'
>>>
```

The methods `lower()` and `upper()` are useful for performing a case-insensitive comparison of two ASCII strings. Listing 1.2 displays the contents of `Compare.py` that uses the `lower()` function to compare two ASCII strings.

LISTING 1.2 Compare.py

```
x = 'Abc'
y = 'abc'

if(x == y):
  print 'x and y: identical'
elif (x.lower() == y.lower()):
  print 'x and y: case insensitive match'
else:
  print 'x and y: different'
```

Since x contains mixed-case letters and y contains lowercase letters, the output of Listing 1.2 is:

```
x and y: case insensitive match
```

Formatting Strings in Python

Python provides the functions `string.lstring()`, `string.rstring()`, and `string.center()` for positioning a text string so that it is left-justified, right-justified, and centered, respectively. As you saw in a previous section, Python also provides the `format()` method for advanced interpolation features.

Now enter the following commands in the Python interpreter:

```
import string

str1 = 'this is a string'
print string.lstring(str1, 10)
print string.rstring(str1, 40)
print string.center(str1,40)
```

The output is shown here:

```
this is a string
                        this is a string
            this is a string
```

UNINITIALIZED VARIABLES AND THE VALUE NONE IN PYTHON

Python distinguishes between an uninitialized variable and the value None. The former is a variable that has not been assigned a value, whereas the latter is a value that indicates "no value." Collections and methods often return the value None, and you can test for the value None in conditional logic (shown in Chapter 2).

The next portion of this chapter shows you how to "slice and splice" text strings with built-in Python functions.

SLICING AND SPLICING STRINGS

Python enables you to extract substrings of a string (called "slicing") using array notation. Slice notation is start:stop:step, where the start, stop, and step values are integers that specify the start value, the end value, and the increment value. The interesting part about slicing in Python is that you can use the value -1, which operates from the right side instead of the left side of a string.

Some examples of slicing a string are:

```
text1 = "this is a string"
print 'First 7 characters:',text1[0:7]
print 'Characters 2-4:',text1[2:4]
print 'Right-most character:',text1[-1]
print 'Right-most 2 characters:',text1[-3:-1]
```

The output from the preceding code block is here:

```
First 7 characters: this is
Characters 2-4: is
Right-most character: g
Right-most 2 characters: in
```

Later in this chapter you will see how to insert a string ("splice") in the middle of another string.

Testing for Digits and Alphabetic Characters

Python enables you to examine each character in a string and then test whether that character is a bona fide digit or an alphabetic character. This section provides a precursor to the regular expressions that are discussed in Chapter 4.

Listing 1.3 displays the contents of CharTypes.py that illustrates how to determine if a string contains digits or characters. In case you are unfamiliar with the conditional "if" statement in Listing 1.3, more detailed information is available in Chapter 2.

LISTING 1.3 CharTypes.py

```
str1 = "4"
str2 = "4234"
str3 = "b"
str4 = "abc"
str5 = "a1b2c3"
```

```
if(str1.isdigit()):
  print "this is a digit:",str1

if(str2.isdigit()):
  print "this is a digit:",str2

if(str3.isalpha()):
  print "this is alphabetic:",str3

if(str4.isalpha()):
  print "this is alphabetic:",str4

if(not str5.isalpha()):
  print "this is not pure alphabetic:",str5

print "capitalized first letter:",str5.title()
```

Listing 1.3 initializes some variables, followed by two conditional tests that check whether or not str1 and str2 are digits using the isdigit() function. The next portion of Listing 1.3 checks if str3, str4, and str5 are alphabetic strings using the isalpha() function.

The output of Listing 1.3 is here:

```
this is a digit: 4
this is a digit: 4234
this is alphabetic: b
this is alphabetic: abc
this is not pure alphabetic: a1b2c3
capitalized first letter: A1B2C3
```

SEARCH AND REPLACE A STRING IN OTHER STRINGS

Python provides methods for searching and also for replacing a string in a second text string.

Listing 1.4 displays the contents of FindPos1.py that shows you how to use the find function to search for the occurrence of one string in another string.

LISTING 1.4 FindPos1.py

```
item1 = 'abc'
item2 = 'Abc'
text = 'This is a text string with abc'

pos1 = text.find(item1)
pos2 = text.find(item2)

print 'pos1=',pos1
print 'pos2=',pos2
```

Listing 1.4 initializes the variables item1, item2, and text and then searches for the index of the contents of item1 and item2 in the string text. The Python find() function returns the column number where the first successful match occurs; otherwise, the `find()` function returns a `-1` if a match is unsuccessful.

The output of Listing 1.4 is here:

```
pos1= 27
pos2= -1
```

In addition to the `find()` method, you can use the `in` operator when you want to test for the presence of an element, as shown here:

```
>>> lst = [1,2,3]
>>> 1 in lst
True
```

Listing 1.5 displays the contents of `Replace1.py` that shows you how to replace one string with another string.

LISTING 1.5 Replace1.py

```
text = 'This is a text string with abc'
print 'text:',text
text = text.replace('is a', 'was a')
print 'text:',text
```

Listing 1.5 starts by initializing the variable text and then printing its contents. The next portion of Listing 1.5 replaces the occurrence of "is a" with "was a" in the string text and then prints the modified string.

The output of Listing 1.5 is here:

```
text: This is a text string with abc
text: This was a text string with abc
```

REMOVE LEADING AND TRAILING CHARACTERS

Python provides the functions `strip()`, `lstrip()`, and `rstrip()` to remove characters in a text string. Listing 1.6 displays the contents of `Remove1.py` that shows you how to search for a string.

LISTING 1.6 Remove1.py

```
text = '   leading and trailing white space   '
print 'text1:','x',text,'y'

text = text.lstrip()
print 'text2:','x',text,'y'

text = text.rstrip()
print 'text3:','x',text,'y'
```

Listing 1.6 starts by concatenating the letter x and the contents of the variable `text` and then printing the result. The second part of Listing 1.6 removes the leading white spaces in the string `text` and then appends the result to the letter `x`. The third part of Listing 1.6 removes the trailing white spaces in the string `text` (note that the leading white spaces have already been removed) and then appends the result to the letter `x`.

The output of Listing 1.6 is here:

```
text1: x    leading and trailing white space    y
text2: x leading and trailing white space    y
text3: x leading and trailing white space y
```

If you want to remove extra white spaces inside a text string, use the `re-place()` function, as discussed in the previous section. The following example illustrates how this can be accomplished; it also contains the `re` module as a "preview" for what you will learn in Chapter 4:

```
import re
text = 'a    b'
a = text.replace(' ', '')
b = re.sub('\s+', ' ', text)

print a
print b
```

The result is here:

```
ab
a b
```

Chapter 2 shows you how to use the `join()` function to remove extra white spaces in a text string.

PRINTING TEXT WITHOUT NEW LINE CHARACTERS

If you need to suppress white space and a new line between objects output with multiple print statements, you can use concatenation or the `write()` function.

The first technique is to concatenate the string representations of each object using the `str()` function prior to printing the result. For example, run the following statement in Python:

```
x = str(9)+str(0xff)+str(-3.1)
print 'x: ',x
```

The output is shown here:

```
x: 9255-3.1
```

The preceding line contains the concatenation of the numbers 9 and 255 (which is the decimal value of the hexadecimal number `0xff`) and `-3.1`.

Incidentally, you can use the str() function with modules and user-defined classes (discussed in Chapter 8). An example involving the Python built-in module sys is here:

```
>>> import sys
>>> print str(sys)
<module 'sys' (built-in)>
```

The second technique for suppressing a new line character involves the write() function, as shown in the following code block:

```
import sys
write = sys.stdout.write
write('123')
write('456\n')
```

The output is here:

```
123456
```

TEXT ALIGNMENT

Python provides the methods ljust(), rjust(), and center() for aligning text. The ljust() and rjust() functions left justify and right justify a text string, respectively, whereas the center() function centers a string. An example is shown in the following code block:

```
text = 'Hello World'
text.ljust(20)
'Hello World '
>>> text.rjust(20)
'         Hello World'
>>> text.center(20)
'    Hello World     '
```

You can use the Python format() function to align text. Use the <, >, or ^ characters, along with a desired width, to right justify, left justify, or center the text, respectively. The following examples illustrate how you can specify text justification:

```
>>> format(text, '>20')
'         Hello World'
>>>
>>> format(text, '<20')
'Hello World         '
>>>
>>> format(text, '^20')
'    Hello World     '
>>>
```

WORKING WITH DATES

Python provides a rich set of date-related functions, which are documented here:

http://docs.python.org/2/library/datetime.html

Listing 1.7 displays the contents of the Python script `Datetime2.py` that displays various date-related values, such as the current date and time; the day of the week, month, and year; and the time in seconds since the epoch (January 1, 1970).

LISTING 1.7 Datetime2.py

```
import time
import datetime


print "Time in seconds since the epoch: %s" %time.time()
print "Current date and time: " ,datetime.datetime.now()
print "Another format: ",datetime.datetime.now().strftime("%y-%m-%d-%H-
%M")


print "Current year:   ",datetime.date.today().strftime("%Y")
print "Month of year: ",datetime.date.today().strftime("%B")
print "Week number of the year:",datetime.date.today().strftime("%W")
print "Weekday of the week:",datetime.date.today().strftime("%w")
print "Day of year:    ",datetime.date.today().strftime("%j")
print "Day of the month: ",datetime.date.today().strftime("%d")
print "Day of week:    ",datetime.date.today().strftime("%A")
```

Listing 1.8 displays the output generated by launching the code in Listing 1.7 and redirecting the output to the file datetime2.out.

LISTING 1.8 datetime2.out

```
Time in seconds since the epoch: 1375144195.66
Current date and time:   2013-07-29 17:29:55.664164
Or like this:   13-07-29-17-29
Current year:   2013
Month of year:   July
Week number of the year:   30
Weekday of the week:  1
Day of year:  210
Day of the month :   29
Day of week:  Monday
```

Python also enables you to perform arithmetic calculations with date-related values, such as the addition of two dates, as shown in the following code block:

```
>>> from datetime import timedelta
>>> a = timedelta(days=2, hours=6)
>>> b = timedelta(hours=4.5)
>>> c = a + b
>>> c.days
```

```
2
>>> c.seconds
37800
>>> c.seconds / 3600
10.5
>>> c.total_seconds() / 3600
58.5
```

Converting Strings to Dates

Listing 1.9 displays the contents of `String2Date.py` that illustrates how to convert a string to a date, and also how to calculate the difference between two dates.

LISTING 1.9 String2Date.py

```
from datetime import datetime

text = '2014-08-13'
y = datetime.strptime(text, '%Y-%m-%d')
z = datetime.now()
diff = z - y
print 'Date difference:',diff
```

The output of Listing 1.9 is shown here:

```
Date difference: -210 days, 18:58:40.197130
```

EXCEPTION HANDLING IN PYTHON

Unlike the case in JavaScript, you cannot add a number and a string in Python. However, you can detect an illegal operation using the `try/except` construct in Python, which is similar to the `try/catch` construct in languages such as JavaScript and Java.

An example of a `try/except` block is:

```
try:
  x = 4
  y = 'abc'
  z = x + y
except:
  print 'cannot add incompatible types:', x, y
```

When you run the preceding code in Python, the `print` statement in the `except` code block is executed, because the variables x and y are of incompatible types.

Earlier in the chapter, you also saw that subtracting two strings throws an exception:

```
>>> 'a' - 'b'
Traceback (most recent call last):
  File "<stdin>", line 1, in <module>
TypeError: unsupported operand type(s) for -: 'str' and 'str'
```

A simple way to handle this situation is to use a `try/except` block:

```
>>> try:
...    print 'a' - 'b'
... except TypeError:
...    print 'TypeError exception while trying to subtract two strings'
... except:
...    print 'Exception while trying to subtract two strings'
...
```

The output from the preceding code block is here:

```
TypeError exception while trying to subtract two strings
```

As you can see, the preceding code block specifies the finer-grained exception called `TypeError`, followed by a "generic" except code block to handle all other exceptions that might occur during the execution of your Python code. This style is similar to the exception handling in Java code.

Listing 1.10 displays the contents of `Exception1.py` that illustrates how to handle various types of exceptions.

LISTING 1.10 Exception1.py

```python
import sys

try:
    f = open('myfile.txt')
    s = f.readline()
    i = int(s.strip())
except IOError as err:
    print("I/O error: {0}".format(err))
except ValueError:
    print("Could not convert data to an integer.")
except:
    print("Unexpected error:", sys.exc_info()[0])
    raise
```

Listing 1.10 contains a `try` block followed by three `except` statements. If an error occurs in the `try` block, the first `except` statement is compared with the type of exception that occurred. If there is a match, then the subsequent print statement is executed and the program terminates. If not, a similar test is performed with the second `except` statement. If neither `except` statement matches the exception, the third `except` statement handles the exception, which involves printing a message and then "raising" an exception.

Note that you can also specify multiple exception types in a single statement, as shown here:

```python
except (NameError, RuntimeError, TypeError):
    print 'One of three error types occurred'
```

The preceding code block is more compact, but it does not tell you which of the three error types occurred. Python allows you to define custom exceptions, but this topic is beyond the scope of this book.

HANDLING USER INPUT

Python enables you to read user input from the command line via the `input()` function or the `raw_input()` function. Typically, you assign user input to a variable, which will contain all characters that users enter from the keyboard. User input terminates when users press the `<return>` key (which is included with the input characters). Listing 1.11 displays the contents of `UserInput1.py` that prompts users for their name and then uses interpolation to display a response.

LISTING 1.11 UserInput1.py

```
userInput = raw_input("Enter your name: ")
print ("Hello, %s, my name is Python" % userInput);
```

The output of Listing 1.11 is here (assuming that the user entered the name Dave):

```
Hello, Dave, my name is Python
```

The `print` statement in Listing 1.11 uses string interpolation via `%s`, which substitutes the value of the variable after the `%` symbol. This functionality is obviously useful when you want to specify something that is determined at run-time.

User input can cause exceptions (depending on the operations that your code performs), so it's important to include exception-handling code.

Listing 1.12 displays the contents of `UserInput2.py` that prompts users for a string and attempts to convert the string to a number in a `try/except` block.

LISTING 1.12 UserInput2.py

```
userInput = raw_input("Enter something: ")

try:
  x = 0 + eval(userInput)
  print 'you entered the number:',userInput
except:
  print userInput,'is a string'
```

Listing 1.12 adds the value 0 to the result of converting a user's input to a number. If the conversion was successful, a message with the user's input is displayed. If the conversion failed, the `except` code block consists of a `print` statement that displays a message.

NOTE *This code sample uses the `eval()` function, which should be avoided so that your code does not evaluate arbitrary (and possibly destructive) commands.*

Listing 1.13 displays the contents of `UserInput3.py` that prompts users for two numbers and attempts to compute their sum in a pair of `try/except` blocks.

LISTING 1.13 UserInput3.py

```
sum = 0

msg = 'Enter a number:'
val1 = raw_input(msg)

try:
  sum = sum + eval(val1)
except:
  print val1,'is a string'

msg = 'Enter a number:'
val2 = raw_input(msg)

try:
  sum = sum + eval(val2)
except:
  print val2,'is a string'

print 'The sum of',val1,'and',val2,'is',sum
```

Listing 1.13 contains two `try` blocks, each of which is followed by an `except` statement. The first `try` block attempts to add the first user-supplied number to the variable `sum`, and the second `try` block attempts to add the second user-supplied number to the previously entered number. An error message occurs if either input string is not a valid number; if both are valid numbers, a message is displayed containing the input numbers and their sum. Be sure to read the caveat regarding the `eval()` function that is mentioned earlier in this chapter.

COMMAND-LINE ARGUMENTS

Python provides a `getopt` module to parse command-line options and arguments and a `sys` module to provide access to any command-line arguments via the `sys.argv`. This serves two purposes:

- sys.argv is the list of command-line arguments
- len(sys.argv) is the number of command-line arguments

Here `sys.argv[0]` is the program name, so if the Python program is called `test.py`, it matches the value of `sys.argv[0]`.

This functionality lets you provide input values for a Python program on the command line instead of providing input values by prompting users for their input.

As an example, consider the script `test.py`, shown here:

```
#!/usr/bin/python
import sys
print 'Number of arguments:',len(sys.argv),'arguments'
print 'Argument List:', str(sys.argv)
```

Now run the above script as follows:

```
python test.py arg1 arg2 arg3
```

This will produce the following result:

```
Number of arguments: 4 arguments.
Argument List: ['test.py', 'arg1', 'arg2', 'arg3']
```

The ability to specify input values from the command line provides useful functionality. For example, suppose that you have a custom Python class that contains the methods add and subtract to add and subtract a pair of numbers.

You can use command-line arguments to specify which method to execute on a pair of numbers, as shown here:

```
python MyClass add 3 5
python MyClass subtract 3 5
```

This functionality is very useful, because you can programmatically execute different methods in a Python class, which means that you can write unit tests for your code as well. Read Chapter 8 to learn how to create custom Python classes.

Listing 1.14 displays the contents of Hello.py that shows you how to use sys.argv to check the number of command-line parameters.

LISTING 1.14 Hello.py
```
import sys

def main():
  if len(sys.argv) >= 2:
    name = sys.argv[1]
  else:
    name = 'World'
  print 'Hello', name

# Standard boilerplate to invoke the main() function
if __name__ == '__main__':
  main()
```

Listing 1.14 defines the main() function that checks the number of command-line parameters; if this value is at least 2, then the variable name is assigned the value of the second parameter. (The first parameter is Hello.py.) Otherwise, name is assigned the value "Hello". The print statement then prints the value of the variable name.

The final portion of Listing 1.14 uses conditional logic to determine whether or not to execute the main() function.

SUMMARY

This chapter showed you how to work with numbers and perform arithmetic operations on numbers and then taught you how to work with strings and use string operations. The next chapter shows you how to work with conditional statements, loops, and user-defined functions in Python.

EXERCISES

Exercise 1: Write a Python script that is a temperature converter from Celsius to Fahrenheit, using this formula: `F = C*9/5 + 32`. In addition, convert from Fahrenheit to Celsius using the formula `C = (F-32) * 5/9`. Test your program with several values for Celsius and Fahrenheit.

Exercise 2: Extend the Python script that you wrote in Exercise 1 to support user input. Make sure that you include exception-handling code in this new version of the script.

Exercise 3: Write a Python script that accepts a line of input text from users and then prints the first and last character of the input text.

Exercise 4: Write a Python script that accepts a line of input text from users and then prints the first word of the input text.

Exercise 5: Write a Python script that accepts a line of input text from users and then checks if the first five characters form a palindrome (words that are the same when you read them from left to right or from right to left). The Python `chr()` function will help you complete this exercise.

CONDITIONAL LOGIC, LOOPS, AND FUNCTIONS

This chapter introduces you to various ways to perform conditional logic in Python, as well as control structures and user-defined functions in Python. Virtually every Python program that performs useful calculations requires some type of conditional logic or control structure (or both). Although the syntax for these Python features is slightly different from that for other languages, the functionality will be familiar to you.

The first part of this chapter contains a brief discussion of operator precedence and reserved words in Python, followed by a discussion of loops and while statements in Python. This section contains an assortment of examples (comparing strings, computing numbers raised to different exponential powers, and so forth) that illustrate various ways that you can use loops and while statements in Python. The second part of this chapter illustrates how to handle if-else conditional logic as well as if-else statements in Python. The third part of this chapter contains examples that involve nested loops and recursion. The final part of this chapter introduces you to user-defined Python functions.

PRECEDENCE OF OPERATORS IN PYTHON

When you have an expression involving numbers, you might remember that multiplication ("*") and division ("/") have higher precedence than addition ("+") or subtraction ("-"). Exponentiation has even higher precedence than these four arithmetic operators.

However, instead of relying on precedence rules, it's simpler (as well as safer) to use parentheses. For example, $(x/y)+10$ is clearer than $x/y+10$, even though they are equivalent expressions.

As another example, the following two arithmetic expressions are equivalent, but the second is less error prone than the first:

```
x/y+3*z/8+x*y/z-3*x
(x/y)+(3*z)/8+(x*y)/z-(3*x)
```

In any case, the following Website contains precedence rules for operators in Python:

http://mathcs.emory.edu/~valerie/courses/fall10/155/resources/op_precedence.html

PYTHON RESERVED WORDS

Every programming language has a set of reserved words, which is a set of words that cannot be used as identifiers, and Python is no exception. The Python reserved words are: and, exec, not, assert, finally, or, break, for, pass, class, from, print, continue, global, raise, def, if, return, del, import, try, elif, in, while, else, is, with, except, lambda, and yield.

If you inadvertently use a reserved word as a variable, you will see an "invalid syntax" error message instead of a "reserved word" error message when you launch the Python code. For example, suppose you create a Python script test1.py with the following code:

```
break = 2
print 'break =', break
```

If you run the preceding Python code, you will see the following output:

```
File "test1.py", line 2
   break = 2
         ^
SyntaxError: invalid syntax
```

However, a quick inspection of the Python code reveals the fact that you are attempting to use the reserved word break as a variable.

WORKING WITH LOOPS IN PYTHON

Python supports for loops, while loops, and range() statements. The following subsections illustrate how you can use each of these constructs.

Python for Loops

Python supports the for loop, whose syntax is slightly different from that in other languages (such as JavaScript and Java).

The following code block shows you how to use a for loop in Python in order to iterate through the elements in a list:

```
>>> x = ['a', 'b', 'c']
>>> for w in x:
...    print w
...
a
b
c
```

The preceding code snippet prints three letters on three separate lines. You can force the output to be displayed on the same line (which will "wrap" if you specify a large enough number of characters) by appending a comma (",") in the print statement, as shown here:

```
>>> x = ['a', 'b', 'c']
>>> for w in x:
...    print w,
...
a b c
```

You can use this type of code when you want to display the contents of a text file in a single line instead of multiple lines.

Python also provides the built-in `reversed()` function, which reverses the direction of the loop, as shown here:

```
>>> a = [1, 2, 3, 4, 5]
>>> for x in reversed(a):
... print(x)
5
4
3
2
1
```

Note that reversed iteration works only if the size of the current object can be determined or if the object implements a __reversed__() special method.

A `for` Loop with `try/except` in Python

Listing 2.1 displays the contents of `StringToNums.py` that illustrates how to calculate the sum of a set of integers that have been converted from strings.

LISTING 2.1: StringToNums.py

```
line = '1 2 3 4 10e abc'
sum  = 0
invalidStr = ""

print 'String of numbers:',line

for str in line.split(" "):
    try:
        sum = sum + eval(str)
    except:
        invalidStr = invalidStr + str + ' '

print 'sum:', sum
if(invalidStr != ""):
  print 'Invalid strings:',invalidStr
else:
  print 'All substrings are valid numbers'
```

Listing 2.1 initializes the variables `line`, `sum`, and `invalidStr` and then displays the contents of `line`. The next portion of Listing 2.1 splits the contents of `line` into words and then uses a `try` block to add the numeric value of each word to the variable `sum`. If an exception occurs, the contents of the current `str` are appended to the variable `invalidStr`. When the loop has finished executing, Listing 2.1 displays the count of the number of occurrences of words that are actually numbers, followed by the list of words that are not numbers.

The output of Listing 2.1 is here:

```
String of numbers: 1 2 3 4 10e abc
sum: 10
Invalid strings: 10e abc
```

Numeric Exponents in Python

Listing 2.2 displays the contents of `Nth-exponent.py` that illustrates how to calculate intermediate powers of a set of integers.

LISTING 2.2: Nth-exponent.py

```
maxPower = 4
maxCount = 4

def pwr(num):
  prod = 1
  for n in range(1,maxPower+1):
    prod = prod*num
    print num,'to the power',n, 'equals',prod
  print '-----------'

for num in range(1,maxCount+1):
    pwr(num)
```

Listing 2.2 contains a function called `pwr()` that accepts a numeric value. This function contains a loop that prints the value of that number raised to the power n, where n ranges between 1 and `maxPower+1`.

The second part of Listing 2.2 contains a `for` loop that invokes the function `pwr()` with the numbers between 1 and `maxPower+1`.

The output of Listing 2.2 is here:

```
1 to the power 1 equals 1
1 to the power 2 equals 1
1 to the power 3 equals 1
1 to the power 4 equals 1
-----------
2 to the power 1 equals 2
2 to the power 2 equals 4
2 to the power 3 equals 8
2 to the power 4 equals 16
-----------
3 to the power 1 equals 3
3 to the power 2 equals 9
3 to the power 3 equals 27
3 to the power 4 equals 81
-----------
```

```
4 to the power 1 equals 4
4 to the power 2 equals 16
4 to the power 3 equals 64
4 to the power 4 equals 256
```

NESTED LOOPS

Listing 2.3 displays the contents of `Triangular1.py` that illustrates how to print a row of consecutive integers (starting from 1), where the length of each row is one greater than that of the previous row.

LISTING 2.3: Triangular1.py

```
max = 8
for x in range(1,max+1):
  for y in range(1,x+1):
    print y,
  print
```

Listing 2.3 initializes the variable `max` with the value 8, followed by an outer `for` loop whose loop variable `x` ranges from 1 to `max+1`. The inner loop has a loop variable `y` that ranges from 1 to `x+1`, which prints the value of `y` during each iteration.

The output of Listing 2.3 is here:

```
1
1 2
1 2 3
1 2 3 4
1 2 3 4 5
1 2 3 4 5 6
1 2 3 4 5 6 7
1 2 3 4 5 6 7 8
```

THE SPLIT() FUNCTION WITH FOR LOOPS

Python supports various useful string-related functions, including the `split()` function and the `join()` function. The `split()` function is useful when you want to tokenize ("split") a line of text into words and then use a `for` loop to iterate through those words and process them accordingly.

The `join()` function does the opposite of `split()`: it "joins" two or more words into a single line. You can easily remove extra spaces in a sentence by using the `split()` function and then invoking the `join()` function, thereby creating a line of text with one white space between any two words.

USING THE SPLIT() FUNCTION TO COMPARE WORDS

Listing 2.4 displays the contents of `Compare1.py` that illustrates how to use the `split` function to compare each word in a text string with another word.

LISTING 2.4 Compare1.py

```
x = 'This is a string that contains abc and Abc'
y = 'abc'
identical = 0
casematch = 0

for w in x.split():
  if(w == y):
    identical = identical + 1
  elif (w.lower() == y.lower()):
    casematch = casematch + 1

if(identical > 0):
 print 'found identical matches:', identical

if(casematch > 0):
 print 'found case matches:', casematch

if(casematch == 0 and identical == 0):
 print 'no matches found'
```

Listing 2.4 uses the `split()` function in order to compare each word in the string x with the word abc. If there is an exact match, the variable `identical` is incremented. If a match does not occur, a case-insensitive match of the current word is performed with the string abc, and the variable `casematch` is incremented if the match is successful.

The output of Listing 2.4 is here:

```
found identical matches: 1
found case matches: 1
```

USING THE `SPLIT()` FUNCTION TO PRINT JUSTIFIED TEXT

Listing 2.5 displays the contents of `FixedColumnCount1.py` that illustrates how to print a set of words from a text string as justified text using a fixed number of columns.

LISTING 2.5: FixedColumnCount1.py

```
import string

wordCount = 0
str1 = 'this is a string with a set of words in it'

print 'left-justified strings:'
print '-----------------------'
for w in str1.split():
   print '%-10s' % w,
   wordCount = wordCount + 1
   if(wordCount % 2 == 0):
      print
print
print
```

```
print 'right-justified strings:'
print '------------------------'
wordCount = 0

for w in str1.split():
    print '%10s' % w,
    wordCount = wordCount + 1
    if(wordCount % 2 == 0):
        print
```

Listing 2.5 initializes the variables wordCount and str1, followed by two for loops. The first for loop prints the words in str1 in left-justified format, and the second for loop prints the words in str1 in right-justified format. In both loops, a linefeed is printed after a pair of consecutive words is printed, which occurs whenever the variable wordCount is even.

The output of Listing 2.5 is here:

```
Left-justified strings:
-----------------------
this        is
a           string
with        a
set         of
words       in
it

Right-justified strings:
-----------------------
      this         is
         a     string
      with          a
       set         of
     words         in
        it
```

USING THE SPLIT() FUNCTION TO PRINT FIXED-WIDTH TEXT

Listing 2.6 displays the contents of FixedColumnWidth1.py that illustrates how to print a text string in a column of fixed width.

LISTING 2.6: FixedColumnWidth1.py
```
import string

left = 0
right = 0
columnWidth = 8

str1 = 'this is a string with a set of words in it and it will be
split into a fixed column width'
strLen = len(str1)

print 'Left-justified column:'
print '----------------------'
```

```
rowCount = strLen/columnWidth
print 'row:',rowCount

for i in range(0,rowCount):
   left  = i*columnWidth
   right = (i+1)*columnWidth-1
   word  = str1[left:right]
   print "%-10s" % word

# check for a 'partial row'
if(rowCount*columnWidth < strLen):
   left  = rowCount*columnWidth-1;
   right = strLen
   word  = str1[left:right]
   print "%-10s" % word
```

Listing 2.6 initializes the integer variable `columnWidth` and the string variable `str1`. The variable `strLen` is the length of `str1`, and `rowCount` is `strLen` divided by `columnWidth`.

The next part of Listing 2.6 contains a loop that prints `rowCount` rows of characters, where each row contains `columnWidth` characters. The final portion of Listing 2.6 prints any "leftover" characters (which in this example are `th`) that make up a partial row.

The newspaper-style output (but without any partial white space formatting) of Listing 2.6 is here:

```
Left-justified column:
----------------------
this is
a strin
 with a
set of
ords in
it and
t will
e split
into a
ixed co
umn wid
th
```

USING THE SPLIT() FUNCTION TO COMPARE TEXT STRINGS

Listing 2.7 displays the contents of `CompareStrings1.py` that illustrates how to determine whether or not the words in one text string are also words in a second text string.

LISTING 2.7 *CompareStrings1.py*

```
text1 = 'a b c d'
text2 = 'a b c e d'

if(text2.find(text1) >= 0):
```

```
    print 'text1 is a substring of text2'
else:
    print 'text1 is not a substring of text2'

subStr = True
for w in text1.split():
    if(text2.find(w) == -1):
        subStr = False
        break

if(subStr == True):
    print 'Every word in text1 is a word in text2'
else:
    print 'Not every word in text1 is a word in text2'
```

Listing 2.7 initializes the string variables `text1` and `text2` and uses conditional logic (which discussed in detail in a subsequent section) to determine whether or not `text1` is a substring of `text2` (and then prints a suitable message).

The next part of Listing 2.7 is a loop that iterates through the individual words in the string `text1` and checks if each of those words is also a word in the string `text2`. If a non-match occurs, the variable `subStr` is set to `False`, followed by the `break` statement that causes an early exit from the loop. The final portion of Listing 2.7 prints the appropriate message based on the value of `subStr`.

The output of Listing 2.7 is here:

```
text1 is not a substring of text2
Every word in text1 is a word in text2
```

USING THE `SPLIT()` FUNCTION TO DISPLAY CHARACTERS IN A STRING

Listing 2.8 displays the contents of `StringChars1.py` that illustrates how to print the characters in a text string.

LISTING 2.8: StringChars1.py

```
text = 'abcdef'
for ch in text:
    print('char:',ch,'ord value:',ord(ch))
print
```

Listing 2.8 is straightforward: a `for` loop iterates through the characters in the string `text` and then prints the character and its `ord` value (which is its corresponding numeric value in ASCII).

The output of Listing 2.8 is here:

```
('char:', 'a', 'ord value:', 97)
('char:', 'b', 'ord value:', 98)
('char:', 'c', 'ord value:', 99)
('char:', 'd', 'ord value:', 100)
('char:', 'e', 'ord value:', 101)
('char:', 'f', 'ord value:', 102)
```

THE `JOIN()` FUNCTION

Another way to remove extraneous spaces is to use the `join()` function, as shown here:

```
text1 = '    there are      extra    spaces   '
print 'text1:',text1

text2 = ' '.join(text1.split())
print 'text2:',text2

text2 = 'XYZ'.join(text1.split())
print 'text2:',text2
```

The `split()` function "splits" a text string into a set of words and also removes the extraneous white spaces. Next, the `join()` function "joins" together the words in the string `text1`, using a single white space as the delimiter. The last code portion of the preceding code block uses the string `XYZ` as the delimiter instead of a single white space.

The output of the preceding code block is here:

```
text1:    there are     extra    spaces
text2: there are extra spaces
text2: thereXYZareXYZextraXYZspaces
```

PYTHON `WHILE` LOOPS

You can define a `while` loop to iterate through a set of numbers, as shown in the following examples:

```
>>> x = 0
>>> while x < 5:
...     print x
...     x = x + 1
...
0
1
2
3
4
5
```

Python uses indentation instead of the curly braces that are used in other languages such as JavaScript and Java.

Although the Python list data structure is not discussed until Chapter 3, you can probably understand the following simple code block, which contains a variant of the preceding `while` loop that you can use when working with lists:

```
lst  = [1,2,3,4]

while lst:
  print 'list:',lst
  print 'item:',lst.pop()
```

The preceding `while` loop terminates when the `1st` variable is empty, and there is no need to explicitly test for an empty list. The output of the preceding code is here:

```
list: [1, 2, 3, 4]
item: 4
list: [1, 2, 3]
item: 3
list: [1, 2]
item: 2
list: [1]
item: 1
```

This concludes the examples that use the `split()` function in order to process words and characters in a text string. The next part of this chapter shows you examples of using conditional logic in Python code.

CONDITIONAL LOGIC IN PYTHON

If you have written code in other programming languages, you have undoubtedly seen `if/then/else` (or `if-elseif-else`) conditional statements. Although the syntax varies between languages, the logic is essentially the same.

The following example shows you how to use `if/elif` statements in Python:

```
>>> x = 25
>>> if x < 0:
...    print 'negative'
... elif x < 25:
...    print 'under 25'
... elif x == 25:
...    print 'exactly 25'
... else:
...   print 'over 25'
...
exactly 25
```

The preceding code block illustrates how to use multiple conditional statements, and the output is exactly what you would expect.

THE `BREAK/CONTINUE/PASS` STATEMENTS

The `break` statement in Python enables you to perform an "early exit" from a loop, whereas the `continue` statement essentially returns to the top of the loop and continues with the next value of the `loop` variable. The `pass` statement is essentially a "do nothing" statement.

Listing 2.9 displays the contents of `BreakContinuePass.py` that illustrates the use of these three statements.

LISTING 2.9: *BreakContinuePass.py*

```
print 'first loop'
for x in range(1,4):
  if(x == 2):
    break
  print x

print 'second loop'
for x in range(1,4):
  if(x == 2):
    continue
  print x

print 'third loop'
for x in range(1,4):
  if(x == 2):
    pass
  print x
```

The output of Listing 2.9 is here:

```
first loop
1
second loop
1
3
third loop
1
2
3
```

COMPARISON AND BOOLEAN OPERATORS

Python supports a variety of Boolean operators, such as `in`, `not in`, `is`, `is not`, `and`, `or`, and `not`. The next several sections discuss these operators and provide some examples of how to use them.

The `in/not in/is/is not` Comparison Operators

The `in` and `not in` operators are used with sequences to check whether a value occurs or does not occur in a sequence.

The operators `is` and `is not` determine whether or not two objects are the same object, which matters only for mutable objects such as lists. All comparison operators have the same priority, which is lower than that of all numerical operators.

Comparisons can be chained. For example, `a < b == c` tests whether a is less than b and moreover whether b equals c.

The `and`, `or`, and `not` Boolean Operators

The Boolean operators `and`, `or`, and `not` have lower priority than comparison operators. The Boolean `and` and `or` are binary operators, whereas the Boolean `not` operator is a unary operator.

Examples are here:

A and B can be true only if both A and B are true
A or B is true if either A or B is true
not (A) is true if and only if A is false

You can also assign the result of a comparison or other Boolean expression to a variable, as shown here:

```
>>> string1, string2, string3 = '', 'b', 'cd'
>>> str4 = string1 or string2 or string3
>>> str4.
'b'
```

The preceding code block initializes the variables string1, string2, and string3, where string1 is an empty string. Next, str4 is initialized via the or operator, and since the first non-null value is string2, the value of str4 is equal to the value of string2, which is the letter b

LOCAL AND GLOBAL VARIABLES

A Python variable is local to a function if it is:

a parameter of the function
on the left-side of a statement in the function
bound to a control structure (such as for, with, and except)

A variable that is referenced in a function but is not local (according to the previous list) is a nonlocal variable. You can specify a variable as nonlocal with this snippet:

```
nonlocal z
```

A variable can be explicitly declared as global with this statement:

```
global z
```

The following code block illustrates the behavior of a global versus a local variable:

```
global z
z = 3

def changeVar(z):
  z = 4
  print 'z in function:',z

print 'first global z:',z

if __name__ == '__main__':
  changeVar(z)
  print 'second global z:',z
```

The output from the preceding code block is here:

```
first global z: 3
z in function: 4
second global z: 3
```

SCOPE OF VARIABLES

The accessibility, or scope, of a variable depends on where that variable has been defined. Python provides two scopes: global and local, with the added "twist" that global is actually a module-level scope (i.e., the current file), and therefore you can have variables with the same name in different files and they will be treated differently.

Local variables are straightforward: they are defined inside a function, and they can be accessed only inside the function where they are defined.

Any variables that are not local variables have global scope, which means that such a variable is "global" *only* with respect to the file where it has been defined and can be accessed anywhere in a file.

In addition, an "unscoped" variable is a variable that has not been defined with an explicit scope, which you will see in the next section.

There are two scenarios to consider regarding variables. First, suppose two files (aka modules), `file1.py` and `file2.py`, have a variable called x and `file1.py` also imports `file2.py`. The question now is how to disambiguate between the variables labeled x in the two different modules. As an example, suppose that `file2.py` contains the following two lines of code:

```
x = 3
print 'unscoped x in file2:',x
```

Suppose that `file1.py` contains the following code:

```
import file2 as file2

x = 5
print 'unscoped x in file1:',x
print 'scoped x from file2:',file2.x
```

Launch `file1.y` from the command line, and you will see the following output:

```
unscoped x in file2: 3
unscoped x in file1: 5
scoped x from file2: 3
```

The second scenario involves a program that contains a local variable and a global variable with the same name. According to the earlier rule, the local variable is used in the function where it is defined and the global variable is used outside of that function.

The following code block illustrates the use of a global and a local variable with the same name:

```
#!/usr/bin/python
# a global variable:
total = 0;

def sum(x1, x2):
    # this total is local:
    total = x1+x2;

    print "Local total : ", total
    return total

# invoke the sum function
sum(2,3);
print "Global total : ", total
```

When the above code is executed, it produces the following result:

```
Local total :    5
Global total :   0
```

As you might have surmised, Python uses a sequence of steps for determining the value of an unscoped variable, as shown here:

1. check the local scope for the name
2. ascend the enclosing scopes and check for the name
3. perform step 2 until the global scope (i.e., module level)
4. if x still hasn't been found, Python checks __builtins__

The following example defines an unscoped variable x and assigns it the value 1, and also shows you that x is a global variable:

```
Python 2.7.5 (default, Dec  2 2013, 18:34:31)
[GCC 4.2.1 Compatible Apple LLVM 4.2 (clang-425.0.28)] on darwin
Type "help", "copyright", "credits" or "license" for more
information.
>>> x = 1
>>> g = globals()
>>> g
{'g': {...}, '__builtins__': <module '__builtin__' (built-in)>,
'__package__': None, 'x': 1, '__name__': '__main__', '__doc__':
None}
>>> g.pop('x')
1
>>> x
Traceback (most recent call last):
  File "<stdin>", line 1, in <module>
NameError: name 'x' is not defined
```

NOTE *You can access the* dicts *that Python uses to track local and global scopes by invoking* locals() *and* globals(), *respectively.*

PASS BY REFERENCE VERSUS VALUE

All parameters (arguments) in the Python language are passed by reference. Thus, if you change what a parameter refers to within a function, the change is reflected in the calling function. For example:

```
def changeme(mylist):
    "This changes a passed list into this function"
    mylist.append([1,2,3,4])
    print "Values inside the function: ", mylist
    return

# Now you can call changeme function
mylist = [10,20,30]
changeme(mylist)
print "Values outside the function: ", mylist
```

Here we are maintaining reference to the passed object and appending values in the same object, and the result is shown here:

```
Values inside the function:   [10, 20, 30, [1, 2, 3, 4]]
Values outside the function:  [10, 20, 30, [1, 2, 3, 4]]
```

The fact that values are passed by reference gives rise to the notion of mutability versus immutability, which is discussed in Chapter 3.

ARGUMENTS AND PARAMETERS

Python differentiates between arguments to functions and parameter declarations in functions: a positional (mandatory) and keyword (optional/default value). This concept is important because Python has operators for packing and unpacking these kinds of arguments.

Python "unpacks" positional arguments from an iterable, as shown here:

```
>>> def foo(x, y):
...    return x - y
...
>>> data = 4,5
>>> foo(data) # only passed one arg
Traceback (most recent call last):
  File "<stdin>", line 1, in <module>
TypeError: foo() takes exactly 2 arguments (1 given)
>>> foo(*data) # passed however many args are in tuple
-1
```

USING A WHILE LOOP TO FIND THE DIVISORS OF A NUMBER

Listing 2.10 displays the contents of Divisors.py, which contains a while loop, conditional logic, and the modulus (%) operator to find the factors of any integer greater than 1 because the initial value of the variable div is 2 (and not 1).

LISTING 2.10 Divisors.py

```
def divisors(num):
  div = 2

  while(num > 1):
    if(num % div == 0):
      print "divisor: ", div
      num = num / div
    else:
      div = div + 1
  print "** finished **"

divisors(12)
```

Listing 2.10 defines a function divisors(), which takes an integer value num and then initializes the variable div with the value 2. The while loop divides num by div if the remainder is 0, and also prints the value of div; if the remainder is not 0, then div is incremented by 1. This while loop continues as long as the value of num is greater than 1.

The output of Listing 2.10 passing the value 12 to the function divisors() is here:

```
divisor:   2
divisor:   2
divisor:   3
** finished **
```

Listing 2.11 displays the contents of Divisors2.py that contains a while loop, conditional logic, and the modulus operator ("%") in order to find the factors of any integer greater than 1.

LISTING 2.11 Divisors2.py

```
def divisors(num):
  primes = ""
  div = 2

  while(num > 1):
    if(num % div == 0):
      divList = divList + str(div) + ' '
      num = num / div
    else:
      div = div + 1
  return divList

result = divisors(12)
print 'The divisors of',12,'are:',result
```

Listing 2.11 is very similar to Listing 2.10; the main difference is that Listing 2.10 constructs the variable divList (which is a concatenated list of the divisors of a number) in the while loop and then returns the value of divList when the while loop has completed.

The output of Listing 2.11 is here:

```
The divisors of 12 are: 2 2 3
```

Using a while Loop to Find Prime Numbers

Listing 2.12 displays the contents of `Divisors3.py` that contains a `while` loop, conditional logic, and the modulus operator in order to count the number of prime factors of any integer greater than 1. If there is only one divisor for a number, then that number is a prime number.

LISTING 2.12 Divisors3.py

```
def divisors(num):
  count = 1
  div = 2
  while(div < num):
    if(num % div == 0):
      count = count + 1
    div = div + 1
  return count

result = divisors(12)

if(result == 1):
  print '12 is prime'
else:
  print '12 is not prime'
```

The output from Listing 2.12 is here:

```
12 is not prime
```

USER-DEFINED FUNCTIONS IN PYTHON

Python provides built-in functions and also enables you to define your own functions.

You can define functions to provide the required functionality. Here are simple rules for defining a function in Python:

- Function blocks begin with the keyword def followed by the function name and parentheses
- Any input arguments should be placed within these parentheses
- The first statement of a function can be an optional statement--the documentation string of the function or docstring
- The code block within every function starts with a colon (:) and is indented
- The statement return [expression] exits a function, optionally passing back an expression to the caller. A return statement with no arguments is the same as a return of None
- if a function does not specify a return statement, the function automatically returns None, which is a special type of value in Python

A very simple custom Python function is here:

```
>>> def func():
...    print 3
```

```
...
>>> func()
3
```

The preceding function is trivial, but it does illustrate the syntax for defining custom functions in Python. The following example is slightly more useful:

```
>>> def func(x):
...     for i in range(0,x):
...         print i
...
>>> func(5)
0
1
2
3
4
```

SPECIFYING DEFAULT VALUES IN A FUNCTION

Listing 2.13 displays the contents of `DefaultValues.py` that illustrates how to specify default values in a function.

LISTING 2.13 DefaultValues.py

```
def numberFunc(a, b=10):
  print (a,b)

def stringFunc(a, b='xyz'):
  print (a,b)

def collectionFunc(a, b=None):
  if(b is None):
      print 'No value assigned to b'

numberFunc(3)
stringFunc('one')
collectionFunc([1,2,3])
```

Listing 2.13 defines three functions, followed by an invocation of each of those functions. The functions `numberFunc()` and `stringFunc()` print a list containing the values of their two parameters, and `collectionFunc()` displays a message if the second parameter is `None`.

The output of Listing 2.13 is here:

```
(3, 10)
('one', 'xyz')
No value assigned to b
```

Returning Multiple Values from a Function

This task is accomplished by the code in Listing 2.14, which displays the contents of `MultipleValues.py`.

LISTING 2.14: MultipleValues.py

```
def MultipleValues():
    return 'a', 'b', 'c'

x, y, z = MultipleValues()

print 'x:',x
print 'y:',y
print 'z:',z
```

The output of Listing 2.14 is here:

```
x: a
y: b
z: c
```

FUNCTIONS WITH A VARIABLE NUMBER OF ARGUMENTS

Python enables you to define functions with a variable number of arguments. This functionality is useful in many situations, such as computing the sum, average, or product of a set of numbers.

For example, the following code block computes the sum of two numbers:

```
def sum(a, b):
    return a + b

values = (1, 2)
s1 = sum(*values)
print 's1 = ', s1
```

The output of the preceding code block is here:

```
s1 =  3
```

However, the sum function in the preceding code block can be used only for two numeric values.

Listing 2.15 displays the contents of `VariableSum1.py` that illustrates how to compute the sum of a variable number of numbers.

LISTING 2.15 VariableSum1.py

```
def sum(*values):
    sum = 0
    for x in values:
        sum = sum + x
    return sum

values1 = (1, 2)
s1 = sum(*values1)
print 's1 = ',s1

values2 = (1, 2, 3, 4)
s2 = sum(*values2)
print 's2 = ',s2
```

Listing 2.15 defines the function sum, whose parameter values can be an arbitrary list of numbers. The next portion of this function initializes sum to 0, and then a for loop iterates through values and adds each of its elements to the variable sum. The last line in the function sum() returns the value of the variable sum.

The output of Listing 2.15 is here:

```
s1 =   3
s2 =   10
```

LAMBDA EXPRESSIONS

Listing 2.16 displays the contents of Lambda1.py that illustrates how to create a simple lambda function in Python.

LISTING 2.16 Lambda1.py
```
add = lambda x, y: x + y

x1 = add(5,7)
x2 = add('Hello', 'Python')

print x1
print x2
```

Listing 2.16 defines the lambda expression add that accepts two input parameters and then returns their sum (for numbers) or their concatenation (for strings).

The output of Listing 2.16 is here:

```
12
HelloPython
```

RECURSION

Recursion is a powerful technique that can provide an elegant solution to various problems. The following subsections contain examples of using recursion to calculate some well-known numbers.

Calculating Factorial Values

The factorial value of a positive integer n is the product of all the integers between 1 and n. The symbol for factorial is the exclamation point ("!"), and some sample factorial values are here:

```
1! = 1
2! = 2
3! = 6
4! = 24
5! = 120
```

The formula for the factorial value of a number is succinctly defined as follows:

```
Factorial(n) = n*Factorial(n-1) for n > 1 and Factorial(1) = 1
```

Listing 2.17 displays the contents of `Factorial.py` that illustrates how to use recursion in order to calculate the factorial value of a positive integer.

LISTING 2.17 Factorial.py

```
def factorial(num):
  if (num > 1):
    return num * factorial(num-1)
  else:
    return 1

result = factorial(5)
print 'The factorial of 5 =', result
```

Listing 2.17 contains the function `factorial` that implements the recursive definition of the factorial value of a number.

The output of Listing 2.17 is here:

```
The factorial of 5 = 120
```

In addition to a recursive solution, there is also an iterative solution for calculating the factorial value of a number.

Listing 2.18 displays the contents of `Factorial2.py` that illustrates how to use the `range()` function in order to calculate the factorial value of a positive integer.

LISTING 2.18 Factorial2.py

```
def factorial2(num):
  prod = 1
  for x in range(1,num+1):
    prod = prod * x
  return prod

result = factorial2(5)
print 'The factorial of 5 =', result
```

Listing 2.18 defines the function `factorial2()` with a parameter num, followed by the variable `prod`, which has an initial value of 1. The next part of `factorial2()` is a `for` loop whose loop variable x ranges between 1 and num+1, and each iteration through that loop multiples the value of `prod` by the value of x, thereby computing the factorial value of num.

The output of Listing 2.18 is here:

```
The factorial of 5 = 120
```

Calculating Fibonacci Numbers

The set of Fibonacci numbers represents some interesting patterns (such as the pattern of a sunflower) in nature, and its recursive definition is here:

```
Fib(0) = 0
Fib(1) = 1
Fib(n) = Fib(n-1) + Fib(n-2) for n >= 2
```

Listing 2.19 displays the contents of fib.py that illustrates how to calculate Fibonacci numbers.

LISTING 2.19 fib.py

```
def fib(num):
  if (num == 0):
    return 1
  elif (num == 1):
    return 1
  else:
    return fib(num-1) + fib(num-2)

result = fib(10)
print 'Fibonacci value of 10 =', result
```

Listing 2.19 defines the fib() function with the parameter num. If num equals 0 or 1, then fib() returns num; otherwise, fib() returns the result of adding fib(num-1) and fib(num-2).

The output of Listing 2.19 is here:

```
Fibonacci value of 10 = 89
```

Calculating the GCD of Two Numbers

The GCD (greatest common divisor) of two positive integers is the largest integer that divides both integers with a remainder of 0. Some values are shown here:

```
gcd(6,2)   = 2
gcd(10,4)  = 2
gcd(24,16) = 8
```

Listing 2.20 uses recursion and Euclid's algorithm in order to find the GCD of two positive integers.

LISTING 2.20 gcd.py

```
def gcd(num1, num2):
  if(num1 % num2 == 0):
    return num2
  elif (num1 < num2):
    print "switching ", num1, " and ", num2
    return gcd(num2, num1)
  else:
    print "reducing", num1, " and ", num2
    return gcd(num1-num2, num2)
```

```
result = gcd(24, 10)
print "GCD of", 24, "and", 10, "=", result
```

Listing 2.20 defines the function gcd() with the parameters num1 and num2. If num1 is divisible by num2, the function returns num2. If num1 is less than num2, then gcd is invoked by switching the order of num1 and num2. In all other cases, gcd() returns the result of computing gcd() with the values num1-num2 and num2.

The output of Listing 2.20 is here:

```
reducing 24   and   10
reducing 14   and   10
switching 4   and   10
reducing 10   and   4
reducing 6   and   4
switching 2   and   4
GCD of 24 and 10 = 2
```

Calculating the LCM of Two Numbers

The LCM (lowest common multiple) of two positive integers is the smallest integer that is a multiple of those two integers. Some values are shown here:

```
lcm(6,2)    = 2
lcm(10,4)   = 20
lcm(24,16)  = 48
```

In general, if x and y are two positive integers, you can calculate their LCM as follows:

```
lcm(x,y) = x/gcd(x,y)*y/gcd(x,y)
```

Listing 2.21 uses the gcd() function that is defined in the previous section in order to calculate the LCM of two positive integers.

LISTING 2.21 lcm.py
```
def gcd(num1, num2):
  if(num1 % num2 == 0):
    return num2
  elif (num1 < num2):
    #print "switching ", num1, " and ", num2
    return gcd(num2, num1)
  else:
    #print "reducing", num1, " and ", num2
    return gcd(num1-num2, num2)

def lcm(num1, num2):
  gcd1 = gcd(num1, num2)
  lcm1 = num1/gcd1*num2/gcd1
  return lcm1

result = lcm(24, 10)
print "The LCM of", 24, "and", 10, "=", result
```

Listing 2.21 defines the function gcd(), which was discussed in the previous section, followed by the function lcm, which takes the parameters num1 and num2. The first line in lcm() computes gcd1, which is the gcd() of num1 and num2. The second line in lcm() computes lcm1, which is num1 divided by three values. The third line in lcm() returns the value of lcm1.

The output of Listing 2.21 is here:

```
The LCM of 24 and 10 = 60
```

SUMMARY

This chapter showed you how to use conditional logic, such as if/elif statements. You also learned how to work with loops in Python, including for loops and while loops. You learned how to compute various values, such as the GCD and of a pair of numbers, and also how to determine whether or not a positive number is prime.

EXERCISES

Exercise 1: Write a Python script that prompts users for a number (representing an hour value) and display that number using a 12-hour clock and also with a 24-hour clock. Make sure that you include exception-handling code, and also print the number as a two-digit number (include a leading zero when necessary).

Exercise 2: Print a report that displays three columns containing the set of numbers from 1 to 10, as well as their squares and their cubes. Right-justify the numbers in each column.

Exercise 3: Modify the Python script in Exercise 2 so that only the odd numbers between 1 and 10 are processed.

Exercise 4: Modify the Python script in Exercise 2 so that only the prime numbers between 1 and 10 are processed.

Exercise 5: Given an array of strings, print a report that displays two columns: the left column contains each word in the array, and the right column contains the same words in reverse.

Exercise 6: Find the longest word and the shortest word in a text string.

Exercise 7: Given a text string, find the position of the even-numbered occurrences of a given word in the text string.

Exercise 8: Given a text string, determine whether or not the entire string is a palindrome.

Exercise 9: Given a text string, find the words (if any) that are palindromes.

Exercise 10: Write a Python script `Triangular2.py` that generates the following output:

```
* # # # # # #
* * # # # # #
* * * # # # #
* * * * # # #
* * * * * # #
* * * * * * #
* * * * * * * #
* * * * * * *
```

Exercise 11: Find the numbers between 1 and 100 that are divisible by 2 or by 3 (or both) but not by any other prime.

Exercise 12: Given a text string, reverse the order of the words and reverse the letters in each word.

Exercise 13: A positive integer is a perfect number if the sum of all of its divisors equals twice the number. For example, 6 is a perfect number because 1+2+3+6 = 2*6. Find the first three perfect numbers.

Exercise 14: Goldbach's conjecture states that every even number greater than 2 can be expressed as the sum of two prime numbers. For each even number greater than 2 and less than 100, find a pair of primes whose sum equals that even number.

Exercise 15: Given a text string, write a Python script that capitalizes the first letter of every word in that text string.

The next chapter delves into various types of data structures that are available in Python.

## CHAPTER 3

PYTHON COLLECTIONS

In Chapters 1 and 2, you learned how to work with numbers and strings, as well as control structures in Python. This chapter discusses Python collections, such as lists (or arrays), sets, tuples, and dictionaries. You will see many short code blocks that will help you rapidly learn how to work with these data structures in Python. After you have finished reading this chapter, you will be in a better position to create more complex Python modules using one or more of these data structures.

The first part of this chapter discusses Python lists and shows you code samples that illustrate various methods that are available for manipulating lists. The second part of this chapter discusses Python sets and how they differ from Python lists. The third part of this chapter discusses Python tuples, and the final part of this chapter discusses Python dictionaries.

WORKING WITH LISTS

Python supports a `list` data type, along with a rich set of list-related functions. Since lists are not typed, you can create a list of different data types, as well as multidimensional lists. The next several sections show you how to manipulate list structures in Python.

Lists and Basic Operations

A Python list consists of comma-separated values enclosed in a pair of square brackets. The following examples illustrate the syntax for defining a list in Python, and also how to perform various operations on a Python list:

```
>>> list = [1, 2, 3, 4, 5]
>>> list
[1, 2, 3, 4, 5]
>>> list[2]
```

```
3
>>> list2 = list + [1, 2, 3, 4, 5]
>>> list2
[1, 2, 3, 4, 5, 1, 2, 3, 4, 5]
>>> list2.append(6)
>>> list2
[1, 2, 3, 4, 5, 1, 2, 3, 4, 5, 6]
>>> len(list)
5
>>> x = ['a', 'b', 'c']
>>> y = [1, 2, 3]
>>> z = [x, y]
>>> z[0]
['a', 'b', 'c']
>>> len(x)
3
```

You can assign multiple variables to a list, provided that the number and type of the variables match the structure. Here is an example:

```
>>> point = [7,8]
>>> x,y = point
>>> x
7
>>> y
8
```

The following example shows you how to assign values to variables from a more complex data structure:

```
>>> line = ['a', 10, 20, (2014,01,31)]
>>> x1,x2,x3,date1 = line
>>> x1
'a'
>>> x2
10
>>> x3
20
>>> date1
(2014, 1, 31)
```

If you want to access the year/month/date components of the date1 element in the preceding code block, you can do so with the following code block:

```
>>> line = ['a', 10, 20, (2014,01,31)]
>>> x1,x2,x3,(year,month,day) = line
>>> x1
'a'
>>> x2
10
>>> x3
20
>>> year
2014
```

```
>>> month
1
>>> day
31
```

If the number and/or structure of the variables does not match the data, an error message is displayed, as shown here:

```
>>> point = (1,2)
>>> x,y,z = point
Traceback (most recent call last):
  File "<stdin>", line 1, in <module>
ValueError: need more than 2 values to unpack
```

If the number of variables that you specify is less than the number of data items, you will see an error message, as shown here:

```
>>> line = ['a', 10, 20, (2014,01,31)]
>>> x1,x2 = line
Traceback (most recent call last):
  File "<stdin>", line 1, in <module>
ValueError: too many values to unpack
```

Reversing and Sorting a List

The Python reverse() method is discussed in more detail later in this chapter, but its purpose is straightforward: this method reverses the contents of a list, as shown here:

```
>>> a = [4, 1, 2, 3]
>>> a.reverse()
[3, 2, 1, 4]
```

The Python sort() method sorts a list:

```
>>> a = [4, 1, 2, 3]
>>> a.sort()
[1, 2, 3, 4]
```

You can sort a list and then reverse its contents, as shown here:

```
>>> a = [4, 1, 2, 3]
>>> a.reverse(a.sort())
[4, 3, 2, 1]
```

Another way to reverse a list is shown here:

```
>>> L = [0,10,20,40]
>>> L[::-1]
[40, 20, 10, 0]
```

Keep in mind that reverse(array) is an iterable and not a list. However, you can convert the reversed array to a list with this code snippet:

```
list(reversed(array)) or L[::-1]
```

Listing 3.1 illustrates how to define an initial list called `list1`, and then use the upper() function to define `list2`, as well as conditional logic to define `list3` and `list4`.

LISTING 3.1: Uppercase1.py

```
list1 = ['a', 'list', 'of', 'words']
list2 = [s.upper() for s in list1]
list3 = [s for s in list1 if len(s) <=2 ]
list4 = [s for s in list1 if 'w' in s ]

print 'list1:',list1
print 'list2:',list2
print 'list3:',list3
print 'list4:',list4
```

The output of Listing 3.1 is here:

```
list1: ['a', 'list', 'of', 'words']
list2: ['A', 'LIST', 'OF', 'WORDS']
list3: ['a', 'of']
list4: ['words']
```

Lists and Arithmetic Operations

The minimum value of a list of numbers is the first number in the sorted list of numbers. If you reverse the sorted list, the first number is the maximum value. As you saw earlier in this chapter, there are several ways to reverse a list, starting with the technique shown in the following code:

```
x = [3,1,2,4]
maxList = x.sort()
minList = x.sort(x.reverse())

min1 = min(x)
max1 = max(x)
print min1
print max1
```

The output of the preceding code block is here:

```
1
4
```

A second (and better) way to sort a list is shown here:

```
minList = x.sort(reverse=True)
```

A third way to sort a list involves the built-in functional version of the `sort()` method, as shown here:

```
sorted(x, reverse=True)
```

The preceding code snippet is useful when you do not want to modify the original order of the list or you want to compose multiple list operations on a single line.

Lists and Filter-Related Operations

Python enables you to filter a list (also called list comprehension), as shown here:

```
mylist = [1, -2, 3, -5, 6, -7, 8]
pos = [n for n in mylist if n > 0]
neg = [n for n in mylist if n < 0]

print pos
print neg
```

You can also specify if-else logic in a filter, as shown here:

```
mylist = [1, -2, 3, -5, 6, -7, 8]
negativeList = [n if n < 0 else 0 for n in mylist]
positiveList = [n if n > 0 else 0 for n in mylist]

print positiveList
print negativeList
```

The output of the preceding code block is here:

```
[1, 3, 6, 8]
[-2, -5, -7]
[1, 0, 3, 0, 6, 0, 8]
[0, -2, 0, -5, 0, -7, 0]
```

SORTING LISTS OF NUMBERS AND STRINGS

Listing 3.2 displays the contents of the Python script Sorted1.py that determines whether or not two lists are sorted.

LISTING 3.2: Sorted1.py

```
list1 = [1,2,3,4,5]
list2 = [2,1,3,4,5]

sort1 = sorted(list1)
sort2 = sorted(list2)

if(list1 == sort1):
  print list1,'is sorted'
else:
  print list1,'is not sorted'

if(list2 == sort2):
  print list2,'is sorted'
else:
  print list2,'is not sorted'
```

Listing 3.2 initializes the lists list1 and list2 and the sorted lists sort1 and sort2, based on the lists list1 and list2, respectively. If list1 equals sort1, then list1 is already sorted; similarly, if list2 equals sort2, then list2 is already sorted.

The output of Listing 3.2 is here:

```
[1, 2, 3, 4, 5] is sorted
[2, 1, 3, 4, 5] is not sorted
```

Note that if you sort a list of character strings the output is case sensitive and that uppercase letters appear before lowercase letters. This is due to the fact that the collating sequence for ASCII places uppercase letters (decimal 65 through decimal 90) before lowercase letters (decimal 97 through decimal 122). The following example provides an illustration:

```
>>> list1 = ['a', 'A', 'b', 'B', 'Z']
>>> print sorted(list1)
['A', 'B', 'Z', 'a', 'b']
```

You can also specify the reverse option so that the list is sorted in reverse order:

```
>>> list1 = ['a', 'A', 'b', 'B', 'Z']
>>> print sorted(list1, reverse=True)
['b', 'a', 'Z', 'B', 'A']
```

You can even sort a list based on the length of the items in the list:

```
>>> list1 = ['a', 'AA', 'bbb', 'BBBBB', 'ZZZZZZZ']
>>> print sorted(list1, key=len)
['a', 'AA', 'bbb', 'BBBBB', 'ZZZZZZZ']
>>> print sorted(list1, key=len, reverse=True)
['ZZZZZZZ', 'BBBBB', 'bbb', 'AA', 'a']
```

You can specify `str.lower` if you want treat uppercase letters as though they are lowercase letters during the sorting operation, as shown here:

```
>>> print sorted(list1, key=str.lower)
['a', 'AA', 'bbb', 'BBBBB', 'ZZZZZZZ']
```

EXPRESSIONS IN LISTS

The following code snippet is similar to a `for` loop but without the colon ":" character that appears at the end of a loop construct. Consider the following example:

```
nums = [1, 2, 3, 4]
cubes = [ n*n*n for n in nums ]

print 'nums: ',nums
print 'cubes:',cubes
```

The output of the preceding code block is here:

```
nums:  [1, 2, 3, 4]
cubes: [1, 8, 27, 64]
```

CONCATENATING A LIST OF WORDS

Python provides the `join()` method for concatenating text strings, as shown here:

```
>>> parts = ['Is', 'SF', 'In', 'California?']
>>> ' '.join(parts)
'Is SF In California?'
>>> ','.join(parts)
'Is,SF,In,California?'
>>> ''.join(parts) 'IsSFInCalifornia?'
```

There are several ways to concatenate a set of strings and then print the result. The following is the most inefficient way to do so:

```
print "This" + " is" + " a" + " sentence"
```

Either of the following is preferred:

```
print "%s %s %s %s" % ("This", "is", "a", "sentence")
print " ".join(["This","is","a","sentence"])
```

THE BUBBLE SORT IN PYTHON

The previous sections contain examples that illustrate how to sort a list of numbers using the `sort()` function. However, sometimes you need to implement different types of sorts in Python. Listing 3.3 displays the contents of `BubbleSort.py` that illustrates how to implement the bubble sort in Python.

LISTING 3.3 BubbleSort.py

```
list1 = [1, 5, 3, 4]

print "Initial list:",list1

for i in range(0,len(list1)-1):
  for j in range(i+1,len(list1)):
   if(list1[i] > list1[j]):
      temp = list1[i]
      list1[i] = list1[j]
      list1[j] = temp

print "Sorted list: ",list1
```

The output of Listing 3.3 is here:

```
Initial list: [1, 5, 3, 4]
Sorted list:  [1, 3, 4, 5]
```

THE PYTHON RANGE() FUNCTION

In Chapter 8, you will learn about iterators in Python, such as `filter()` and `map()`. In this section you will learn about the Python `range()` function, which you can use to iterate through a list, as shown here:

```
>>> for i in range(0,5):
...    print i
...
0
1
2
3
4
```

You can use a `for` loop to iterate through a list of strings, as shown here:

```
>>> x
['a', 'b', 'c']
>>> for w in x:
...    print w
...
a
b
c
```

You can use a `for` loop to iterate through a list of strings and provide additional details, as shown here:

```
>>> x
['a', 'b', 'c']
>>> for w in x:
...    print len(w), w
...
1 a
1 b
1 c
```

The preceding output displays the length of each word in the list x, followed by the word itself.

Counting Digits, Uppercase Letters, and Lowercase Letters

Listing 3.4 displays the contents of the Python script `CountCharTypes.py` that counts the occurrences of digits and letters in a string.

LISTING 3.4 CountCharTypes.py
```
str1 = "abc4234AFde"
digitCount = 0
alphaCount = 0
upperCount = 0
lowerCount = 0
```

```
for i in range(0,len(str1)):
  char = str1[i]
  if(char.isdigit()):
   #print "this is a digit:",char
    digitCount += 1
  elif(char.isalpha()):
   #print "this is alphabetic:",char
    alphaCount  += 1
    if(char.upper() == char):
      upperCount  += 1
    else:
      lowerCount  += 1

print 'Original String:   ',str1
print 'Number of digits:  ',digitCount
print 'Total alphanumeric:',alphaCount
print 'Upper Case Count:  ',upperCount
print 'Lower Case Count:  ',lowerCount
```

Listing 3.4 initializes counter-related variables, followed by a loop (with loop variable i) that iterates from 0 to the length of the string str1. The string variable char is initialized with the letter at index i of the string str1. The next portion of the loop uses conditional logic to determine whether char is a digit or an alphabetic character; in the latter case, the code checks whether the character is uppercase or lowercase. In all cases, the values of the appropriate counter-related variables are incremented.

The output of Listing 3.4 is here:

```
Original String:    abc4234AFde
Number of digits:   4
Total alphanumeric: 7
Upper Case Count:   2
Lower Case Count:   5
```

ARRAYS AND THE APPEND() FUNCTION

Although Python does have an array type (import array), which is essentially a heterogeneous list, the array type has no advantages over the list type other than a slight saving in memory use.

You can also define heterogeneous arrays:

```
a = [10, 'hello', [5, '77']]
```

You can append a new element to an element inside a list:

```
>>> a = [10, 'hello', [5, '77']]
>>> a[2].append('abc')
>>> a
[10, 'hello', [5, '77', 'abc']]
```

You can assign simple variables to the elements of a list, as shown here:

```
myList = [ 'a', 'b', 91.1, (2014, 01, 31) ]
x1, x2, x3, x4 = myList
```

```
print 'x1:',x1
print 'x2:',x2
print 'x3:',x3
print 'x4:',x4
```

The output of the preceding code block is here:

```
x1: a
x2: b
x3: 91.1
x4: (2014, 1, 31)
```

The Python `split()` function is more convenient (especially when the number of elements is unknown or variable) than the preceding sample, and you will see examples of the `split()` function in the next section.

WORKING WITH LISTS AND THE `SPLIT()` FUNCTION

You can use the Python `split()` function to split the words in a text string and populate a list with those words. An example is here:

```
>>> x = "this is a string"
>>> list = x.split()
>>> list
['this', 'is', 'a', 'string']
```

A simple way to print the list of words in a text string is shown here:

```
>>> x = "this is a string"
>>> for w in x.split():
...     print w
...
this
is
a
string
```

You can search for a word in a string as follows:

```
>>> x = "this is a string"
>>> for w in x.split():
...     if(w == 'this'):
...         print "x contains this"
...
x contains this
...
```

COUNTING WORDS IN A LIST

Python provides the `Counter` class, which enables you to count the words in a list. Listing 3.5 displays the contents of `CountWord2.py` that displays the top three words with greatest frequency.

LISTING 3.5: CountWord2.py

```python
from collections import Counter

mywords = ['a', 'b', 'a', 'b', 'c', 'a', 'd', 'e', 'f', 'b']

word_counts = Counter(mywords)
topThree = word_counts.most_common(3)
print(topThree)
```

Listing 3.5 initializes the variable `mywords` with a set of characters and then initializes the variable `word_counts` by passing `mywords` as an argument to `Counter`. The variable `topThree` is an array containing the three most common characters (and their frequency) that appear in `mywords`.

The output of Listing 3.5 is here:

```
[('a', 3), ('b', 3), ('c', 1)]
```

Because of the manner in which the data is represented internally, words with equal frequency are not necessarily displayed in alphabetical order. In Listing 3.5, try changing the number 3 to the number 5 in order to illustrate this point.

ITERATING THROUGH PAIRS OF LISTS

Python supports operations on pairs of lists, which means that you can perform vector-like operations, such as the following:
Multiply every list element by 3:

```python
>>> list1 = [1, 2, 3]
>>> [3*x for x in list1]
[3, 6, 9]
```

Create a new list with pairs of elements consisting of the original element and the original element multiplied by 3:

```python
>>> list1 = [1, 2, 3]
>>> [[x, 3*x] for x in list1]
[[1, 3], [2, 6], [3, 9]]
```

Compute the product of every pair of numbers from two lists:

```python
>>> list1 = [1, 2, 3]
>>> list2 = [5, 6, 7]
>>> [a*b for a in list1 for b in list2]
[5, 6, 7, 10, 12, 14, 15, 18, 21]
```

Calculate the sum of every pair of numbers from two lists:

```python
>>> list1 = [1, 2, 3]
>>> list2 = [5, 6, 7]
>>> [a+b for a in list1 for b in list2]
[6, 7, 8, 7, 8, 9, 8, 9, 10]
```

Calculate the pair-wise product of two lists:

```
>>> [list1[i]*list2[i] for i in range(len(list1))]
[8, 12, -54]
```

OTHER LIST-RELATED FUNCTIONS

Python provides additional functions that you can use with lists, such as `append()`, `insert()`, `delete()`, `pop()`, and `extend()`. Python also supports the functions `index()`, `count()`, `sort()`, and `reverse()`. Examples of these functions are illustrated in the following code block.

Define a Python list (notice that duplicates are allowed):

```
>>> a = [1, 2, 3, 2, 4, 2, 5]
```

Display the number of occurrences of 1 and 2:

```
>>> print a.count(1), a.count(2)
1 3
```

Insert -8 in position 3:

```
>>> a.insert(3,-8)
>>> a
[1, 2, 3, -8, 2, 4, 2, 5]
```

Remove occurrences of 3:

```
>>> a.remove(3)
>>> a
[1, 2, -8, 2, 4, 2, 5]
```

Remove occurrences of 1:

```
>>> a.remove(1)
>>> a
[2, -8, 2, 4, 2, 5]
```

Append 19 to the list:

```
>>> a.append(19)
>>> a
[2, -8, 2, 4, 2, 5, 19]
```

Print the index of 19 in the list:

```
>>> a.index(19)
6
```

Reverse the list:

```
>>> a.reverse()
>>> a
[19, 5, 2, 4, 2, -8, 2]
```

Sort the list:

```
>>> a.sort()
>>> a
[-8, 2, 2, 2, 4, 5, 19]
```

Extend list a with list b:

```
>>> b = [100,200,300]
>>> a.extend(b)
>>> a
[-8, 2, 2, 2, 4, 5, 19, 100, 200, 300]
```

Remove the first occurrence of 2:

```
>>> a.pop(2)
2
>>> a
[-8, 2, 2, 4, 5, 19, 100, 200, 300]
```

Remove the last item of the list:

```
>>> a.pop()
300
>>> a
[-8, 2, 2, 4, 5, 19, 100, 200]
```

Now that you understand how to use list-related operations, the next section shows you how to use a Python list as a stack.

USING A LIST AS A STACK AND AS A QUEUE

A stack is a "Last In First Out" (LIFO) data structure with push() and pop() functions for adding and removing elements, respectively. The most recently added element in a stack is in the top position, and therefore the first element that can be removed from the stack.

The following code block illustrates how to create a stack and also how to remove and append items to a stack in Python.

Create a Python list (which we'll use as a stack):

```
>>> s = [1,2,3,4]
```

Append 5 to the stack:

```
>>> s.append(5)
>>> s
[1, 2, 3, 4, 5]
```

Remove the last element from the stack:

```
>>> s.pop()
5
>>> s
[1, 2, 3, 4]
```

A queue is a "First In First Out" (FIFO) data structure with `insert()` and `pop()` functions for inserting and removing elements, respectively. The most recently added element in a queue is in the top position and therefore is the last element that can be removed from the queue.

The following code block illustrates how to create a queue and also how to insert and append items to a queue in Python.

Create a Python list (which we'll use as a queue):

```
>>> q = [1,2,3,4]
```

Insert 5 at the beginning of the queue:

```
>>> q.insert(0,5)
>>> q
[5, 1, 2, 3, 4]
```

Remove the first element from the queue:

```
>>> q.pop(0)
5
>>> q
[5, 2, 3, 4]
```

The preceding code uses `q.insert(0, 5)` to insert at the beginning and `q.pop()` to remove from the end. However, keep in mind that the `insert()` operation is slow in Python: inserting at 0 requires copying all the elements in the underlying array "to the right" by one position. Therefore, use `collections.deque` with `coll.appendleft()` and `coll.pop()`, where `coll` is an instance of the `Collection` class.

The next section shows you how to work with vectors in Python.

WORKING WITH VECTORS

A vector is a one-dimensional array of values, and you can perform vector-based operations, such as addition, subtraction, and inner or "dot" product. Listing 3.6 displays the contents of `MyVectors.py` that illustrates how to perform vector-based operations.

LISTING 3.6: MyVectors.py

```
v1 = [1,2,3]
v2 = [1,2,3]
v3 = [5,5,5]

s1 = [0,0,0]
d1 = [0,0,0]
p1 = 0

print "Initial Vectors"
print 'v1:',v1
print 'v2:',v2
print 'v3:',v3
```

```
for i in range(len(v1)):
    d1[i] = v3[i] - v2[i]
    s1[i] = v3[i] + v2[i]
    p1    = v3[i] * v2[i] + p1

print "After operations"
print 'd1:',d1
print 's1:',s1
print 'p1:',p1
```

Listing 3.6 starts with the definition of three lists in Python, each of which represents a vector. The lists d1 and s1 represent the difference of v2 and the sum v2, respectively. The number p1 represents the "inner product" (also called the "dot product") of v3 and v2.

The output of Listing 3.6 is here:

```
Initial Vectors
v1: [1, 2, 3]
v2: [1, 2, 3]
v3: [5, 5, 5]
After operations
d1: [4, 3, 2]
s1: [6, 7, 8]
p1: 30
```

WORKING WITH MATRICES

A two-dimensional matrix is a two-dimensional array of values, and you can easily create such a matrix. For example, the following code block illustrates how to access different elements in a 2D matrix:

```
mm = [["a","b","c"],["d","e","f"],["g","h","i"]];
print 'mm:        ',mm
print 'mm[0]:     ',mm[0]
print 'mm[0][1]:',mm[0][1]
```

The output from the preceding code block is here:

```
mm:        [['a', 'b', 'c'], ['d', 'e', 'f'], ['g', 'h', 'i']]
mm[0]:     ['a', 'b', 'c']
mm[0][1]: b
```

Listing 3.7 displays the contents of My2DMatrix.py that illustrates how to create and populate one two-dimensional matrix.

LISTING 3.7: My2DMatrix.py

```
rows = 3
cols = 3

my2DMatrix = [[0 for i in range(rows)] for j in range(rows)]
print 'Before:',my2DMatrix

for row in range(rows):
  for col in range(cols):
```

```
        my2DMatrix[row][col] = row*row+col*col
print 'After: ',my2Dmatrix
```

Listing 3.7 initializes the variables `rows` and `cols` and then uses them to create the `rows x cols` matrix my2Dmatrix, whose values are initially 0. The next part of Listing 3.7 contains a nested loop that initializes the element of my-2DMatrix whose position is `(row,col)` with the value `row*row+col*col`. The last line of code in Listing 3.7 prints the contents of `my2DArray`.

The output of Listing 3.7 is here:

```
Before:  [[0, 0, 0], [0, 0, 0], [0, 0, 0]]
After:   [[0, 1, 4], [1, 2, 5], [4, 5, 8]]
```

THE NUMPY LIBRARY FOR MATRICES

The NumPy library (which you can install via `pip`) has a matrix object for manipulating matrices in Python. The following examples illustrate some of the features of NumPy.

Initialize a matrix m and then display its contents:

```
>>> import numpy as np
>>> m = np.matrix([[1,-2,3],[0,4,5],[7,8,-9]])
>>> m
matrix([[ 1,  -2,  3],
        [ 0,   4,  5],
        [ 7,   8, -9]])
```

The next snippet returns the transpose of matrix m:

```
>>> m.T
matrix([[ 1,  0,  7],
        [-2,  4,  8],
        [ 3,  5, -9]])
```

The next snippet returns the inverse of matrix m (if it exists):

```
>>> m.I
matrix([[ 0.33043478,  -0.02608696,  0.09565217],
        [-0.15217391,   0.13043478,  0.02173913],
        [ 0.12173913,   0.09565217, -0.0173913 ]])
```

The next snippet defines a vector y and then computes the product m*v:

```
>>> v = np.matrix([[2],[3],[4]])
>>> v
matrix([[2],[3],[4]])
>>> m * v
matrix([[ 8],[32],[ 2]])
```

The next snippet imports the `numpy.linalg` subpackage and then computes the determinant of the matrix m:

```
>>> import numpy.linalg
>>> numpy.linalg.det(m)
-229.99999999999983
```

The next snippet finds the eigenvalues of the matrix m:

```
>>> numpy.linalg.eigvals(m)
array([-13.11474312, 2.75956154, 6.35518158])
```

The next snippet finds solutions to the equation m*x = v:

```
>>> x = numpy.linalg.solve(m, v)
>>> x
matrix([[ 0.96521739],
        [ 0.17391304],
        [ 0.46086957]])
```

In addition to the preceding samples, the NumPy package provides additional functionality, which you can find by performing an Internet search for articles and tutorials.

QUEUES

Earlier in this chapter you learned how to treat a list as a queue. However, Python provides the collections module that contains an actual queue object.

The following code snippets illustrate how to define and use a queue in Python.

```
>>> from collections import deque
>>> q = deque('',maxlen=10)
>>> for i in range(10,20):
...    q.append(i)
...
>>> print q
deque([10, 11, 12, 13, 14, 15, 16, 17, 18, 19], maxlen=10)
```

The next section shows you how to use tuples in Python.

TUPLES (IMMUTABLE LISTS)

Python supports a data type called a *tuple* (often pronounced either tupple or toople) that consists of comma-separated values without brackets. (Square brackets are for lists, round brackets are for arrays, and curly braces are for dictionaries.) Various examples of Python tuples are here:

http://docs.python.org/2/tutorial/datastructures.html#tuples-and-sequences

The following code block illustrates how to create a tuple and create new tuples from an existing type in Python.

Define a Python tuple t as follows:

```
>>> t = 1,'a', 2,'hello',3
>>> t
(1, 'a', 2, 'hello', 3)
```

Display the first element of t:

```
>>> t[0]
1
```

Create a tuple v containing 10, 11, and t:

```
>>> v = 10,11,t
>>> v
(10, 11, (1, 'a', 2, 'hello', 3))
```

Try modifying an element of t (which is immutable):

```
>>> t[0] = 1000
Traceback (most recent call last):
  File "<stdin>", line 1, in <module>
TypeError: 'tuple' object does not support item assignment
```

Python "deduplication" is useful because you can remove duplicates from a set and obtain a list, as shown here:

```
>>> lst = list(set(lst))
```

> **NOTE** *The "in" operator on a list to be searched is* O(n), *whereas the "in" operator in a set is* O(1).*j*

The next section discusses Python sets.

SETS

A Python set is an unordered collection that does not contain duplicate elements. Use curly braces or the set() function to create sets. set objects support set-theoretic operations such as union, intersection, and difference.

> **NOTE** set() *is required to create an empty set, because* { } *creates an empty dictionary.*

The following code block illustrates how to work with a Python set. Create a list of elements:

```
>>> l = ['a', 'b', 'a', 'c']
```

Create a set from the preceding list:

```
>>> s = set(l)
>>> s
set(['a', 'c', 'b'])
```

Test if an element is in the set:

```
>>> 'a' in s
True
```

```
>>> 'd' in s
False
>>>
```

Create a set from a string:

```
>>> n = set('abacad')
>>> n
set(['a', 'c', 'b', 'd'])
>>>
```

Subtract n from s:

```
>>> s - n
set([])
```

Subtract s from n:

```
>>> n - s
set(['d'])

>>>
```

Find the union of s and n:

```
>>> s | n
set(['a', 'c', 'b', 'd'])
```

Find the intersection of s and n:

```
>>> s & n
set(['a', 'c', 'b'])
```

The exclusive-or of s and n:

```
>>> s ^ n
set(['d'])
```

The next section shows you how to work with Python dictionaries.

DICTIONARIES

Python has a key/value structure called a "dict" that is a hash table (perform an Internet search to find a detailed explanation if you are unfamiliar with hash tables). A Python dictionary (and hash tables in general) can retrieve the value of a key in constant time, regardless of the number of entries in the dictionary. (The same is true for sets.) You can think of a set as essentially just the keys (not the values) of a dict implementation.

The contents of a dict can be written as a series of key:value pairs, as shown here:

```
dict1 = {key1:value1, key2:value2, ... }
```

An "empty dict" is just an empty pair of curly braces ("{ }").

Creating a Dictionary

A Python dictionary (or hash table) contains of colon-separated key/value bindings inside a pair of curly braces, as shown here:

```
dict1 = {}
dict1 = {'x' : 1, 'y' : 2}
```

The preceding code snippet defines `dict1` as an empty dictionary and then adds two key/value bindings.

Displaying the Contents of a Dictionary

You can display the contents of `dict1` with the following code:

```
>>> dict1 = {'x':1,'y':2}
>>> dict1
{'y': 2, 'x': 1}
>>> dict1['x']
1
>>> dict1['y']
2
>>> dict1['z']
Traceback (most recent call last):
  File "<stdin>", line 1, in <module>
KeyError: 'z'
```

NOTE *Key/value bindings for a `dict` and a `set` are not necessarily stored in the same order in which you defined them.*

Python dictionaries also provide the `get` method of retrieving key values:

```
>>> dict1.get('x')
1
>>> dict1.get('y')
2
>>> dict1.get('z')
```

As you can see, the Python `get` method returns `None` (which is displayed as an empty string) instead of an error when referencing a key that is not defined in a dictionary.

You can also use `dict` "comprehensions" to create dictionaries from expressions, as shown here:

```
>>> {x: x**3 for x in (1, 2, 3)}
{1: 1, 2: 8, 3: 37}
```

Checking for Keys in a Dictionary

You can check for the presence of a key in a dictionary as follows:

```
>>> 'x' in dict1
True
>>> 'z' in dict1
False
```

Use square brackets for finding or setting a value in a dictionary. For example, dict ['abc'] finds the value associated with the key "abc." Strings, numbers, and tuples as key values, and you can use any type as the value for the key.

If you access a value that is not in the dictionary, Python throws a KeyError. Consequently, use the "in"" operator to check if the key is in the dictionary. Alternatively, use dict.get(key), which returns the value of None if the key is not present. You can even use the expression get(key, notfound-string) to specify the value to return if a key is not found.

Deleting Keys from a Dictionary

Launch the Python interpreter and enter the following commands:

```
>>> MyDict = {'x' : 5, 'y' : 7}
>>> MyDict['z'] = 13
>>> MyDict
{'y': 7, 'x': 5, 'z': 13}
>>> del MyDict['x']
>>> MyDict
{'y': 7, 'z': 13}
>>> MyDict.keys()
['y', 'z']
>>> MyDict.values()
[13, 7]
>>> 'z' in MyDict
True
```

Iterating through a Dictionary

The following code snippet shows you how to iterate through a dictionary:

```
MyDict = {'x' : 5, 'y' : 7, 'z' : 13}

for key, value in MyDict.iteritems():
    print key, value
```

The output from the preceding code block is here:

```
y 7
x 5
z 13
```

Interpolating Data from a Dictionary

The modulus operator substitutes values from a Python dictionary into a string by name. Listing 3.8 contains an example of doing so.

LISTING 3.8: InterpolateDict1.py

```
hash = {}
hash['beverage'] = 'coffee'
hash['count'] = 3

# %d for int, %s for string
s = 'Today I drank %(count)d cups of %(beverage)s' % hash
```

The output of Listing 3.8 is here:

```
Today I drank 3 cups of coffee
```

DICTIONARY FUNCTIONS AND METHODS

Python provides various functions and methods for a Python dictionary, such as cmp(), len(), and str(), that compare two dictionaries, return the length of a dictionary, and display a string representation of a dictionary, respectively.

You can also manipulate the contents of a Python dictionary using the functions clear() to remove all elements, copy() to return a shallow copy, get() to retrieve the value of a key, items() to display the (key, value) pairs of a dictionary, keys() to displays the keys of a dictionary, and values() to return the list of values of a dictionary.

ORDERED DICTIONARIES

Regular Python dictionaries iterate over key/value pairs in arbitrary order. Python 2.7 introduced a new OrderedDict class in the collections module. The OrderedDict API (Application Programming Interface) provides the same interface as regular dictionaries but iterates over keys and values in a guaranteed order depending on when a key was first inserted:

```
>>> from collections import OrderedDict
>>> d = OrderedDict([('first', 1),
...                  ('second', 2),
...            '     ('third', 3)])
>>> d.items()
[('first', 1), ('second', 2), ('third', 3)]
```

If a new entry overwrites an existing entry, the original insertion position is left unchanged:

```
>>> d['second'] = 4
>>> d.items()
[('first', 1), ('second', 4), ('third', 3)]
```

Deleting an entry and reinserting it will move it to the end:

```
>>> del d['second']
>>> d['second'] = 5
>>> d.items()
[('first', 1), ('third', 3), ('second', 5)]
```

Sorting Dictionaries

Python enables you to sort the entries in a dictionary. For example, you can modify the code in the preceding section to display the alphabetically sorted words and their associated word count.

Python Multi-Dictionaries

You can define entries in a Python dictionary so that they reference lists or other types of Python structures. Listing 3.9 displays the contents of `Multi-Dictionary1.py` that illustrates how to define more complex dictionaries.

LISTING 3.9: MultiDictionary1.py

```
from collections import defaultdict

d = {'a' : [1, 2, 3], 'b' : [4, 5]}
print 'firsts:',d

d = defaultdict(list)
d['a'].append(1)
d['a'].append(2)
d['b'].append(4)
print 'second:',d

d = defaultdict(set)
d['a'].add(1)
d['a'].add(2)
d['b'].add(4)
print 'third:',d
```

Listing 3.9 starts by defining the dictionary d and printing its contents. The next portion of Listing 3.9 specifies a list-oriented dictionary and then modifies the values for the keys a and b. The final portion of Listing 3.9 specifies a set-oriented dictionary and then modifies the values for the keys a and b as well.

The output of Listing 3.9 is here:

```
first: {'a': [1, 2, 3], 'b': [4, 5]}
second: defaultdict(<type 'list'>, {'a': [1, 2], 'b': [4]})
third: defaultdict(<type 'set'<, {'a': set([1, 2]), 'b':
set([4])})
```

The next section discusses other Python sequence types that have not been discussed in previous sections of this chapter.

OTHER SEQUENCE TYPES IN PYTHON

Python supports seven sequence types: `str`, `unicode`, `list`, `tuple`, `bytearray`, `buffer`, and `xrange`.

You can iterate through a sequence and retrieve the position index and corresponding value at the same time using the `enumerate()` function.

```
>>> for i, v in enumerate(['x', 'y', 'z']):
...     print i, v
...
0 x
1 y
2 z
```

Bytearray objects are created with the built-in function `bytear-ray()`. Although buffer objects are not directly supported by Python syntax, you can create them via the built-in `buffer()` function.

Objects of type `xrange` are created with the `xrange()` function. An `xrange` object is similar to a buffer in the sense that there is no specific syntax to create them. Moreover, `xrange` objects do not support operations such as slicing, concatenation, or repetition.

At this point you have seen all the Python types that you will encounter in the remaining chapters of this book, so it makes sense to discuss mutable and immutable types in Python, which is the topic of the next section.

MUTABLE AND IMMUTABLE TYPES IN PYTHON

Python represents its data as objects. Some of these objects (such as lists and dictionaries) are mutable, which means you can change their content without changing their identity. Objects such as integers, floats, strings, and tuples that cannot be changed. The key point to understand is the difference between changing the value and assigning a new value to an object: you cannot change a string, but you can assign it a different value. You can verify the preceding statement by checking the `id` value of an object, as shown in Listing 3.10.

LISTING 3.10 *Mutability.py*

```
s = "abc"
print 'id #1:', id(s)
print 'first char:', s[0]

try:
  s[0] = "o"
except:
  print 'Cannot perform reassignment'

s = "xyz"
print 'id #2:',id(s)
s += "uvw"
print 'id #3:',id(s)
```

The output of Listing 3.10 is here:

```
id #1: 4297972672
first char: a
Cannot perform reassignment
id #2: 4299809336
id #3: 4299777872
```

Thus, a Python type is immutable if its value cannot be changed (even though it's possible to assign a new value to such a type); otherwise, a Python type is mutable. The Python immutable objects are of the types `byte`, `complex`, `float`, `int`, `str`, and `tuple`. On the other hand, dictionaries, lists, and sets are mutable. The key in a hash table must be an immutable type.

Since strings are immutable in Python, you cannot insert a string in the "middle" of a given text string unless you construct a second string using concatenation. For example, suppose you have the string:

```
"this is a string"
```

and you want to create the following string:

```
"this is a longer string"
```

The following Python code block illustrates how to perform this task:

```
text1 = "this is a string"
text2 = text1[0:10] + "longer" + text1[9:]
print 'text1:',text1
print 'text2:',text2
```

The output of the preceding code block is here:

```
text1: this is a string
text2: this is a longer string
```

THE TYPE() FUNCTION

The type() primitive returns the type of any object, including Python primitives, functions, and user-defined objects. The following code sample displays the type of an integer and a string:

```
var1 = 123
var2 = 456.78
print "type var1: ",type(var1)
print "type var2: ",type(var2)
```

The output of the preceding code block is here:

```
type var1:   <type 'int'>
type var2:   <type 'float'>
```

SUMMARY

This chapter showed you how to work with various Python data types. In particular, you learned about tuples, sets, and dictionaries. Next you learned how to work with lists and how to use list-related operations to extract sublists. You also learned how to about mutable and immutable data types in Python, as well as the type() function.

EXERCISES

Exercise 1: Write a Python script that counts the words in a list, but without using the Counter class.

Exercise 2: Given a list, write a Python script that displays all the elements in the list that are also lists.

Exercise 3: Write a Python script that "flattens" a list so that every item in the list is a top-level item. You can use recursion and the code from the previous exercise.

Exercise 4: Given a list of words, write a Python script to capitalize the first letter in each word in that list.

Exercise 5: Given a list of words, write a Python script to that counts the frequency of letters and digits. Use a Python dictionary to store the letters and the digits, and then display their frequency in descending order.

Exercise 6: Given a list of words, find the frequency of all the substrings of each word and display them in order of decreasing frequency. For example, the substring the occurs with the highest frequency in the list ['the', 'them', 'then', 'these']

## CHAPTER 4

REGULAR EXPRESSIONS

This chapter introduces you to regular expressions, which is a very powerful language feature in Python. Since regular expressions are available in other programming languages (such as JavaScript and Java), the knowledge that you gain from the material in this chapter will be useful to you outside of Python. This chapter contains a mixture of code blocks and complete code samples, with varying degrees of complexity, that are suitable for beginners as well as people who have had some exposure to regular expressions. In fact, you have probably used (albeit simple) regular expressions in a command line on a laptop, whether it be in Windows-based, Unix-based, or Linux-based systems. In this chapter, you will learn how to define and use more complex regular expressions than the regular expressions that you have used from the command line. Recall that in Chapter 1 you learned about some basic meta characters, and you can use them as part of regular expressions to perform sophisticated search-and-replace operations involving text strings and text files.

The first part of this chapter shows you how to define regular expressions with digits and letters (uppercase as well as lowercase), and also how to use character classes in regular expressions.

The second portion discusses the Python `re` module, which contains several useful methods, such as the `re.match()` method for matching groups of characters, the `re.search()` method to perform searches in character strings, and the `findAll()` method to find all matching substrings. You will also learn how to use character classes (and how to group them) in regular expressions.

The final portion of this chapter contains an assortment of code samples, such as modifying text strings, splitting text strings with the `re.split()` method, and substituting text strings with the `re.sub()` method.

One additional point about this chapter: you will encounter many concepts and facets of regular expressions that might make you feel overwhelmed with the density of the material if you are a novice. However, practice and repetition will help you become comfortable with regular expressions.

WHAT ARE REGULAR EXPRESSIONS?

Regular expressions are referred to as REs, regexes, or regex patterns, and they enable you to specify expressions that can match specific "parts" of a string. For instance, you can define a regular expression to match a single character or digit, a telephone number, a zip code, or an email address. You can use meta characters and character classes (defined in the next section) as part of regular expressions to search text documents for specific patterns. As you learn more about REs, you will find other ways to use them as well.

The `re` module (added in Python 1.5) provides Perl-style regular expression patterns. Note that earlier versions of Python provided the `regex` module that was removed in Python 2.5. The `re` module provides an assortment of methods (discussed later in this chapter) for searching text strings or replacing text strings, which is similar to the basic search/and replace functionality that is available in word processors (but usually without regular expression support). The `re` module also provides methods for splitting text strings based on regular expressions.

Before delving into the methods in the `re` module, you need to learn about meta characters and character classes, which are the topic of the next section.

META CHARACTERS IN PYTHON

Python supports a set of meta characters, most of which are the same as the meta characters in other scripting languages such as Perl, as well as programming languages such as JavaScript and Java. The complete list of meta characters in Python is here:

```
. ^ $ * + ? { } [ ] \ | ( )
```

The meaning of the preceding meta characters is here:

- ? (matches 0 or 1): the expression a? matches the string a (but not ab)
- * (matches 0 or more): the expression a* matches the string aaa (but not baa)
- + (matches 1 or more): the expression a+ matches aaa (but not baa)
- ^ (beginning of line): the expression ^[a] matches the string abc (but not bc)
- $ (end of line): [c]$ matches the string abc (but not cab)
- . (a single dot): matches any character (except newline)

Sometimes you need to match the meta characters themselves rather than their representations, which can be done in two ways. The first way involves "escaping" their symbolic meaning with the backslash ("\") character. Thus, the sequences \?, *, \+, \^, \$, and \. represent the literal characters instead of their symbolic meaning. You can also "escape" the backslash character with the sequence "\\". If you have two consecutive backslash characters, you need an additional backslash for each of them, which means that "\\\\" is the "escaped" sequence for "\\".

The second way is to list the meta characters inside a pair of square brackets. For example, [+?] treats the two characters "+" and "?" as literal characters instead of meta characters. The second approach is obviously more compact and less prone to error. (It's easy to forget a backslash in a long sequence of meta characters.) As you might surmise, the methods in the re module support meta characters.

NOTE *When the "^" character is to the left (and outside) of a sequence in square brackets (such as ^[A-Z]), it "anchors" the regular expression to the beginning of a line, whereas when the "^" character is the first character inside a pair of square brackets, it negates the regular expression (such as [^A-Z]) inside the square brackets.*

The interpretation of the "^" character in a regular expression depends on its location in that regular expression, as shown here:

"^[a-z]" means any string that starts with any lowercase letter

"[^a-z]" means any string that does *not* contain any lowercase letters

"^[^a-z]" means any string that starts with anything *except* a lowercase letter

"^[a-z]$" means a single lowercase letter

"^[^a-z]$" means a single character (including digits) that is *not* a lowercase letter

As a quick preview of the re module that is discussed later in this chapter, the re.sub() method enables you to remove characters (including meta characters) from a text string. For example, the following code snippet removes all occurrences of the forward slash ("/") and the plus sign ("+") from the variable str:

```
>>> import re
>>> str  = "this string has a / and + in it"
>>> str2 = re.sub("[/]+","",str)
>>> print 'original:',str
original: this string has a / and + in it
>>> print 'replaced:',str2
replaced: this string has a  and + in it
```

We can easily remove occurrences of other meta characters in a text string by listing them inside square brackets, just as we have done in the preceding code snippet.

Listing 4.1 displays the contents of `RemoveMetaChars1.py` that illustrates how to remove other meta characters from a line of text.

LISTING 4.1: RemoveMetaChars1.py

```
import re

text1 = "meta characters ? and / and + and ."
text2 = re.sub("[/\.*?=+]+","",text1)

print 'text1:',text1
print 'text2:',text2
```

The regular expression in Listing 4.1 might seem daunting if you are new to regular expressions, but let's demystify its contents by examining the entire expression and then the meaning of each character. First of all, the term `[/\.*?=+]` matches a forward slash ("/"), a dot ("."), a question mark ("?"), an equals sign ("="), or a plus sign ("+"). Notice that the dot is preceded by a backslash character. Doing so "escapes" the meaning of the dot meta character (which matches any single non-white-space character) and treats it as a literal character.

Thus, the term `[/\.*?=+]+` means "one or more occurrences of any of the meta characters--treated as literal characters--inside the square brackets."

Consequently, the expression `re.sub("[/\.*?=+]+","",text1)` matches any occurrence of the previously listed meta characters and then replaces them with an empty string in the text string specified by the variable `text1`.

The output of Listing 4.1 is here:

```
text1: meta characters ? and / and + and .
text2: meta characters  and  and  and
```

Later in this chapter you will learn about other functions in the `re` module that enable you to modify and split text strings.

CHARACTER SETS IN PYTHON

A single digit in base 10 is a number between 0 and 9, inclusive, represented by the sequence `[0-9]`. Similarly, a lowercase letter can be any letter between a and z, represented by the sequence `[a-z]`. An uppercase letter can be any letter between A and Z, represented by the sequence `[A-Z]`.

The following code snippets illustrate how to specify sequences of digits and sequences of character strings using a shorthand notation that is much simpler than specifying every matching digit:

`[0-9]` matches a single digit
`[0-9][0-9]` matches 2 consecutive digits
`[0-9]{3}` matches 3 consecutive digits
`[0-9]{2,4}` matches 2, 3, or 4 consecutive digits

[0-9]{5,} matches 5 or more consecutive digits
^[0-9]+$ matches a string consisting solely of digits

You can define similar patterns using uppercase or lowercase letters in a way that is much simpler than explicitly specifying every lowercase letter or every uppercase letter:

[a-z][A-Z] matches a single lowercase letter that is followed by one uppercase letter

[a-zA-Z] matches any upper or lowercase letter

Working with "^" and "\"

The purpose of the "^" character depends on its context in a regular expression. For example, the following expression matches a text string that starts with a digit:

^[0-9].

However, the following expression matches a text string that does *not* start with a digit, because of the "^" meta character that is at the beginning of an expression in square brackets as well as the "^" meta character that is to the left (and outside) of the expression in square brackets (which you learned in a previous note):

^[^0-9]

Thus, the "^" character inside a pair of matching square brackets ("[]") negates the expression immediately to its right that is also located inside the square brackets.

Other examples involving the backslash meta character are here:

\.H.* matches the string .Hello
H.* matches the string Hello
H.*\. matches the string Hello.
.ell. matches the string Hello
.* matches the string Hello
\..* matches the string .Hello

CHARACTER CLASSES IN PYTHON

Character classes are convenient expressions that are shorter and simpler than their "bare" counterparts that you saw in the previous section. Some convenient character sequences that express patterns of digits and letters are:

\d matches a single digit
\w matches a single character (digit or letter)
\s matches a single white space (space, new line, return, or tab)
\b matches a boundary between a word and a nonword (such as meta-characters)

\n, \r, and \t represent a new line, a return, and a tab, respectively
\ "escapes" any character (except for \n, \r, and \t)

Based on the preceding definitions, \d+ matches one or more digits and
\w+ matches one or more characters; both of these are more compact expressions to use than character sets. In addition, we can reformulate the expressions in the previous section:

\d is the same as [0-9] and \D is the same as [^0-9]
\s is the same as [\t\n\r\f\v], and it matches any non-white-space
   character, whereas \S is the opposite (it matches [^ \t\n\r\f\v])
\w is the same as [a-zA-Z0-9_], and it matches any alphanumeric character, whereas \W is the opposite (it matches [^a-zA-Z0-9_])

Additional examples are here:

\d{2} is the same as [0-9][0-9]
\d{3} is the same as [0-9]{3}
\d{2,4} is the same as [0-9]{2,4}
\d{5,} is the same as [0-9]{5,}
^\d+$ is the same as ^[0-9]+$

The curly braces ("{ }") are called *quantifiers*, and they specify the number
(or range) of characters in the expressions that precede them.

MATCHING CHARACTER CLASSES WITH THE RE MODULE

The re module provides the following methods for matching and searching one or more occurrences of a regular expression in a text string:

match(): Determine if the RE matches at the *beginning* of the string
search(): Scan through a string, looking for *any* location where the RE
   matches
findall(): Find *all* substrings where the RE matches and return them
   as a list
finditer(): Find all substrings where the RE matches and return them
   as an iterator

NOTE *The* match() *function matches the pattern only to the start of string.*

The next section shows you how to use the match() function in the re
module.

USING THE RE.MATCH() METHOD

The re.match() method attempts to match an RE pattern in a text
string (with optional flags), and it has the following syntax:

```
re.match(pattern, string, flags=0)
```

The `pattern` parameter is the regular expression that you want to match in the `string` parameter. The `flags` parameter allows you to specify multiple flags using the bitwise OR operator that is represented by the pipe (" | ") symbol.

The `re.match` method returns a match object on success and `None` on failure. Use the `group(num)` or `groups()` function of the match object to get a matched expression:

`group(num=0)` Return an entire match (or a specific subgroup num)
`groups()` Return all matching subgroups in a tuple (or empty if there aren't any)

> **NOTE** *The re.match() method matches patterns only from the start of a text string, which is different from the re.search() method discussed later in this chapter.*

The following code block illustrates how to use the `group()` function in regular expressions:

```
>>> import re
>>> p = re.compile('(a(b)c)de')
>>> m = p.match('abcde')
>>> m.group(0)
'abcde'
>>> m.group(1)
'abc'
>>> m.group(2)
'b'
```

Notice that the higher the number inside the `group()` method, the deeper the matching nested expression, relative to the initial regular expression.

Listing 4.2 displays the contents of `MatchGroup1.py` that illustrates how to use the `group()` function to match an alphanumeric text string and an alphabetic string.

LISTING 4.2 MatchGroup1.py

```
import re

line1 = 'abcd123'
line2 = 'abcdefg'
mixed = re.compile(r"^[a-z0-9]{5,7}$")
line3 = mixed.match(line1)
line4 = mixed.match(line2)

print 'line1:',line1
print 'line2:',line2
print 'line3:',line3
print 'line4:',line4
print 'line5:',line4.group(0)

line6 = 'a1b2c3d4e5f6g7'
mixed2 = re.compile(r"^([a-z]+[0-9]+){5,7}$")
line7 = mixed2.match(line6)
```

```
print 'line6:',line6
print 'line7:',line7.group(0)
print 'line8:',line7.group(1)

line9 = 'abc123fgh4567'
mixed3 = re.compile(r"^([a-z]*[0-9]*){5,7}$")
line10 = mixed3.match(line9)
print 'line9:',line9
print 'line10:',line10.group(0)
```

The output of Listing 4.2 is here:

```
line1: abcd123
line2: abcdefg
line3: <_sre.SRE_Match object at 0x100485440>
line4: <_sre.SRE_Match object at 0x1004854a8>
line5: abcdefg
line6: a1b2c3d4e5f6g7
line7: a1b2c3d4e5f6g7
line8: g7
line9: abc123fgh4567
line10: abc123fgh4567
```

Notice that the variables line3 and line7 involve two similar but different regular expressions. The variable mixed specifies a sequence of lowercase letters followed by digits, where the length of the text string is also between 5 and 7. The string 'abcd123' satisfies all of these conditions.

On the other hand, mixed2 specifies a pattern consisting of one or more pairs, each containing one or more lowercase letters followed by one or more digits, where the length of the matching pairs is also between 5 and 7. In this case, the string 'abcd123' as well as the string 'a1b2c3d4e5f6g7' both satisfy these criteria.

The third regular expression, mixed3, allows for multiple matching pairs, where each pair consists of zero or more occurrences of lowercase letters and zero or more occurrences of a digit, and also that the number of such pairs is between 5 and 7. As you can see from the output, the regular expression in mixed3 matches lowercase letters and digits in any order.

In the preceding example, the regular expression specified a range for the length of the string, which involves a lower limit of 5 and an upper limit of 7. However, you can also specify a lower limit without an upper limit or an upper limit without a lower limit.

Listing 4.3 displays the contents of MatchGroup2.py that illustrates how to specify a regular expression and the group() function to match an alphanumeric text string and an alphabetic string.

LISTING 4.3 MatchGroup2.py

```
import re

alphas = re.compile(r"^[abcde]{5,}")
line1 = alphas.match("abcde").group(0)
line2 = alphas.match("edcba").group(0)
```

```
line3 = alphas.match("acbedf").group(0)
line4 = alphas.match("abcdefghi").group(0)
line5 = alphas.match("abcdefghi abcdef")

print 'line1:',line1
print 'line2:',line2
print 'line3:',line3
print 'line4:',line4
print 'line5:',line5
```

Listing 4.3 initializes the variable alphas as a regular expression that matches any string that starts with one of the letters a through e and consists of at least five characters. The next portion of Listing 4.3 initializes the four variables line1, line2, line3, and line4 by means of the alphas RE that is applied to various text strings. These four variables are set to the first matching group by means of the expression group(0).

The output of Listing 4.3 is here:

```
line1: abcde
line2: edcba
line3: acbed
line4: abcde
line5: <_sre.SRE_Match object at 0x1004854a8>
```

Listing 4.4 displays the contents of MatchGroup3.py that illustrates how to use a regular expression with the group() function to match words in a text string.

LISTING 4.4 MatchGroup3.py

```
import re

line = "Giraffes are taller than elephants";

matchObj = re.match( r'(.*) are(\.*)', line, re.M|re.I)

if matchObj:
    print "matchObj.group()   : ", matchObj.group()
    print "matchObj.group(1) : ", matchObj.group(1)
    print "matchObj.group(2) : ", matchObj.group(2)
else:
    print "matchObj does not match line:", line
```

The output of Listing 4.4 is here:

```
matchObj.group()   :  Giraffes are
matchObj.group(1) :  Giraffes
matchObj.group(2) :
```

Listing 4.4 contains a pair of delimiters separated by a pipe symbol. The first delimiter is re.M, for "multi-line" in order to match more than a single line (although this example contains only a single line of text), and the second delimiter is re.I, for "ignore case" (during the pattern-matching operation).

The re.match() method supports additional delimiters, as discussed in the next section.

OPTIONS FOR THE RE.MATCH() METHOD

The match() method supports various optional modifiers that affect the type of matching that will be performed. As you saw in the previous example, you can also specify multiple modifiers separated by the OR ("|") symbol. Additional modifiers that are available for RE are shown here:

re.I: Perform case-insensitive matches (see previous section)

re.L: Interpret words according to the current locale

re.M: Make $ match the end of a line and makes ^ match the start of any line

re.S: Make a period (".") match any character (including a newline)

re.U: Interpret letters according to the Unicode character set

Experiment with these modifiers by writing Python code that uses them in conjunction with different text strings.

MATCHING CHARACTER CLASSES WITH THE RE.SEARCH() METHOD

As you saw earlier in this chapter, the re.match() method matches only from the beginning of a string, whereas the re.search() method can successfully match a substring anywhere in a text string.

The re.search() method takes two arguments: a regular expression pattern and a string. Then it searches for the specified pattern in the given string. The search() method returns a match object (if the search was successful) or None.

As a simple example, the following code searches for the pattern tasty followed by a five-letter word:

```
import re

str = 'I want a tasty pizza'
match = re.search(r'tasty \w\w\w\w\w', str)

if match:
  ## 'found tasty pizza'
  print 'found', match.group()
else:
  print 'Nothing tasty here'
```

The output of the preceding code block is here:

```
found tasty pizza
```

The following code block further illustrates the difference between the `re.match()` method and the `re.search()` method:

```
>>> import re
>>> print re.search('this', 'this is the one').span()
(0, 4)
>>>
>>> print re.search('the', 'this is the one').span()
(8, 11)
>>> print re.match('this', 'this is the one').span()
(0, 4)
>>> print re.match('the', 'this is the one').span()
Traceback (most recent call last):
  File "<stdin>", line 1, in <module>
AttributeError: 'NoneType' object has no attribute 'span'
```

MATCHING CHARACTER CLASSES WITH THE `FINDALL()` METHOD

Listing 4.5 displays the contents of the Python script `RegEx1.py` that illustrates how to define simple character classes that match various text strings.

LISTING 4.5: RegEx1.py

```
import re

str1 = "123456"
matches1 = re.findall("(\d+)", str1)
print 'matches1:',matches1

str1 = "123456"
matches1 = re.findall("(\d\d\d)", str1)
print 'matches1:',matches1

str1 = "123456"
matches1 = re.findall("(\d\d)", str1)
print 'matches1:',matches1

print
str2 = "1a2b3c456"
matches2 = re.findall("(\d)", str2)
print 'matches2:',matches2

print
str2 = "1a2b3c456"
matches2 = re.findall("\d", str2)
print 'matches2:',matches2

print
str3 = "1a2b3c456"
matches3 = re.findall("(\w)", str3)
print 'matches3:',matches3
```

Listing 4.5 contains simple regular expressions (which you have seen already) for matching digits in the variables `str1` and `str2`. The final code block of Listing 4.5 matches every character in the string `str3`, effectively "splitting" `str3` into a list in which each element consists of one character.

The output from Listing 4.5 is here; notice the blank lines after the first three output lines:

```
matches1: ['123456']
matches1: ['123', '456']
matches1: ['12', '34', '56']

matches2: ['1', '2', '3', '4', '5', '6']

matches2: ['1', '2', '3', '4', '5', '6']

matches3: ['1', 'a', '2', 'b', '3', 'c', '4', '5', '6']
```

Finding Capitalized Words in a String

Listing 4.6 displays the contents of the Python script `FindCapitalized.py` that illustrates how to define simple character classes that match various text strings.

LISTING 4.6: *FindCapitalized.py*

```
import re

str = "This Sentence contains Capitalized words"
caps = re.findall(r'[A-Z][\w\.-]+', str)

print 'str: ',str
print 'caps:',caps
```

Listing 4.6 initializes the string variable `str` and the RE `caps` that matches any word that starts with a capital letter because the first portion of `caps` is the pattern `[A-Z]` that matches any capital letter between `A` and `Z`, inclusive.

The output of Listing 4.6 is here:

```
str:  This Sentence contains Capitalized words
caps: ['This', 'Sentence', 'Capitalized']
```

ADDITIONAL MATCHING FUNCTION FOR REGULAR EXPRESSIONS

After invoking any of the methods `match()`, `search()`, `findAll()`, or `finditer()`, you can invoke additional methods on the "matching object." An example of this functionality using the `match()` method is here:

```
import re

p1 = re.compile('[a-z]+')
m1 = p1.match("hello")
```

In the preceding code block, the p1 object represents the compiled regular expression for one or more lowercase letters and the "matching object" m1 supports the following methods:

group() : Return the string matched by the RE
start() : Return the starting position of the match
end() : Return the ending position of the match
span() Return a tuple containing the (start, end) positions of the match

As a further illustration, Listing 4.7 displays the contents of Search-Function1.py that illustrates how to use the search() method and the group() method.

LISTING 4.7 SearchFunction1.py

```
import re

line = "Giraffes are taller than elephants";

searchObj = re.search( r'(.*) are(\.*)', line, re.M|re.I)

if searchObj:
   print "searchObj.group()  : ", searchObj.group()
   print "searchObj.group(1) : ", searchObj.group(1)
   print "searchObj.group(2) : ", searchObj.group(2)
else:
   print "searchObj does not match line:", line
```

Listing 4.7 contains the variable line that represents a text string, and the variable searchObj is an RE involving the search() method and pair of pipe-delimited modifiers (discussed in more detail in the next section). If searchObj is not null, the if/else conditional code in Listing 4.7 displays the contents of the three groups resulting from the successful match with the contents of the variable line.

The output from Listing 4.7 is here:

```
searchObj.group()  :  Giraffes are
searchObj.group(1) :  Giraffes
searchObj.group(2) :
```

GROUPING CHARACTER CLASSES IN REGULAR EXPRESSIONS

In addition to the character classes that you have seen earlier in this chapter, you can specify sub-expressions of character classes.

Listing 4.8 displays the contents of Grouping1.py that illustrates how to use the search() method.

LISTING 4.8: Grouping1.py

```
import re

p1 = re.compile('(ab)*')
```

```
print 'match1:',p1.match('abababababab').group()
print 'span1: ',p1.match('abababababab').span()

p2 = re.compile('(a)b')
m2 = p2.match('ab')
print 'match2:',m2.group(0)
print 'match3:',m2.group(1)
```

Listing 4.8 starts by defining the RE p1 that matches zero or more occurrences of the string ab. The first print statement displays the result of using the match() function of p1 (followed by the group() function) against a string, and the result is a string. This illustrates the use of "method chaining," which eliminates the need for an intermediate object (as shown in the second code block). The second print statement displays the result of using the match() function of p1, followed by applying the span() function, against a string. In this case the result is a numeric range (see output below).

The second part of Listing 4.8 defines the RE p2 that matches an optional letter a followed by the letter b. The variable m2 invokes the match method on p2 using the string ab. The third print statement displays the result of invoking group(0) on m2, and the fourth print statement displays the result of involving group(1) on m2. Both results are substrings of the input string ab. Recall that group(0) returns the highest-level match that occurred and group(1) returns a more "specific" match that occurred, such as one that involves the parentheses in the definition of p2. The higher the value of the integer in the expression group(n), the more specific the match.

The output from Listing 4.8 is here:

```
match1: abababababab
span1:  (0, 10)
match2: ab
match3: a
```

USING CHARACTER CLASSES IN REGULAR EXPRESSIONS

This section contains some examples that illustrate how to use character classes to match various strings and also how to use delimiters to split a text string. For example, one common date string involves a date format of the form MM/DD/YY. Another common scenario involves records with a delimiter that separates multiple fields. Usually such records contain one delimiter, but as you will see, Python makes it very easy to split records using multiple delimiters.

Matching Strings with Multiple Consecutive Digits

Listing 4.9 displays the contents of the Python script MatchPatterns1. py that illustrates how to define simple regular expressions to split the contents of a text string based on the occurrence of one or more consecutive digits.

Although the regular expressions \d+/\d+/\d+ and \d\d/\d\d/\d\d\d\d both match the string 08/13/2014, the first regular expression matches more patterns than the second regular expression, which is an "exact match" with respect to the number of matching digits that are allowed.

LISTING 4.9 MatchPatterns1.py

```python
import re

date1 = '02/28/2013'
date2 = 'February 28, 2013'

# Simple matching: \d+ means match one or more digits
if re.match(r'\d+/\d+/\d+', date1):
  print('date1 matches this pattern')
else:
  print('date1 does not match this pattern')

if re.match(r'\d+/\d+/\d+', date2):
  print('date2 matches this pattern')
else:
  print('date2 does not match this pattern')
```

The output from launching Listing 4.9 is here:

```
date1 matches this pattern
date2 does not match this pattern
```

Reversing Words in Strings

Listing 4.10 displays the contents of the Python script ReverseWords1.py that illustrates how to reverse a pair of words in a string.

LISTING 4.10 ReverseWords1.py

```python
import re

str1 = 'one two'
match = re.search('([\w.-]+) ([\w.-]+)', str1)

str2 = match.group(2) + ' ' + match.group(1)
print 'str1:',str1
print 'str2:',str2
```

The output from Listing 4.10 is here:

```
str1: one two
str2: two one
```

Now that you understand how to define regular expressions for digits and letters, let's look at some more sophisticated regular expressions. For example, the following expression matches a string that is any combination of digits, uppercase letters, and lowercase letters (i.e., no special characters):

```
^[a-zA-Z0-9]$
```

Here is the same expression rewritten using character classes:

```
^[\w\W\d]$
```

MODIFYING TEXT STRINGS WITH THE RE MODULE

The Python re module contains several methods for modifying strings. The split() method uses a regular expression to "split" a string into a list. The sub() method finds all substrings where the regular expression matches and then replaces them with a different string. The subn() performs the same functionality as sub() and also returns the new string and the number of replacements. The following subsections contains examples that illustrate how to use the functions split(), sub(), and subn() in regular expressions.

SPLITTING TEXT STRINGS WITH THE RE.SPLIT() METHOD

Listing 4.11 displays the contents of the Python script RegEx2.py that illustrates how to define simple regular expressions to split the contents of a text string.

LISTING 4.11 RegEx2.py

```
import re

line1 = "abc def"
result1 = re.split(r'[\s]', line1)
print 'result1:',result1

line2 = "abc1,abc2:abc3;abc4"
result2 = re.split(r'[,:;]', line2)
print 'result2:',result2

line3 = "abc1,abc2:abc3;abc4 123 456"
result3 = re.split(r'[,:;\s]', line3)
print 'result3:',result3
```

Listing 4.11 contains three blocks of code, each of which uses the split() method in the re module to tokenize three different strings. The first regular expression specifies a white space, the second regular expression specifies three punctuation characters, and the third regular expression specifies the combination of the first two regular expressions.

The output of Listing 4.11 is here:

```
result1: ['abc', 'def']
result2: ['abc1', 'abc2', 'abc3', 'abc4']
result3: ['abc1', 'abc2', 'abc3', 'abc4', '123', '456']
```

SPLITTING TEXT STRINGS USING DIGITS AND DELIMITERS

Listing 4.12 displays the contents of SplitCharClass1.py that illustrates how to use a regular expression consisting of a character class, the " . " character, and a white space to split the contents of two text strings.

LISTING 4.12 SplitCharClass1.py

```
import re

line1 = '1. Section one 2. Section two 3. Section three'
line2 = '11. Section eleven 12. Section twelve 13. Section
thirteen'

print re.split(r'\d+\. ', line1)
print re.split(r'\d+\. ', line2)
```

Listing 4.12 contains two text strings that can be split using the same regular expression "\d+\. ". Note that if you use the expression "\d\. ", only the first text string will split correctly.

The output of Listing 4.12 is here:

```
['', 'Section one ', 'Section two ', 'Section three']
['', 'Section eleven ', 'Section twelve ', 'Section thirteen']
```

SUBSTITUTING TEXT STRINGS WITH THE RE.SUB() METHOD

Earlier in this chapter, you saw a preview of using the sub() method to remove all the meta characters in a text string. The following code block illustrates how to use the re.sub() method to substitute alphabetic characters in a text string.

```
>>> import re
>>> p = re.compile( '(one|two|three)')
>>> p.sub( 'some', 'one book two books three books')
'some book some books some books'
>>>
>>> p.sub( 'some', 'one book two books three books', count=1)
'some book two books three books'
```

The following code block uses the re.sub() method to insert a line feed after each alphabetic character in a text string:

```
>>> line = 'abcde'
>>> line2 = re.sub('', '\n', line)
>>> print 'line2:',line2
line2:
a
b
c
d
e
```

MATCHING THE BEGINNING AND THE END OF TEXT STRINGS

Listing 4.13 displays the contents of the Python script RegEx3.py that illustrates how to find substrings using the startswith() function and the endswith() function.

LISTING 4.13: RegEx3.py

```
import re

line2 = "abc1,Abc2:def3;Def4"
result2 = re.split(r'[,:;]', line2)

for w in result2:
  if(w.startswith('Abc')):
    print 'Word starts with Abc:',w
  elif(w.endswith('4')):
    print 'Word ends with 4:',w
  else:
    print 'Word:',w
```

Listing 4.13 starts by initializing the string line2 (with punctuation characters as word delimiters) and the RE result2 that uses the split() function with a comma, colon, and semicolon as "split delimiters" to tokenize the string variable line2.

The output of Listing 4.13 is here:

```
Word: abc1
Word starts with Abc: Abc2
Word: def3
Word ends with 4: Def4
```

Listing 4.14 displays the contents of the Python script MatchLines1.py that illustrates how to find substrings using character classes.

LISTING 4.14 MatchLines1.py

```
import re

line1 = "abcdef"
line2 = "123,abc1,abc2,abc3"
line3 = "abc1,abc2,123,456f"

if re.match("^[A-Za-z]*$", line1):
  print 'line1 contains only letters:',line1

# better than the preceding snippet:
line1[:-1].isalpha()
  print 'line1 contains only letters:',line1

if re.match("^[\w]*$", line1):
  print 'line1 contains only letters:',line1

if re.match(r"^[^\W\d_]+$", line1, re.LOCALE):
  print 'line1 contains only letters:',line1
print

if re.match("^[0-9][0-9][0-9]", line2):
  print 'line2 starts with 3 digits:',line2

if re.match("^\d\d\d", line2):
  print 'line2 starts with 3 digits:',line2
```

```
print

if re.match(".*[0-9][0-9][0-9][a-z]$", line3):
  print 'line3 ends with 3 digits and 1 char:',line3

if re.match(".*[a-z]$", line3):
  print 'line3 ends with 1 char:',line3
```

Listing 4.14 starts by initializing the three string variables line1, line2, and line3. The first RE contains an expression that matches any line containing uppercase or lowercase letters or both:

```
if re.match("^[A-Za-z]*$", line1):
```

The following two snippets also test for the same thing:

```
line1[:-1].isalpha()
```

The preceding snippet starts from the rightmost position of the string and checks if each character is alphabetic. The next snippet checks if line1 can be tokenized into words (which contain only alphabetic characters):

```
if re.match("^[\w]*$", line1):
```

The next portion of Listing 4.14 checks if a string contains three consecutive digits:

```
if re.match("^[0-9][0-9][0-9]", line2):
  print 'line2 starts with 3 digits:',line2

if re.match("^\d\d\d", line2):
```

The first snippet uses the pattern [0-9] to match a digit, whereas the second snippet uses the expression \d to match a digit.

The output of Listing 4.14 is here:

```
line1 contains only letters: abcdef
line1 contains only letters: abcdef
line1 contains only letters: abcdef
line1 contains only letters: abcdef

line2 starts with 3 digits: 123,abc1,abc2,abc3
line2 starts with 3 digits: 123,abc1,abc2,abc3
```

COMPILATION FLAGS

Compilation flags modify the manner in which regular expressions work. Flags are available in the re module as a long name (such as IGNORECASE) and as a short, one-letter form (such as I). The short form is the same as that for the flags in pattern modifiers in Perl. You can specify multiple flags by using the "|" symbol. For example, re.I | re.M sets both the I and M flags.

You can check the online Python documentation regarding all the available compilation flags in Python.

COMPOUND REGULAR EXPRESSIONS

Listing 4.15 displays the contents of `MatchMixedCase1.py` that illustrates how to use the pipe ("|") symbol to specify two regular expressions in the same `match()` function.

LISTING 4.15 MatchMixedCase1.py

```
import re

line1 = "This is a line"
line2 = "That is a line"

if re.match("^[Tt]his", line1):
  print 'line1 starts with This or this:'
  print line1
else:
  print 'no match'

if re.match("^This|That", line2):
  print 'line2 starts with This or That:'
  print line2
else:
  print 'no match'
```

Listing 4.15 starts with two string variables `line1` and `line2`, followed by an `if/else` conditional code block that checks if `line1` starts with the RE `[Tt]his`, which matches the string `This` as well as the string `this`.

The second conditional code block checks if `line2` starts with the string `This` or the string `That`. Notice the "^" meta character, which in this context anchors the RE to the beginning of the string.

The output of Listing 4.15 is here:

```
line1 starts with This or this:
This is a line
line2 starts with This or That:
That is a line
```

COUNTING CHARACTER TYPES IN A STRING

You can use a regular expression to check whether a character is a digit, a letter, or some other type of character. Listing 4.16 displays the contents of `CountDigitsAndChars.py` that performs this task.

LISTING 4.16 CountDigitsAndChars.py

```
import re

charCount  = 0
digitCount = 0
```

```
otherCount = 0

line1 = "A line with numbers: 12 345"

for ch in line1:
   if(re.match(r'\d', ch)):
      digitCount = digitCount + 1
   elif(re.match(r'\w', ch)):
      charCount = charCount + 1
   else:
      otherCount = otherCount + 1

print 'charcount:',charCount
print 'digitcount:',digitCount
print 'othercount:',otherCount
```

Listing 4.16 initializes three numeric counter-related variables, followed by the string variable `line1`. The next part of Listing 4.16 contains a `for` loop that processes each character in the string `line1`. The body of the `for` loop contains a conditional code block that checks whether the current character is a digit, a letter, or some other non-alphanumeric character. Each time there is a successful match, the corresponding `count-related` variable is incremented.

The output of Listing 4.16 is here:

```
charcount: 16
digitcount: 5
othercount: 6
```

REGULAR EXPRESSIONS AND GROUPING

You can also "group" subexpressions and even refer to them symbolically. For example, the following expression matches zero or one occurrence of three consecutive letters or digits:

```
^([a-zA-Z0-9]{3,3})?
```

The following expression matches a telephone number (such as 650-555-1212) in the USA:

```
^\d{3,3}[-]\d{3,3}[-]\d{4,4}
```

The following expression matches a zip code (such as `67827` or `94343-4005`) in the USA:

```
^\d{5,5}([-]\d{4,4})?
```

The following code block partially matches an email address:

```
str = 'john.doe@google.com'
   match = re.search(r'\w+@\w+', str)
   if match:
     print match.group()   ## 'doe@google'
```

Exercise: Use the preceding code block as a starting point to define a regular expression for email addresses.

SIMPLE STRING MATCHES

Listing 4.17 displays the contents of the Python script RegEx4.py that illustrates how to define regular expressions that match various text strings.

LISTING 4.17 RegEx4.py

```
import re

searchString = "Testing pattern matches"

expr1 = re.compile( r"Test" )
expr2 = re.compile( r"^Test" )
expr3 = re.compile( r"Test$" )
expr4 = re.compile( r"\b\w*es\b" )
expr5 = re.compile( r"t[aeiou]", re.I )

if expr1.search( searchString ):
    print '"Test" was found.'

if expr2.match( searchString ):
    print '"Test" was found at the beginning of the line.'

if expr3.match( searchString ):
    print '"Test" was found at the end of the line.'

result = expr4.findall( searchString )

if result:
    print 'There are %d words(s) ending in "es":' % \
        ( len( result ) ),

    for item in result:
        print " " + item,

print

result = expr5.findall( searchString )
if result:
    print 'The letter t, followed by a vowel, occurs %d times:' % \
        ( len( result ) ),

    for item in result:
        print " "+item,

print
```

Listing 4.17 starts with the variable searchString that specifies a text string, followed by the REs expr1, expr2, and expr3. The RE expr1 matches the string Test that occurs anywhere in searchString, whereas expr2 matches Test if it occurs at the beginning of searchString and expr3 matches `Test` if it occurs at the end of `searchString`. The RE expr4 matches words that end in the letters `es`, and the RE expr5 matches the letter `t` followed by a vowel.

The output of Listing 4.17 is here:

```
"Test" was found.
"Test" was found at the beginning of the line.
There are 1 words(s) ending in "es":  matches
The letter t, followed by a vowel, occurs 3 times:  Te  ti  te
```

ADDITIONAL TOPICS FOR REGULAR EXPRESSIONS

In addition to the Python-based search/replace functionality that you have seen in this chapter, you can also perform a greedy search and substitution. Perform an Internet search to learn what these features are and how to use them in Python code.

SUMMARY

This chapter showed you how to create various types of regular expressions. First you learned how to define primitive regular expressions using sequences of digits, lowercase letters, and uppercase letters. Next you learned how to use character classes, which are more convenient, simpler expressions that can perform the same functionality. You also learned how to use the Python `re` library to compile regular expressions and then use them to see if they match substrings of text strings.

EXERCISES

Exercise 1: Given a text string, find the list of words (if any) that start or end with a vowel, and treat upper- and lowercase vowels as distinct letters. Display this list of words in alphabetical order and also in descending order based their frequency.

Exercise 2: Given a text string, find the list of words (if any) that contain lowercase vowels or digits or both but no uppercase letters. Display this list of words in alphabetical order and also in descending order based their frequency.

Exercise 3: There is a spelling rule in English specifying "'i' is before 'e,' except after 'c,'" (and sometimes after 's') which means that "receive" is correct but "recieve" is incorrect. Write a Python script that checks for incorrectly spelled words in a text string.

Exercise 4: Subject pronouns cannot follow a preposition in the English language. Thus, "between you and me" and "for you and me" are correct, whereas "between you and I" and "for you and I" are incorrect. Write a Python script that checks for incorrect grammar in a text string, and search for the prepositions "between," "for," and "with." In addition, search for the subject pronouns "I," "you," "he," and "she." Modify and display the text with the correct grammar.

Exercise 5: Find the words in a text string whose length is at most 4 and then print all the substrings of those characters. For example, if a text string contains the word "text," print the strings "t," "te," "tex," and "text."

CHAPTER 5

FILES AND STREAMS

This chapter shows you how to work with files and how to perform various file-related operations in Python.

The first part of this chapter discusses file modes, file permissions, and file descriptors. The second part of this chapter shows you how to create a file, how to read data from a file, and how to write data to a file. The third part of this chapter shows you how to perform various input and output operations and also how to simulate relational data with CSV files.

FILE-RELATED MODULES IN PYTHON

Python provides modules with functions that enable you to manipulate text files and binary files on a file system. Python allows you to create files, update their contents, and also delete files. For example, you can open a text file in which each row contains customer-related data, such as a purchase order or line item. You can specify a delimiter to split each row into its constituent parts (such as first name, last name, and so forth) and then use Python functions to compute totals and sort lines by an input field (such as last name). In addition, you can use conditional logic, loops, and regular expressions to assist you in processing the data in the associated text files.

Python provides several libraries for working with the file system, such as os, os.path, and shutil. The os and os.path-related modules include functions for accessing the file system, whereas the shutil module enables you to copy files. The os module contains the following methods (among others):

os.listdir(dir): Lists filenames in a directory
os.path.join(dir, filename): Returns the path of a filename
os.path.abspath(path): Returns an absolute path
os.path.dirname(path): Returns the directory of a file

os.path.basename(path): Returns the filename

os.path.exists(path): Returns "true" if path exists

os.mkdir(dir_path): Creates a directory

os.makedirs(dir_path): Creates multiple directories

shutil.copy(source-path, dest-path): Copies a file to a destination

Later in this chapter you will see examples that illustrate how to use some of these Python methods.

FILE MODES

Python enables you to open files in read-only mode, write-only mode, and also read-write mode by specifying the flags "r", "w", and "rw", respectively. You can open a text file by specifying the option "t", so the preceding modes become "rt", "wt", and "rwt". Later in the chapter you will learn how to perform these file-related operations and also how to create a file and delete a file.

The example in this section shows you how to determine various attributes of a file, as well as its file permissions (read, write, and execute). Listing 5.1 displays the contents of FileStat.py that determines the file-related permissions of a file.

LISTING 5.1 FileStat.py

```
import os
import stat

filename = "DirList1.py"
stat = os.stat(filename)

print 'stat:',stat

readPerm  = os.access(filename, os.R_OK)
writePerm = os.access(filename, os.W_OK)
execPerm  = os.access(filename, os.X_OK)

print 'readPerm:',readPerm
print 'writePerm:',writePerm
print 'execPerm:',execPerm
```

Listing 5.1 starts by initializing the variable filename and then uses the os.stat() method to obtain file-related information. The next part of Listing 5.1 determines if the specified file has read, write, or execute permissions. The output from Listing 5.1 is here:

```
stat: posix.stat_result(st_mode=33188, st_ino=38440377,
st_dev=16777218L, st_nlink=1, st_uid=501, st_gid=20, st_size=75,
st_atime=1375647321, st_mtime=1375309857, st_ctime=1375309857)
readPerm: True
writePerm: True
execPerm: False
```

CHANGING FILE PERMISSIONS

You can change the permissions of a file via the chmod() function, as shown in the following code:

```
import os

filename = "DirList3.py"
mode = 0444

# method #1:
os.chmod(filename, mode)

# method #2:
#os.chmod(filename, stat.S_IRUSR|stat.S_IRGRP|stat.S_IROTH)
```

The preceding code contains three constants in the stat module:

S_IRUSR is 0400, S_IRGRP is 040, and S_IROTH is 4. When you perform a bitwise OR operation, the result is 0444.

Open a command shell and type the command ls -l DirList3.py, and you will see the new permissions for the file.

WORKING WITH FILE DESCRIPTORS

You can redirect standard out and standard error from the command line as follows:

```
python MyScript.py 1>stdout 2>stderr
```

You can redirect stderr and stdout to the same file as follows:

```
python MyScript.py 2>&1 1>stdout
```

You can redirect stderr to nowhere with this code snippet:

```
python MyScript.py 1>stdout 2>/dev/null
```

The equivalent Python code block for redirecting standard out is here:

```
import os
f = open(os.devnull, 'w')
sys.stdout = f
```

CREATING AND DELETING TEXT FILES

You can create a file with the "w" option, as shown here:

```
>>> f.closed
>>>    with open('somefile', 'wt') as f:
...    f.write('Hello Python\n')
...
```

The with statement (introduced in Python 2.5) in the preceding code fragment automatically closes the file after the associated code block has completed execution, which makes for cleaner and more compact code.

You can check if a file exists with this code block:

```
import os

myfile="abc"

if os.path.exists(myfile):
  print 'File',myfile,'already exists'
else:
  print 'File',myfile,'does not exist'
```

If you want to delete a file, first check if it exists and then remove the file, as shown in Listing 5.2 below that displays the contents of DeleteFile1.py.

LISTING 5.2: DeleteFile1.py

```
import os

myfile="abc"

if os.path.exists(myfile):
  print 'File',myfile,'exists: deleting it'
  os.remove(myfile)
else:
  print 'File',myfile,'does not exist'
```

You can remove an empty directory with this command:

```
os.rmdir()
```

You can delete a directory and all its contents with this code:

```
import shutil
shutil.rmtree()
```

The shutil module contains other useful functions that enable you to copy a file, copy a directory tree, and so forth.

WORKING WITH PATHNAMES

Listing 5.3 displays the contents of Pathnames1.py that illustrates how to obtain various components of a fully qualified filename.

LISTING 5.3 Pathnames1.py

```
import os

#specify the full path to a file
file = '/Users/ocampesato/myfile.csv'

if os.path.exists(file):
  print 'File',file,'exists'
```

```
else:
  print 'File',file,'does not exist'

# Get the last component of the file
print 'basename:', os.path.basename(file)
#'myfile.csv'

# Get the directory name
print 'directory:', os.path.dirname(file)
#'/Users/ocampesato'

# Join path components together
print 'join:',os.path.join('tmp', 'myfile', os.path.
basename(file))
#'/tmp/myfile/data.csv'

# Expand the user's home directory
file = '~/myfile.csv'
print 'expanded:',file

print 'expand user:',os.path.expanduser(file)
#'/Users/ocampesato/myfile.csv'

# Split the file extension
file = '/Users/ocampesato/myfile.csv'
print 'split:', os.path.splitext(file)
#('~/data', '.csv')
```

Listing 5.3 starts by specifying the file myfile.csv in the home directory and then uses intuitively named Python functions to extract information such as the basename and dirname of the file.

The output from Listing 5.3 is here:

```
File /Users/ocampesato/myfile.csv exists
basename: myfile.csv
directory: /Users/ocampesato
join: tmp/myfile/myfile.csv
expanded: ~/myfile.csv
expand user: /Users/ocampesato/myfile.csv
split: ('/Users/ocampesato/myfile', '.csv')
```

REDIRECTING STANDOUT OUTPUT TO A FILE

The following code snippet redirects the output of the print command to a file:

```
import sys

filename = 'outputfile'
sys.stdout = open(filename, 'w')
print 'test'
```

The preceding code opens the file outputfile in write mode and then prints the string "test" in the file. Alternatively, you can create a Python script Redirect1.py with the following line:

```
print 'test'
```

Redirect the output with this command:

```
python Redirect1.py > outputfile
```

READING DATA FROM A FILE

The following command opens a file in "read" mode:

```
f = open('sample.txt', 'r')
```

The following command reads two consecutive lines from a file:

```
>>> f.readline()
>>> f.readline()
```

The following command reads all lines in a file (provided that it is executed before any other commands that read from a file):

```
>>> f.readlines()
```

The following code snippet reads (at most) size characters from a file:

```
>>> f.read(size)
```

Counting Lines and Characters in a File

There are several ways to read the contents of a text file.
The following code snippet shows you how to read the contents of a text file:

```
f = open('sample.txt', 'rt')
data = f.read()
print data
f.close()
```

The following code block illustrates one of the shortest ways to open a text file and display its contents:

```
with open('sample.txt', 'rt') as f: data = f.read()
print data
```

A slightly longer technique that displays the line number of each line in a text file is here:

```
count = 1
with open('sample.txt', 'rt') as f:
  for line in f:
    print "Line",count,":",line
    count = count + 1
```

Listing 5.4 displays the contents of CountChars.py that illustrates how read the entire contents of a file into a variable, print the lines, and also print the total number of characters.

LISTING 5.4 CountChars.py

```
# specify a filename
filename = 'sample.txt'

# Open file in read-only mode
file = open(filename, 'rt')

# read entire contents of the file
str = file.read()

# display the contents of the file
print 'file contents:',str
print 'character count:',len(str)
```

Listing 5.4 opens the text file sample.txt in "read" mode, initializes the variable str with the contents of sample.txt, and then prints the value of the variable str.

One interesting way to count the number of lines in a file is here:

```
lineCount = sum(1 for line in open(filename))
```

Yet another way to determine the line count is here:

```
lines = file.read().split("\n")
print "line count:",len(lines)
```

DISPLAYING THE CONTENTS OF A TEXT FILE IN REVERSE

In Chapter 2, you learned how to print the items in a list in reverse, and Listing 5.5 displays the contents of FileBackward.py that shows you how to print the contents of a file in reverse.

LISTING 5.5: FileBackward.py

```
# Print a file backwards
f = open('somefile')
for line in reversed(list(f)):
  print(line, end='')
```

Keep in mind that converting an iterable into a list as shown could consume a lot of memory if it's large.

WRITING DATA TO A TEXT FILE

The following code snippet shows you how to write a text string to a file using the with option:

```
text1 = 'a string of text'
with open('sample2.txt', 'wt') as f: f.write(text1)
```

Listing 5.6 displays the contents of WriteMode.py that illustrates how to open a file in write mode.

LISTING 5.6 WriteMode.py

```
# specify a filename
filename = 'sample2.txt'

# Open file in write-only mode
file = open(filename, 'w')

# define a text string
str = "put me in a file"

# write the string to the file
file.write(str)
```

Note that the `write` operation in Listing 5.6 is destructive: the contents of the variable `str` overwrite the current contents of the file `sample2.txt`. If you want to append data to a file, you must open the file in append mode, as shown here:

```
file = open(filename, 'at')
```

The following command writes the contents of the variable `str` to a file and displays the number of characters that were written to the file:

```
>>> f.write(str)
15
```

You can also append a blank line after each line of text, as shown here:

```
>>> f.write('This is a test\n')
15
```

Non-strings must be converted to a string before writing them to a file:

```
>>> value = ('the answer', 42)
>>> s = str(value)
>>> f.write(s)
18
```

You can append text to a file by using the "`at`" mode, as shown here:

```
text2 = 'a string of text2'
with open('sample.txt', 'at') as f: f.write(text2)
```

Working with Binary Files

The following code snippet reads the contents of a binary file:

```
with open('binaryfile.bin', 'rb') as f: data = f.read()
```

The following code snippet writes to a binary file:

```
with open('binaryfile.bin', 'wb') as f: f.write(b'Hello Python')
```

CREATING A TEMPORARY TEXT FILE

Listing 5.7 displays the contents of `CreateTemporaryFile.py` that illustrates how to create a temporary file in Python.

LISTING 5.7 CreateTemporaryFile.py
```
import os, tempfile

text = b"hello python"

def temp_opener(name, flag, mode=0o777):
    return os.open(name, flag | os.O_TEMPORARY, mode)

with tempfile.NamedTemporaryFile() as f:
    f.write(text)
    f.flush()
    with open(f.name, "rb", opener=temp_opener) as f:
        assert f.read() == text

assert not os.path.exists(f.name)
```

Listing 5.7 starts by defining the contents of the binary string `text`, followed by the function `temp_opener` that opens a file whose name is `name`, using the OR value of `flag` and `os.O_TEMPORARY`.

The next portion of Listing 5.7 writes the contents of the variable `text` to the temporary file and then flushes its contents to complete the `write` operation. The final portion of Listing 5.7 then opens the file `f.name` and compares its contents with the contents of the temporary file.

FINDING AND SETTING THE FILE LOCATION

The following command specifies the current position in a file (measured in bytes from the beginning of the file) of a previously created file object `f`:

```
f.tell()
```

The following command changes the position of a file object:

```
f.seek(offset, from_what)
```

The actual position is calculated by adding the value of `offset` to a reference point that is determined by the value of the `from_what` argument. Specifically, a value of 0 for `from_what` (which is the default value) measures from the beginning of the file; a value of 1 uses the current file position, and a value of 2 uses the end of the file as the reference point. If you omit the variable `from_what`, the default is to start from the beginning of the file as the reference point.

```
>>> f = open('workfile', 'rb+')
>>> f.write(b'0123456789abcdef')
```

```
16
# Go to the fourth byte in the file
>>> f.seek(4)
4
# Read the next byte
>>> f.read(1)
b'5'
# Go to the third byte before the end
>>> f.seek(-3, 2)
13
# Read the next byte
>>> f.read(1)
b'd'
```

Recall that you can open a text file without using a "b" in the mode string. In addition, you can perform only a seek operation that starts from the beginning of a text file. There is one exception: a seek from the beginning to the end of a text file. Make sure that you invoke f.close() to explicitly close a file, which also releases system resources associated with that open file.

This is what happens if you attempt to use a file that has been closed:

```
>>> f.close()
>>> f.read()
Traceback (most recent call last):
  File "<stdin>", line 1, in ?
ValueError: I/O operation on closed file
```

Use the with keyword when working with file objects, because this ensures that the file is properly closed, even if an exception is raised during the processing of the file. This approach is also shorter than writing equivalent try-except code blocks.

```
>>> with open('workfile', 'r') as f:
...     read_data = f.read()
>>> f.closed
True
```

CHECKING FILE TYPES

You can use the following code block to check for the existence of a file:

```
>>> import os
>>> os.path.exists('/etc/passwd')
True
>>> os.path.exists('/tmp/pizza')
False
>>>
```

The following code block checks if the specified path references a file:

```
>>> # Is a regular file
>>> os.path.isfile('/etc/passwd')
True
```

The following code block checks if the specified path references a directory:

```
>>> # Is a directory
>>> os.path.isdir('/etc/passwd')
False
>>> # Is a symbolic link
>>> os.path.islink('/usr/local/bin/python3')
True
>>> # Get the file linked to
>>> os.path.realpath('/usr/local/bin/python3')
'/usr/local/bin/python3.3'
>>>
```

The following code block obtains the file size and the timestamp of /etc/passwd:

```
>>> os.path.getsize('/etc/passwd')
3669
>>> os.path.getmtime('/etc/passwd')
1272478234.0
>>> import time
>>> time.ctime(os.path.getmtime('/etc/passwd'))
'Wed Apr 28 13:10:34 2010'
>>>
```

WORKING WITH DIRECTORIES

Python provides some useful convenience functions for listing the contents of a directory. Listing 5.8 displays the contents of DirList1.py that displays all the files (including subdirectories) of the current directory with a mere three lines of code.

LISTING 5.8 DirList1.py

```
import os


filenames = os.listdir('.')
print 'Directory list:', filenames
```

The actual output of Listing 5.8 varies, because it obviously depends on the contents of the current directory (". ").

Listing 5.9 displays the contents of DirList2.py that displays the contents of a directory, along with additional information about each entry.

LISTING 5.9 DirList2.py

```
import os
from fnmatch import fnmatch, fnmatchcase

matchCount = 0
otherCount = 0

filenames = os.listdir('.')
for f in filenames:
```

```
  if(fnmatch(f, '*.txt')):
    print 'file ends in txt:',f
    matchCount = matchCount + 1
  else:
    otherCount = otherCount + 1

print 'matching file count:',matchCount
print 'other file count:',otherCount
```

Listing 5.9 initializes two integer variables and then initializes the variable filenames with the list of filenames in the current directory. The next portion of Listing 5.9 iterates through the list of filenames and uses conditional logic to determine whether to increment the variable matchCount (for files that have a "txt" suffix) or otherCount (for all other files).

The output from launching Listing 5.9 is here:

```
file ends in txt: good-info.txt
file ends in txt: sample.txt
file ends in txt: sample2.txt
file ends in txt: sample3.txt
matching file count: 4
other file count: 21
```

Listing 5.10 displays the contents of DirList3.py that uses the glob function to find a set of files in a directory, along with additional information about each entry.

LISTING 5.10 DirList3.py

```
import os
import os.path
import glob

# list of files with a 'py' suffix
pyfiles = glob.glob('*.py')

# file sizes and modification dates ·
name_sz_date = [(name, os.path.getsize(name), os.path.getmtime(name))
                for name in pyfiles]

for name, size, mtime in name_sz_date:
  print 'name, size, mtime:', name, size, mtime

# Alternative: Get file metadata
#file_metadata = [(name, os.stat(name)) for name in pyfiles]
#for name, meta in file_metadata:
#  print(name, meta.st_size, meta.st_mtime)
```

Listing 5.10 uses the Python glob module to initialize the variable pyfiles with the files (in the current directory) that have a "py" suffix. Next, the variable name_sz_date is initialized with name, size, and modification time mtime of each file in pyfiles. The final portion of Listing 5.10 contains a simple loop that prints that information.

A partial output of Listing 5.10 is here:

```
name, size, mtime: ArrayToVars.py 131 1375219446.0
name, size, mtime: ArrayToVars2.py 237 1375219544.0
name, size, mtime: average.py 174 1375214431.0
name, size, mtime: ChangeFilePerm1.py 261 1375648268.0
name, size, mtime: CompareFiles.py 238 1376108233.0
name, size, mtime: CountLinesChars.py 276 1376106100.0
name, size, mtime: CreatePipe.py 280 1375651077.0
name, size, mtime: CreateTempFile.py 334 1375649253.0
name, size, mtime: DeleteFile1.py 268 1379292890.0
```

Listing 5.11 displays the contents of the Python script MyDir.py that defines a function that displays the full path of every file in a directory.

LISTING 5.11 MyDir.py

```
## Display the filenames in a directory
## with their relative and absolute paths

def MyDir (dir):
  filenames = os.listdir(dir)

  for filename in filenames:
    print filename  ## foo.txt

    ## dir/foo.txt (relative to current dir)
    print os.path.join(dir, filename)

    print os.path.abspath(os.path.join(dir, filename))

displaydir('/Users/jsmith/Downloads')
```

Listing 5.11 contains a Python function called MyDir() that takes a directory as an argument. The variable filenames is initialized with the contents of the directory dir, followed by a for loop that iterates through the files in the given directory to print the name of each file, its relative path, and its full path.

Change the path in the last line of code in Listing 5.11 to your home directory on your laptop, and then launch the code from the command line. After a few moments you will see the list of filenames and their locations, depending on the actual contents of the directory.

COUNTING THE WORDS IN A TEXT FILE

Listing 5.12 displays the contents of WordCount.py that counts the words in a text file.

LISTING 5.12 WordCount.py

```
words = dict()

with open('sample.txt', 'rt') as f:
```

```
for line in f:
  for w in line.split():
    try:
      if(words[w] == 0):
        words[w] = 1
      else:
        words[w] = words[w] + 1
    except:
      words[w] = 1

for key in words: print(key, words[key])
```

Listing 5.12 defines the dictionary words and then opens the text file `sample.txt` in read mode. The next portion of Listing 5.12 contains a nested pair of loops. The outer `for` loop iterates through the text file, and the loop variable `line` represents a single line of text in the file. The inner `for` loop splits the variable `line` into words, using the loop variable `w` to iterate through the words in `line`.

The next portion of Listing 5.12 contains conditional logic to increment the number of occurrences of each word w in the current line. The final code snippet consists of a `for` loop that prints each key (which is a word in the text file) and its value (the number of occurrences of that key).

Obviously, the output from Listing 5.12 depends on the contents of the file `sample.txt` that you can populate with some data.

SEARCH FOR A STRING IN A FILE

Listing 5.13 displays the contents of `FindStringInFile.py` that illustrates how to search for a string in a text file.

LISTING 5.13 FindStringInFile.py

```
str = 'line'
with open('sample.txt', 'rt') as f:
  print 'Matching Lines:'
  for line in f:
    pos1 = line.find(str)
    if(pos1 >= 0):
      print '###',line
```

Listing 5.13 initializes the variable `str` with the value `line` and then opens the text file `sample.txt` in read mode. Next, a `for` loop iterates through the lines in the text file and prints the lines that contain the string `line`.

Create a text file `sample.txt` and populate the file with sample data, and then launch the code in Listing 5.13 to see the results.

EMULATING THE UNIX GREP COMMAND

This section shows you how to search for a string in a set of files that are in a specific directory. You can read the documentation regarding the other features of the `grep` command.

Listing 5.14 displays the contents of MyGrep1.py that illustrates how to search for a string in a set of text files.

LISTING 5.14 MyGrep1.py

```
import os

def FindStringInFile(f):
  str = 'line'
  with open(f, 'rt') as f:
    print 'Matching Lines:'
    for line in f:
      pos1 = line.find(str)
      if(pos1 >= 0):
        print '###',line

filenames = os.listdir('.')

for f in filenames:
# if(f is file):
    print 'Searching file:',f
    FindStringInFile(f)
```

Listing 5.14 contains a function FindStringInFile() that accepts a filename f and then prints the lines of text that contain the string "line" (similar to the previous section). The next portion of Listing 5.14 populates the variable filenames with names of the files in the current directory. The final portion of Listing 5.14 iterates through the list of filenames and invokes FindStringInFile() with each filename. Create a text file sample.txt and populate the file with sample data, and then launch the code in Listing 5.14 to see the results.

The next part of this chapter shows you an example of working with a comma-separated-value (CSV) file and a file that contains data values that span ranges of columns (which is different from a CSV file).

WORKING WITH CSV FILES

Listing 5.15 displays the contents of PurchaseOrder.csv, and Listing 5.16 displays the contents of PurchaseOrder.py that illustrates how to read the contents of the CSV file in Listing 5.15.

LISTING 5.15 PurchaseOrder.csv

```
Name,UnitPrice,Quantity,Date
"Radio",54.99,2,"01/22/2013"
"DVD",15.99,1,"01/25/2013"
"Laptop",650.00,1,"01/24/2013"
"CellPhone",150.00,1,"01/28/2013"
```

The first line in Listing 5.15 contains a list of names for each column of data. The subsequent lines in Listing 5.15 consist of comma-separated values that correspond to the comma-separated names in the first row of the CSV file.

LISTING 5.16 PurchaseOrder.py

```python
import csv
import string

totalCost = 0
unitPrice = 0
itemQuantity = 0
fieldWidth = 20

print 'Purchase Order Total'
with open('PurchaseOrder.csv') as f:
  f_csv = csv.reader(f)
  headers = next(f_csv)

  for row in f_csv:
    # process each row

    unitPrice = float(row[1])
    itemQuantity = int(row[2])
    lineItemPrice = unitPrice*itemQuantity
    totalCost = totalCost + lineItemPrice

    print 'Item:',string.ljust(row[0], fieldWidth),
    print 'Cost:',lineItemPrice

  print 'Total cost:',totalCost
```

Listing 5.16 initializes some variables and then opens the file `Purchase-Order.csv` as a CSV file. The next part of Listing 5.16 initializes the variable `f_csv` that contains the column names for the data, followed by a loop that iterates through each row of data in the CSV file.

The variables `unitPrice` and `itemQuantity` are initialized from the data in each row of the CSV file and is used to calculate the `lineItemPrice` that is then added to the `totalCost` variable. Notice that the item and associated cost are printed for each row of data during each iteration of the loop. The final `print` statement displays the total cost for all the items in the CSV file.

The output from launching the code in Listing 5.16 is here:

```
Purchase Order Total
Item: Radio              Cost: 108.98
Item: DVD                Cost: 15.99
Item: Laptop             Cost: 650.00
Item: CellPhone          Cost: 150.00
Total cost: 925.97
```

WORKING WITH DATA FILES

A data file is a text file that contains data items in a range of columns. This type of file is different from a CSV file because it contains positional data items instead of data items that are separated by a delimiter.

Listing 5.17 displays the contents of Data.txt, and Listing 5.18 displays the contents of ReadDataFile.py that illustrates how to read the contents of the data file in Listing 5.17.

LISTING 5.17 Data.txt

```
#Data items defined in these columns:
#1-5:    Organization name
#10-19: Accounting Cycle
#22-28: Internal Routing
#30-48: Credit Card Number

#12345678901234567890123456789012345678901234567890
ORG11    12/23/2012   ASDF2XF 1234-9245-1244-0097
ORG12    01/15/2013   ASDF2XF 3234-9245-1244-0098
ORG24    11/20/2012   BBDF2XF 1234-9245-1244-0093
ORG33    02/15/2013   RBDF2XF 3234-9245-1244-0092
```

The first part of Listing 5.17 contains a set of comments that indicate the column range for four items, and the second part of Listing 5.17 contains sample data in the specified columns.

LISTING 5.18 ReadDataFile.py

```python
import re

#1-5:    Organization name
#10-19: Accounting Cycle
#22-28: Internal Routing
#30-48: Credit Card Number

filename = 'data.txt'
with open(filename, 'rt') as f:
  for line in f:
    if re.match(r'^$', line):
      pass # print 'skipping empty line'
    elif re.match(r'^[#]', line):
      pass # print 'skipping comment:',line
    else:
      orgName  = line[0:5]
      AccCycle = line[9:19]
      IntRoute = line[21:28]
      CCNumber = line[29:48]
      print 'line:',orgName, AccCycle, IntRoute, CCNumber
```

Listing 5.18 opens the data file in Listing 5.17 in "read" mode. The subsequent loop uses conditional logic to skip blank lines (which match the pattern "^$") as well as comment lines (which start with the "#" character).

The final code block in Listing 5.18 involves lines that contain valid data (located in the specified columns). This code block initializes the variables orgName, AccCycle, IntRoute, and CCNumber. The print statement in this code block simply prints the values of the preceding four variables; however, you would replace these variables with variables that represent the data in your CSV file, and update the application-specific logic accordingly.

The output of launching the code in Listing 5.18 is here:

```
line: ORG11 12/23/2012 ASDF2XF 1234-9245-1244-0097
line: ORG12 01/15/2013 ASDF2XF 3234-9245-1244-0098
line: ORG24 11/20/2012 BBDF2XF 1234-9245-1244-0093
line: ORG33 02/15/2013 RBDF2XF 3234-9245-1244-0092
```

The next portion of this chapter shows you a Python script that reads data from three text files that simulate the contents of three tables in a relational database. Although you would use an actual database in a working system, this code sample shows you how to solve this type of problem.

SIMULATING RELATIONAL DATA

This section shows you how to read data from several files to keep track of a small database of customers, their purchases, and the details of their purchases that are stored in three text files.

Listing 5.19 displays the contents of the `MasterOrders.txt` text file that contains three columns for each row of data (a `master` id, a `customer` id, and a date field).

LISTING 5.19: MasterOrders.txt

```
M10000 C1000 12/15/2012
M11000 C2000 12/15/2012
M12000 C3000 12/15/2012
```

Listing 5.20 displays the contents of the `Customers.txt` text file that contains five columns for each row of data (a customer id, a first name, a last name, a city, a state, and a zip code).

LISTING 5.20: Customers.txt

```
C1000 John Smith LosAltos California 94002
C2000 Jane Davis MountainView California 94043
C3000 Billy Jones HalfMoonBay California 94040
```

Listing 5.21 displays the contents of the `PurchaseOrders.txt` text file that contains five columns for each row of data (a customer id, a product name, a price, a quantity field, and a date field).

LISTING 5.21: PurchaseOrders.txt

```
C1000 Radio 54.99 2 01/22/2013
C1000 DVD 15.99 5 01/25/2013
C2000 Laptop 650.00 1 01/24/2013
C3000 CellPhone 150.00 2 01/28/2013
```

Listing 5.22 displays the contents of the Python script `MasterDetails. py` that processes the three data files `MasterOrders.txt`, `Customers. txt`, and `PurchaseOrders.txt`.

LISTING 5.22: *MasterDetails.py*

```
# initialize variables for the three main files
MasterOrders="MasterOrders.txt"
CustomerDetails="Customers.txt"
PurchaseOrders="PurchaseOrders.txt"

MastOrderIdDict      = {}
CustomerDetailsDict  = {}
PurchaseOrdersDict   = {}

# iterate through the "customer details"
with open(CustomerDetails, 'rt') as f:
  for line in f:
    items = line.split()
    custDetailsId = items[0]
    CustomerDetailsDict[custDetailsId] = line

# iterate through the "purchase orders"
with open(PurchaseOrders, 'rt') as f:
  for line in f:
    items = line.split()
    poDetailsId = items[0]
    PurchaseOrdersDict[poDetailsId] = line

# iterate through the "master table"
with open(MasterOrders, 'rt') as f:
  for line in f:
    items = line.split()
    mastOrderId = items[1]

    # get the customer information
    custDetails = CustomerDetailsDict[mastOrderId]

    # get the id from the previous line
    custDetailsArr = custDetails.split()
    custDetailsId = custDetailsArr[0]

    # get the customer PO from the PO file
    custPOLine = PurchaseOrdersDict[custDetailsId]
    custPOArr = custPOLine.split()
    custPO=custPOArr[0]

    # print the details of the customer
    print 'Customer', mastOrderId,':'
    print 'Customer Details:',custDetails
    print 'Purchase Orders:',custPOLine
    print '----------------------'
```

Listing 5.22 contains the three text files whose data is shown in Listings 5.19, 5.20, and 5.21. The next portion of Listing 5.22 initializes three dictionaries that correspond to the preceding text files. The next two sections of Listing 5.22 contain code that reads the contents of CustomerDetails and PurchaseOrders and populates their associated dictionaries.

The final portion of code in Listing 5.22 contains a loop that iterates through the rows in MasterOrders. The variable line represents each row of data, and the variable items represents the individual pieces of data in each row. For example, the mastOrderId variable is initialized as the first item in the items variable:

```
mastOrderId = items[1]
```

The customer-related details for this value are obtained from the CustomerDetailsDict dictionary as follows:

```
custDetails = CustomerDetailsDict[mastOrderId]
```

Next, the customer details array is initialized from the custDetails variable, and the first value in this array is the key that enables us to obtain purchase order information:

```
custDetailsArr = custDetails.split()
custDetailsId = custDetailsArr[0]
```

The following code block obtains purchase order details for the current row in the MasterOrders file:

```
custPOLine = PurchaseOrdersDict[custDetailsId]
custPOArr = custPOLine.split()
custPO=custPOArr[0]
```

The final block of code prints the customer-related details:

```
# print the details of the customer
print 'Customer', mastOrderId,':'
print 'Customer Details:',custDetails
print 'Purchase Orders:',custPOLine
print '----------------------'
```

The output from launching the code in Listing 5.22 is here:

```
Customer C1000 :
Customer Details: C1000 John Smith LosAltos California 94002

Purchase Orders: C1000 DVD 15.99 5 01/25/2013

----------------------
Customer C2000 :
Customer Details: C2000 Jane Davis MountainView California 94043

Purchase Orders: C2000 Laptop 650.00 1 01/24/2013

----------------------
Customer C3000 :
Customer Details: C3000 Billy Jones HalfMoonBay California 94040

Purchase Orders: C3000 CellPhone 150.00 2 01/28/2013

----------------------
```

SUMMARY

This chapter introduced you to file modes, file permissions, and file descriptors. Then you learned about file operations, such as reading, writing, creating, and deleting files. Next you learned how to simulate a relational database in Python by reading the contents of three text files and generating a report. You also learned how to work with streams and saw examples of stream-oriented Python scripts.

EXERCISES

Exercise 1: Write a Python script that capitalizes every word in a text file.

Exercise 2: Write a Python script that counts the number of capitalized words in each line of a text file.

Exercise 3: Write a Python script that reads the lines from a text file and then creates another text file whose contents are the list of lines in reverse order.

Exercise 4: Write a Python script that counts the frequency of the words in a text file. Use a Python dictionary to store the words and then display their frequency in descending order.

Exercise 5: Given a text file, write a Python script that counts the frequency of letters and digits. Use a Python dictionary to store the letters and the digits, and then display their frequency in descending order.

## CHAPTER 6

WORKING WITH JSON AND XML

This chapter gives you an overview of using Python with JavaScript Object Notation (JSON) data and XML documents. JSON is a very popular data format for storing data in NoSQL databases. If you plan to create Web applications, you will see JSON used extensively in code that involves NodeJS, Express, and MongoDB. By contrast, XML is an older (and definitely more verbose) data format that is still used in many situations, which warrants its inclusion in this chapter.

The first part of this chapter contains basic examples of JSON-based data, followed by some Python scripts that manipulate JSON-based data. The second (and somewhat shorter) part of this chapter shows you examples of XML documents, along with Python scripts for extracting data from XML documents. You can also read an Appendix that shows you how to use both Java and Python with Document Object Model (DOM) (a stream-oriented parser) and Simple API for XML (SAX) to manipulate XML documents.

Although you will probably be working frequently with JSON, this section gives you some additional concepts that you will encounter when dealing with XML-based documents. However, if you do not anticipate any need to learn more about XML, you can skip this section without any loss of continuity.

JSON DATA, PYTHON OBJECTS, AND JAVASCRIPT OBJECTS

JSON is an acronym for JavaScript Object Notation, and its homepage is here:

http://json.org/

According to this Website, JSON is built on two structures:

1. A collection of name/value pairs. In various languages, this is realized as an object, record, struct, dictionary, hash table, keyed list, or associative array.

2. An ordered list of values. In most languages, this is realized as an array, vector, list, or sequence.

JSON does not have objects, and therefore JSON cannot store JavaScript functions or comments. Both JavaScript and Python support JSON parsers.

Despite the similarity in syntax, JSON-based data is actually represented as a dictionary in Python, as shown by this example:

```
json1 = {'a' : 2, 'b' : 3}
dict1 = dict([('a', 2), ('b', 3)]);
```

A JSON module is available for Python, because Python does not use JSON natively. You can convert JSON data into Python data, as shown here:

```
>>> import json
>>> json.loads('{"x":7}')
{u'x': 7}
```

An example of JSON data involving data elements of different lengths is here:

```
[{'one':'1', 'two':'2', 'three':'3'}, {{'four':'4', 'five':'5'}]
```

Note that JSON data cannot contain functions or comment lines, both of which are supported in JavaScript.

A JavaScript object is a data type that is meaningful only in JavaScript. An example of a JavaScript object containing data and a comment line is here:

```
var obj1 = {
    // a comment line
    a: 1,
    b: 2
};
```

Another example of a JavaScript object, this time with a function, is here:

```
var obj1 = {
    a: 1,
    b: 2,
    startme : {
        return 'hello'
    }
};
```

Neither of the preceding JavaScript objects is directly "convertible" to valid JSON data.

Create and Print a JSON String

The following code snippet defines and prints a JSON string:

```
import json
```

```
data = [{'one':'1', 'two':'2', 'three':'3'}]
print 'data:', (data)
```

The output from the preceding code snippet is here:

```
data: [{'three': '3', 'two': '2', 'one': '1'}]
```

Notice that the order of the elements in the output is different from the order in which the elements are defined. This difference occurs because the JSON-based data is stored in a Python dict, which has no concept of order.

The JSON dumps() Function

The json.dumps method takes a Python data structure and returns a JSON string, as shown in Listing 6.1 that displays the contents of Ordered.py.

LISTING 6.1 Ordered.py

```
import json
from collections import OrderedDict

data = OrderedDict({'one':'1', 'two':'2', 'three':'3'})

print 'data1:',data
print 'data2:',json.dumps(data, sort_keys=False)
print 'data3:',json.dumps(data, sort_keys=True)
```

The output of Listing 6.1 is here:

```
data1: OrderedDict([('three', '3'), ('two', '2'), ('one', '1')])
data2: {"three": "3", "two": "2", "one": "1"}
data3: {"one": "1", "three": "3", "two": "2"}
```

The JSON loads() Function

The opposite of the json.dumps() function is the json.loads() function that takes a JSON string and returns it as a Python data structure, as shown in Listing 6.2.

LISTING 6.2 Loads.py

```
import json
from collections import OrderedDict

data = OrderedDict({'one':'1', 'two':'2', 'three':'3'})
json_encoded = json.dumps(data, sort_keys=False)
json_decoded = json.loads(json_encoded)

print 'encoded:',json_encoded
print 'decoded:',json_decoded

print 'one:',json_decoded['one']
print 'two:',json_decoded['two']
```

The output of Listing 6.2 is here:

```
encoded: {"three": "3", "two": "2", "one": "1"}
decoded: {u'one': u'1', u'three': u'3', u'two': u'2'}
one: 1
two: 2
```

JSON Data Versus Python Dictionary

The format of JSON data and that of a Python dictionary are very similar. For example, consider Listing 6.3 that displays the contents of `DictAndJ-SON.py`, which converts JSON data to Python data and then back to JSON data again.

LISTING 6.3 DictAndJSON.py

```python
import json

data = [{'one': '1'}, {'two': '2'}]
result1 = json.dumps(data)
print 'result1:',result1

result2 = json.loads('[{"one": "1"}, {"two": "2"}]')
print 'result2:',result2
```

Note the string type in the first line of output and the list of dictionaries in the second line of output:

```
result1: [{"one": "1"}, {"two": "2"}]
result2: [{u'one': u'1'}, {u'two': u'2'}]
```

PRETTY-PRINTING JSON DATA

The ability to pretty-print (display in a readable format) data in Python is useful because the hierarchical representation makes it easier for readers to see the structure of the data. Here is a simple code snippet in the Python interpreter:

```python
>>> import json
>>> print json.dumps({'4': 5, '6': 7}, sort_keys=True,
...                   indent=4, separators=(',', ': '))
```

Here is the pretty-printed version of the data in the preceding code snippet:

```
{
    "4": 5,
    "6": 7
}
```

The following code sample also uses the `dumps()` method to pretty-print Python data. Listing 6.4 displays the contents of `ReadJSON1.py` that shows you how to access specific elements and print their associated values.

LISTING 6.4 ReadJSON1.py

```
import json

json_input = '{ "one": 1, \
               "two": { "list":[{"item":"A"},{"item":"B"}]}}'

try:
    decoded = json.loads(json_input)

    # pretty printing of json-formatted string
    print json.dumps(decoded, sort_keys=True, indent=4)

    print "Item #1: ", decoded['one']
    print "Item #2: ", decoded['two']['list'][1]['item']

except (ValueError, KeyError, TypeError):
    print "JSON format error"
```

Listing 6.4 declares the variable `json_input` that specifies a slightly more complex data structure, followed by a `try/except` block that uses the Python `loads()` method to convert the data into a Python data structure. The next portion of code first prints all of the data followed by the value of the first data element, and then "drills down" into the data structure to display the value of one of the "leaf nodes."

The output of Listing 6.5 is here:

```
{
    "one": 1,
    "two": {
        "list": [
            {
                "item": "A"
            },
            {
                "item": "B"
            }
        ]
    }
}
Item #1:  1
Item #1:  B
```

ITERATING THROUGH JSON DATA IN PYTHON

Sometimes you know the structure of the elements of JSON-based data, in which case you can explicitly use the names of the fields. However, there are occasions when you need to iterate through JSON data even when you do not know the structure of that JSON data.

Listing 6.5 displays the contents of `IterateJSONFields.py` that iterates through the values of a JSON string and prints them.

LISTING 6.5 IterateJSONFields.py

```
import json

json1 = {"values": [["iPhone", 450]], "cost": "HIGH", "type":
["Mobile", "SmartPhone"]}

print 'json1:',json1
print

for obj in json1:
  #print 'obj:',obj, 'json1[obj]:',json1[obj]
  print 'obj: %-10s' % obj, 'json1[obj]:',json1[obj]
```

Listing 6.5 defines the variable json1 that contains three key/value pairs, followed by a for loop that iterates through the keys to print each key and its value.

The output of Listing 6.5 is here:

```
json1: {'type': ['Mobile', 'SmartPhone'], 'cost': 'HIGH', 'values':
[['iPhone', 450]]}

obj: type       json1[obj]: ['Mobile', 'SmartPhone']
obj: cost       json1[obj]: HIGH
obj: values     json1[obj]: [['iPhone', 450]]
```

RETRIEVING A JSON STRING FROM A WEBSITE

Python makes it easy to process JSON-based data that is returned from a Website.

Listing 6.6 displays the contents of UrlJSON1.py that iterates through the values of a JSON string and prints them.

NOTE requests *is a third-party library that you must install on your machine (use* pip *or* easy_install).

LISTING 6.6 UrlJSON1.py

```
import requests

url = 'http://echo.jsontest.com/key/value/one/two'

try:
    json1 = requests.get(url).json()
    print 'json1:',json1
except:
    print 'An error occurred converting data to JSON'
    #raise ValueError("No JSON object could be decoded")
```

Listing 6.6 contains the variable url that specifies a Website that returns a JSON-based string. The try/except block assigns the returned string to the variable json1 and then prints its value. If an error occurs, the except handler prints an error message.

The output of Listing 6.6 is here:

```
json1: {u'key': u'value', u'one': u'two'}
```

MERGING TWO JSON-BASED DATA STRINGS

JSON-based data can be obtained in various ways, such as a response from a Web service, from a text file, or from a database, and sometimes you need to aggregate those JSON-based strings.

Listing 6.7 displays the contents of `CombineJSON1.py` that merges two JSON strings into a single JSON string.

LISTING 6.7 CombineJSON1.py

```python
import json

obj1 = {"a1": 1, "a2": 2, "a3": 3}
obj2 = {"a4": 4, "a5": 5, "a6": 6}

data1 = { 'obj1' : obj1, 'obj2' : obj2 }
json.dumps(data1,indent=2)
print data1
print

data2 = [ obj1, obj2 ]
json.dumps(data2,indent=2)
print data2
```

The first part of Listing 6.7 defines the variables `obj1` and `obj2`, each of which contains JSON-based data. The next part of Listing 6.7 defines `data1` as JSON data consisting of the "union" of `obj1` and `obj2`. The variable `data1` is supplied to the `dumps()` method and then printed. The `data2` variable is initialized as an array consisting of `obj1` and `obj2` and then passed to the `dumps()` method and also printed.

The output of Listing 6.7 is here:

```
{'obj1': {'a1': 1, 'a3': 3, 'a2': 2}, 'obj2': {'a5': 5, 'a4': 4,
'a6': 6}}

[{'a1': 1, 'a3': 3, 'a2': 2}, {'a5': 5, 'a4': 4, 'a6': 6}]
```

COMBINING DICTIONARIES WITH JSON-BASED DATA

Listing 6.8 displays the contents of `CombineDicts1.py` that merges two Python dictionaries into a third dictionary and also a JSON object.

LISTING 6.8 CombineDicts1.py

```python
import json

dict1 = {"cost":"HIGH", "type":["Mobile", "SP"], \
        "values":[["Android", 250]]}
```

```
dict2 = {"cost":"HIGH", "type":["Mobile", "SP"], \
         "values":[["iPhone",  450]]}

# combines dictionaries that have
# identical cost and type values
def combine(dict1, dict2):
  if dict1['cost'] == dict2['cost'] and \
     dict1['type'] == dict2['type']:
     return {
         'cost': dict1['cost'],
         'type': dict1['type'],
         'values': dict1['values'] + dict2['values']
     }

result1 = combine(dict1, dict2)
result2 = json.dumps(combine(dict1, dict2))

print 'dict1["cost"]:',dict1["cost"]
print 'dict1["type"]:',dict1["type"]
print 'dict1["values"]:',dict1["values"]
print
print 'dict2["cost"]:',dict2["cost"]
print 'dict2["type"]:',dict2["type"]
print 'dict2["values"]:',dict2["values"]
print
print 'result2:',result2
```

Listing 6.8 defines two Python dictionaries dict1 and dict2, followed by the Python function combine() that merges two dictionaries. Conditional logic determines whether or not the two dictionaries have the same values for the cost and type fields; if so, the combine() method returns a JSON string with three fields: a cost field, a type field, and a values field. The cost field and the type field match those of the two dictionaries, and the values field equals the "sum" of the values fields in the two dictionaries. Since the values field contains a string, the "sum" is actually the concatenation of the contents of the two values fields.

The output of Listing 6.8 is here:

```
dict1["cost"]: HIGH
dict1["type"]: ['Mobile', 'SP']
dict1["values"]: [['Android', 250]]

dict2["cost"]: HIGH
dict2["type"]: ['Mobile', 'SP']
dict2["values"]: [['iPhone', 450]]

result2: {"values": [["Android", 250], ["iPhone", 450]], "cost":
"HIGH", "type": ["Mobile", "SP"]}
```

MANIPULATING THE FIELDS IN JSON DATA

JSON-based data can be obtained in various ways, such as by invoking a Web service, from a text file, or from a database. Sometimes you need to aggregate those JSON-based strings.

Listing 6.9 displays the contents of `ManipulateJSON1.py` that shows you how to use a loop to iterate through the elements of a JSON string to create new JSON strings.

LISTING 6.9 ManipulateJSON1.py

```
import json

data1 = [{"b1": "c11", "b2": "c22"},
         {"b1": "d33", "b2": "d44"},
         {"b1": "e33", "b2": "e44"}]

rowCount = 1
result = []

for line in data1:
    row = {}
    row['F1'] = line['b1']
    row['F2'] = line['b2']
    result.append(row)
    print 'row',rowCount,':',row
    rowCount = rowCount + 1

print
print 'data1:',data1
print
print 'result:',result

print
for x in result:
    newRow1 = [x['F2'], x['F1']]
    newRow2 = {x['F2'], x['F1']}
    print 'new row 1:',newRow1
    print 'new row 2:',newRow2
```

Listing 6.9 starts with the definition of a JSON string `data1`, the numeric variable `rowCount`, and the list variable `result`. The next portion of Listing 6.9 contains a `for` loop that iterates through each top-level element in `data1` and then constructs (and also prints) two corresponding JSON strings from each top-level element in `data1`.

The output of Listing 6.9 is here:

```
row 1 : {'F1': 'c11', 'F2': 'c22'}
row 2 : {'F1': 'd33', 'F2': 'd44'}
row 3 : {'F1': 'e33', 'F2': 'e44'}

data1: [{'b1': 'c11', 'b2': 'c22'}, {'b1': 'd33', 'b2': 'd44'}, {'b1':
'e33', 'b2': 'e44'}]

result: [{'F1': 'c11', 'F2': 'c22'}, {'F1': 'd33', 'F2': 'd44'}, {'F1':
'e33', 'F2': 'e44'}]

new row 1: ['c22', 'c11']
new row 2: set(['c22', 'c11'])
new row 1: ['d44', 'd33']
```

```
new row 2: set(['d33', 'd44'])
new row 1: ['e44', 'e33']
new row 2: set(['e33', 'e44'])
```

READING JSON-BASED TEXT FILES

In Chapter 5, you learned how to read the contents of a text file, and in this section you will learn how to retrieve JSON-based data that is stored in a text file.

Listing 6.10 displays the contents of `ReadFileJSON1.py` that iterates through each row of data in a text file to construct a JSON string that is the concatenation of the JSON data in each row of the text file.

LISTING 6.10 ReadFileJSON1.py

```
import json

jsonFile = "file.json"
data = []
with open(jsonFile) as f:
  for line in f:
    print 'Line:',line
    data.append(json.loads(line))

print 'data:',data
```

Listing 6.10 initializes the variable `jsonFile` with the filename `file.json` (displayed immediately after the output for Listing 6.10) and also initializes the variable `data` as an empty list. The next portion of Listing 6.10 uses the "with" construct to do two things: 1) open the file `file.json` and 2) set up a loop. Each loop iteration accesses a row of data in `file.json` and appends that data to the variable `data`. When the loop is finished, the code prints the value of the `data` variable.

The output of Listing 6.10 is here:

```
Line: {"F1": "c11", "F2": "c22"}

Line: {"F1": "d33", "F2": "d44"}

Line: {"F1": "e33", "F2": "e44"}
```

The following code block displays the contents of `file.json`.

```
{"F1": "c11", "F2": "c22"}
{"F1": "d33", "F2": "d44"}
{"F1": "e33", "F2": "e44"}

data: [{u'F1': u'c11', u'F2': u'c22'}, {u'F1': u'd33', u'F2':
u'd44'}, {u'F1': u'e33', u'F2': u'e44'}]
```

NOTE *You must use double quotes instead of single quotes in a text file containing JSON-based data.*

Although the data in Listing 6.10 is in single-row format, data can span multiple rows.

WRITING JSON-BASED TEXT FILES

Listing 6.11 displays the contents of `WriteFileJSON1.py` that illustrates how to write JSON-based data to a text file.

LISTING 6.11 WriteFileJSON1.py

```
import json

outfile = "jsondata.txt"
data = {"F1": "c11", "F2": "c22"}
print 'data:',data

with open(outfile, 'w') as outfile:
  print 'printing data'
  json.dump(data, outfile)
```

Listing 6.11 contains the variable `outfile` that specifies the file `json-data.txt` and the variable `data` that contains JSON-based data. The next portion of Listing 6.11 prints the value of `data`, followed by a `with` statement that opens the file `jsondata.txt` in write mode and then writes the contents of `data` to `jsondata.txt`.

The output of `WriteFileJSON1.py` is here:

```
{"F1": "c11", "F2": "c22"}
```

PYTHON AND CSV FILES

JSON supports a variety of data structures. A JavaScript "object" is comparable to a Python `dict` (with string keys), and a JavaScript "array" is comparable to a Python "list." In addition, you can nest them, provided that the final "leaf" elements are numbers or strings. A CSV file essentially represents only a two-dimensional table, with an optional first row of column names that identify the fields in each row of data. The first "header" row makes it possible to treat the CSV data as a list of `dicts`, instead of a list of lists.

You can store an array of arrays or an array of objects (all of which have the same keys) as a CSV file; however, you cannot store an arbitrary JSON structure in a CSV file.

WRITING JSON-BASED DATA TO A CSV FILE

Listing 6.12 displays the contents of `JSONToCSV.py` that illustrates how to write JSON-based data to a CSV file.

LISTING 6.12 JSONToCSV.py

```
import json, csv

pairs ="""[
    {"fname": "jane", "lname": "edwards"},
    {"fname": "john", "lname": "smith"},
```

```
      {"fname": "jill", "lname": "jones"}
] """

rows = json.loads(pairs)
with open('firstlastnames.csv', 'wb+') as f:
    dict_writer = csv.DictWriter(f, fieldnames=['fname', 'lname'])
    dict_writer.writeheader()
    dict_writer.writerows(rows)
```

Listing 6.12 defines the variable `pairs` containing data. Note that the triple quote is a document string that differs from a comment, because such a string is accessible as a string in Python code.

The next portion of Listing 6.12 initializes the variable `rows` with Python data, followed by a `with` statement that opens the file `firstlastnames.csv` in `write` mode. The body of the `with` statement initializes a `dict_writer` and then writes the header information (fname and lname), followed by the data in the `rows` variable, to the output file.

The contents of `firstlastnamepairs.csv` is here:

```
fname,lname
jane,edwards
john,smith
jill,jones
```

CONVERTING CSV FILES TO JSON

Listing 6.13 displays the contents of the CVS file `csvtojson.csv`, and Listing 6.14 displays the contents of `CSVToJSON.py` that illustrates how to read the contents of `csvtojson.csv` and convert its contents to a JSON string.

LISTING 6.13 csvtojson.csv
```
height,weight,age
150, 45, 22
100, 35, 8
180, 90, 38
```

LISTING 6.14 CSVToJSON.py
```
import json, csv

mycsvfile="csvtojson.csv"

f = open(mycsvfile,'r')
reader = csv.DictReader(f)

out = json.dumps([row for row in reader])
print 'result:',out
```

Listing 6.14 imports the `json` and `csv` modules and then initializes the variable `mycsvfile` with the value `csvtojson.csv` (displayed in Listing

6.13). The next portion of Listing 6.14 opens the CSV file in "read" mode and passes a reference to this file to the `DictReader()` method of the `csv` module. The final portion of Listing 6.14 invokes the `dumps()` method of the `json` module to read each line from the CSV file and convert the result to a JSON string that is printed on the screen.

The output of Listing 6.14 is here:

```
result: [{"age": " 22", "weight": " 45", "height": "150"}, {"age":
" 8", "weight": " 35", "height": "100"}, {"age": " 38", "weight":
" 90", "height": "180"}]
```

The preceding example demonstrates how easily you can read the contents of CSV files and convert the contents to a JSON string.

THE SIMPLEJSON TOOLKIT

The open source toolkit `simplejson` is a simple, fast, complete, correct and extensible JSON encoder and decoder for Python 2.5+ and Python 3.3+. It is pure Python code with no dependencies, but it includes an optional C extension for a serious speed boost. You can download this toolkit here:

https://pypi.python.org/pypi/simplejson/

The latest documentation for `simplejson` can be read online here:

http://simplejson.readthedocs.org/

`simplejson` is the externally maintained development version of the `json` library included with Python 2.6 and Python 3.0, but it maintains backward compatibility with Python 2.5.

The encoder can be specialized to provide serialization in any kind of situation, without any special support by the objects to be serialized (somewhat like `pickle`).

The decoder can handle incoming JSON strings of any specified encoding (but UTF-8 is used by default).

This concludes the JSON portion of this chapter. The remainder of this chapter discusses XML documents and how you can work with them in Python.

WHAT IS XML?

An XML document contains data values that are organized in a hierarchical fashion. One important difference is that database schemas can model many-to-many relationships, such as the many-to-many relationship that exists between a `students` entity and a classes `entity`. XML documents are strictly one-to-many, with a single root node. People sometimes make the analogy that XML is to data what Java is to code: both are portable, which means that you avoid the problems that are inherent in proprietary systems.

WHY USE XML?

The flexibility of XML makes it useful for business-oriented Web applications. In addition, configuration files in the open-source world are often XML documents. Even Android-based mobile applications use XML documents to define data. Many well-known application servers also use XML-based configuration files. The Ant utility and the Maven utility both XML-based files for defining tasks.

Moreover, you can use XSL style sheets to convert XML documents into HTML pages, SVG documents, PDFs, or other XML documents. XSL is a language for extracting information from data arranged in a tree-like fashion. Although its purpose is conceptually straightforward, there is a significant learning curve associated with acquiring a mastery of XSL.

Despite the widespread use of XML, there is still a significant amount of non-XML business data that resides in columns of relational tables or in text files. This chapter provides examples of Python scripts that can convert text files or database data into XML documents. Once you have created an XML document containing your data, you can avail yourself of the many XML tools that exist today.

A tremendous amount of data in the business world and the scientific community does not use an XML format. To give you some perspective, roughly 80 to 90 percent of all software programs were written in either COBOL or Fortran by the early 1990's. Consequently, data integration and/or migration can be a complex problem. The movement toward XML as a standard for data representation is intended to simplify the problem of exchanging data among systems.

You probably already know that XML is ubiquitous in the Java world, yet you might be asking yourself what all the fuss is about XML. In very broad terms, XML is to data what relational theory is to databases: both provide a standardized mechanism for representing data. A non-trivial database schema would consist of a set of tables in which there is some type of parent/child (or master/detail) relationship whereby data can be viewed hierarchically.

The official source for XML is the URL *http:// w3c.org*, which also contains a link to other XML-related technologies (including SVG). A search on Google for "XML-related" will return many Web pages.

Another useful resource is the following Website that lists various Python toolkits for processing XML, and its homepage is here:

http://wiki.python.org/moin/PythonXml

A SIMPLE XML DOCUMENT

Listing 6.15 displays the contents of `Simple1.xml`, an XML document containing user-related information.

LISTING 6.15 Simple1.xml

```xml
<?xml version="1.0"?>
<user id="1000">
  <firstname>John</firstname>
  <lastname>Smith</lastname>
</user>
```

Listing 6.15 contains a simple XML document that consists of a parent XML `<user>` element with attribute `id` (whose value is `1000`) and two child XML elements that specify the first and last names `John` and `Smith`, respectively.

A QUICK VIEW OF THE DOM

DOM is an acronym for Document Object Model, which is a tree-like representation of an XML file that is constructed in the RAM of your machine. A DOM contains the text of an XML document, as well as additional structure for the DOM itself, which means that a DOM can be several times larger than the XML document itself. Depending on your system, a large document might be "only" 100 megabytes; for the majority of systems, a file of 100 gigabytes is considered large. One disadvantage of using a DOM pertains to performance-related issues and memory contention for very large documents.

An alternative to a DOM structure is SAX, which will be discussed later in this chapter. Note that while SAX-based parsing of an XML document consumes much less memory, you will need to write additional code for accessing the parts of an XML document and you will lose the ability to traverse an in-memory structure that reflects the contents of an XML document (which is what a DOM provides). You will probably find DOM easier to use, but you may be forced to use SAX when performance and document size preclude the use of DOM.

Another advantage of a DOM representation of a document is the ease with which you can traverse a DOM using methods whose names are used consistently in different languages. For example, the method `setAttribute()` is the same in Python, Perl, PHP, ECMAScript, and Java.

In simplified terms, you can follow these guidelines:

- use DOM when element manipulation is required
- use SAX for one-time processing of documents
- use etree for Pythonic XML manipulation

Another point to note is that `lxml` (not discussed in this chapter) is a third-party library and therefore not part of the standard library; in the former case you would use `lxml.tree`, and in the latter case you would use `xml.etree`.

READING XML DOCUMENTS WITH PYTHON

Listing 6.16 displays the contents of the XML document `Employee1.xml`, and Listing 6.17 displays the contents of the Python script `Employee1.py` that reads the contents of `Employee1.xml`.

LISTING 6.16 Employee1.xml

```xml
<?xml version="1.0"?>
<users>
  <user id="1000"
    name="John Smith"
    userid="jsmith" />
  <user id="2000"
    name="Jane Edwards"
    userid="jedwards" />
  <user id="3000"
    name="Tom Jones"
    userid="tjones" />
</users>
```

Listing 6.16 contains an XML `<users>` element that is the root element of the document, which also contains three XML `<user>` child nodes, each of which specifies three attributes: `id`, `name`, and `userid`.

LISTING 6.17 Employee1.py

```python
import xml.dom.minidom
from xml.dom.minidom import Node

userCount = 0

myDocument = xml.dom.minidom.parse("Employee2.xml")

for node in myDocument.getElementsByTagName("user"):
  userCount += 1

    username = node.getAttribute("name")
    userid   = node.getAttribute("userid")

    print "User Name:   "+username
    print "User Id:     "+userid

print "User count: "+str(userCount)
```

Notice the `str()` function for converting a number to a string. If you concatenate a string and number without a conversion, you will get an error.

Listing 6.17 is a simple Python script that uses the `getElementsByTag-Name()` method for retrieving each XML `<user>` element:

```
myDocument.getElementsByTagName("user"):
```

Listing 6.17 also uses the method `getAttribute()` for retrieving an attribute of a node:

```
userName = node.getAttribute("name")
```

The output of `Employee1.py` is shown here:

```
User Name:   John Smith
User Id:     jsmith
User Name:   Jane Edwards
```

```
User Id:    jedwards
User Name:  Tom Jones
User Id:    tjones
User count: 3
```

FINDING XML ELEMENT CONTENTS WITH A DOM PARSER

Listing 6.18 displays the contents of the XML document `Employee2.xml`, and Listing 6.19 displays the contents of the Python script `Employee2.py` that parses `Employee2.xml`.

LISTING 6.18 Employee2.xml

```
<?xml version="1.0"?>
<users>
  <user id="1000">
   <name>John Smith</name>
   <userid>jsmith</userid>
  </user>
  <user id="2000">
   <name>Jane Edwards</name>
   <userid>jedwards</userid>
  </user>
  <user id="3000">
   <name>Tom Jones</name>
   <userid>tjones</userid>>
  </user>
</users>
```

The key difference is that the XML `<user>` element contains two XML child elements called `<name>` and `<userid>` that are defined as attributes in `Employee1.xml`.

LISTING 6.19 Employee2.py

```
import xml.dom.minidom
from xml.dom.minidom import Node

userCount = 0

myDocument = xml.dom.minidom.parse("Employee2.xml")

for node in myDocument.getElementsByTagName("user"):
  userCount += 1

  for subNode in node.childNodes:
    if(subNode.nodeType == subNode.ELEMENT_NODE):
      nodeName = subNode.nodeName

      if(subNode.firstChild != None):
        nodeContents = subNode.firstChild.nodeValue

        if(nodeName == "name"):
          userName = nodeContents;
```

```
      elif(nodeName == "userid"):
          userid  =  nodeContents;

  print "User Name:   "+userName
  print "User Id:     "+userid
  print "-------------------\n"

print "User count:  "+str(userCount)
```

The output of `Employee2.py` is here:

```
User Name:   John Smith
User Id:     jsmith
-------------------

User Name:   Jane Edwards
User Id:     jedwards
-------------------

User Name:   Tom Jones
User Id:     tjones
-------------------

User count:  3
```

TRANSFORMING XML DOCUMENTS WITH PYTHON

In general, you can use attributes or elements for specifying data in an XML document, or you can use a combination of attributes and elements. The specific structure that you use will depend on the purpose or the meaning of the data in the context of an XML document.

Regardless of the structure that you use, you might find it necessary to create a different structure for your XML document. You can perform this transformation using an XSL (Extensible Stylesheet Language) stylesheet (which is a topic that is beyond the scope of this book), or you can use a Python script. If you need to write Python scripts to transform XML documents, perform an online search and you will find code samples that illustrate how this can be accomplished.

Keep in mind that the use of Python for this task differs substantially from using XSL, which uses declarative stylesheets that are applied to XML documents. If you are already familiar with XSL transforms and you have already developed a library of custom stylesheets, then you have a strong incentive to continue using your current code base. On the other hand, if you are unfamiliar with XSL transforms and you do not have sufficient time to acquire the necessary expertise, then Python provides a very attractive alternative.

A QUICK INTRODUCTION TO SAX (SIMPLE API FOR XML)

Earlier in the chapter you learned that SAX-based parsing offers an alternative to DOM when you are working with extremely large XML documents. So how does SAX work?

By way of a very simplified analogy, imagine yourself sitting at the side of a highway, where you need to do three things: report via your cell phone the license plate of every passing truck, the information written on the side of each truck, and the rear license plate of each truck. (Most vehicles have only one license plate, so this analogy is imperfect). Moreover, you are not required to keep track of vehicles once that have driven past your location, nor do you need to "scan ahead" for vehicles that are approaching your location; your reporting responsibility pertains solely to the truck that is currently driving past you.

Similarly, SAX-based parsing involves event-based information for the start of an element, the text in an element, and the end of an element. You also define functions whenever you need to insert custom code to do some extra processing for any of these events. These functions are called "call-back" functions (or methods). Although there are other events that you can detect during SAX-based parsing, the start/text/end events are sufficient for you to parse an XML document, which will be demonstrated in the next section.

Chapter 8 contains an example of defining a custom Python class that uses a SAX parser on an XML document.

Python Tools for XML

The following Website contains a list of various Python-based tools for XML:

https://wiki.python.org/moin/PythonXml

This Website contains links with information about Python support for XML in standard Python libraries (such as the `xml.eTree` package) and external packages, such as `lxml`, `PyXB`, `PyXSD`, and `PyXML`.

SUMMARY

This chapter introduced you to JSON-based data and methods of converting such data to Python data. Next you learned about XML documents and how you can use Python to create such documents, and also how to read their contents. You also learned about DOM-based and SAX-based parsing of XML documents.

EXERCISES

Exercise 1: Create a text string of words and then write a Python script to create a JSON string whose contents are the words in the text string. You need to think of a way to define the key/value pairs (where the value is set to each word in the text string).

Exercise 2: Create a JSON-based string consisting of stock quotes and stock values, and then write a Python script to convert the JSON data to an XML document using attributes or elements (or both) to represent each field in the JSON data.

Exercise 3: Write a Python script that converts the XML document that you created in Exercise 2 into the original JSON-based string.

Exercise 4: Use the following URL to retrieve JSON-based data for a weather forecast:

http://api.openweathermap.org/data/2.5/forecast?q=London, us&mode=json

Read the JSON-based data and calculate the average temperature during the 1500 to 1800 time slot.

Exercise 5: Repeat Exercise 3 using this URL to retrieve XML-based data for a weather forecast:

http://api.openweathermap.org/data/2.5/forecast?q=London, us&mode=xml

Read the XML-based data and calculate the average temperature during the 1500 to 1800 time slot.

## CHAPTER 7

DATA VISUALIZATION AND GRAPHICS

This chapter discusses various Python modules for data visualization, as well as Python modules for manipulating SVG. The information about the Python modules in this chapter is presented in a short and concise manner so that you can quickly decide which modules are useful for your work, and then you can find online resources to help you learn more about those modules.

The first portion of this chapter contains a short description of the Python modules `matplotlib`, `numpy`, `pylab`, and `scipy`. These modules are designed for scientific calculations, so they provide many Python functions that are well suited for statistical analysis and data analysis. They also enable you to generate render various charts that you can save as PNG files on the file system.

The second part of this chapter discusses TkInter, which is a toolkit for graphical user interface (GUI) development. This section contains some code samples for rendering user interface components and generating bar charts.

The third part of this chapter discusses Python toolkits for managing SVG. You will learn about the `svgwrite` toolkit, which consists of a Python script for generating SVG documents. You will also learn about a Python-based toolkit for D3.js (a very popular open-source data visualization toolkit).

One interesting technology (unrelated to Python) is R, which is a package for statisticians. Currently there appears to be some initiative for creating Python modules that provide similar functionality. If you are going to participate in projects that require analysis of statistical data, then you stand to benefit from learning about the Python modules that are discussed in this chapter.

Before delving into the various Python modules in this chapter, let's take a quick look at how to use `IPython` (discussed in Chapter 1) with some of these modules.

IPYTHON

IPython supports interactive data processing and GUI toolkits, and you can download a stable version as well as a development version of IPython from its homepage:

http://ipython.org/

After downloading and installing IPython, you can launch IPython with this command in a command shell:

```
ipython [options] files
```

NOTE *For Python3, use* `ipython3` *in place of* `ipython`.

You can launch IPython with qt via the following command:

```
ipython --gui=qt
```

You can launch IPython by first loading matplotlib and qt via the following command:

```
ipython --matplotlib qt
```

Navigate to the IPython homepage to learn more about features and details of the IPython notebook.

PYTHON MODULES FOR STATISTICAL AND SCIENTIFIC CALCULATIONS

There are various Python modules for generating plots and performing scientific and numeric calculations, such as Matplotlib, NumPy, Pylab, and SciPy.

In brief, these modules provide the following functionalities:

- The matplotlib module is a single module for managing data and generating plots
- The numPy module provides an array type (that augments Python) that is useful for numeric calculations, along with routines for finding eigenvectors
- pylab is a module for generating and saving plots
- sciPy is a module containing routines for scientific work such as computing numeric integrals, solving differential equations, and working with sparse matrices

Fortunately, a large collection of numeric and scientific code based on the preceding modules is also available, which you can use to reduce the complexity of your code.

Installing `matplotlib`, `numPy`, and `scipy`

Use `pip` to install `numPy`, `matplotlib`, and `scipy` for the code sample in this section (`scipy` is used elsewhere) by executing the following commands from the command line:

```
pip install numpy
pip install scipy
pip install matplotlib
```

The following code will work in Python if the preceding modules have been installed correctly:

```
import numpy
import scipy
import matplotlib
```

WHAT IS MATPLOTLIB?

`matplotlib` is a very extensive plotting library for Python, and the NumPy module is its numerical extension. `matplotlib` provides API for embedding plots into applications using toolkits such as `GTK Qt`, `wxPython`, and so forth. `Matplotlib` also contains the `matplotlib.pyplot` module and the `Pylab` module for plots.

The `pyplot` interface is suited for plots in Python scripts, whereas the `pylab` interface is suited for interactive calculations and plotting. If you launch the `Ipython` shell with the `-pylab` option, it will import everything from `pylab`, which makes plotting fully interactive.

`pylab` combines the `pyplot` functionality with the `numpy` functionality in a single namespace, which provides an environment similar to `matlab`.

WORKING WITH NUMPY

NumPy is designed for manipulating homogeneous multidimensional arrays, which means that the elements in such arrays are all of the same type. Numpy refers to dimensions as "axes," and the number of axes is called the "rank."

As a simple example, `[1,2,3]` represents a point in 3D space that:

1) is an array of length 3
2) has one axis
3) is an array of rank 1 because of 2)

As a second example, `[[1,2,3], [4,5,6]]` represents an array in 3D space that:

1) is two-dimensional
2) has a first dimension of length 2

3) has a second dimension of length 3

4) is an array of rank 2 because of 2)

If you can represent an element as an m x n matrix, then the value of m (the number of rows) is the axis and the value of n (the number of columns) is the rank. You can use this analogy to help you remember the difference between an axis and rank.

numpy provides the function array() for creating arrays, with an option for specifying the type of each element in the array, as shown here:

```
>>> from numpy import *
>>> arr1 = array([1,2,3])
>>> arr1
array([1, 2, 3])
>>> arr2 = array([1,2,3], dtype=float)
>>> arr2
array([ 1.,   2.,   3.])
>>> arr3 = zeros((2,3))
>>> arr3
array([[ 0.,   0.,   0.],
       [ 0.,   0.,   0.]])
```

To create sequences of numbers, NumPy provides the function arange(), analogous to the range() function, that returns arrays instead of lists.

```
>>> arange( 10, 30, 5 )
array([10, 15, 20, 25])
>>> arange( 0, 2, 0.3 )                    # it accepts float arguments
array([ 0. ,   0.3, 0.6,  0.9, 1.2, 1.5,  1.8])
```

The numpy function reshape() allows you to change the display of an array of elements by "reshaping" them, as shown here:

```
>>> from numpy import *
>>> a = arange(1,21)
>>> print a
[ 1  2  3  4  5  6  7  8  9 10 11 12 13 14 15 16 17 18 19 20]
>>> b = arange(1,21).reshape(4,5)
>>> print b
[[ 1  2  3  4  5]
 [ 6  7  8  9 10]
 [11 12 13 14 15]
 [16 17 18 19 20]]
>>> c = arange(1,21).reshape(2,2,5)
>>> print c
[[[ 1  2  3  4  5]
  [ 6  7  8  9 10]]

 [[11 12 13 14 15]
  [16 17 18 19 20]]]
```

Another very useful function is linspace(initial, final, count) that can generate a list of numbers in an arithmetic progression consisting of count numbers, where the first number has the value `initial`, the last number has the value `final`, and the difference between any pair of consecutive numbers is the same and equal to the quantity `(final-initial)/count`. Some examples are here:

```
>> from numpy import *
>>> linspace(0,10,5)
array([ 0. ,   2.5,   5. ,   7.5,  10. ])
>> linspace(20,30,11)
array([ 20.,  21.,  22.,  23.,  24.,  25.,  26.,  27.,  28.,  29.,
30.])
```

You can use the `linspace()` function to define a set of points for plotting functions, as shown here:

```
>>> x = linspace(0, 2*pi, 360)
>>> y = cos(x)
```

Later in this chapter you will see an example of plotting trigonometric functions.

The next section shows you how to use the `pylab` module to render some trigonometric functions.

WORKING WITH PYLAB

`pylab` also contains an `arange()` function (similar to the one in `numpy`) and a `plot()` function that enables you to plot functions. You can also label the horizontal and vertical axes and then use the `savefig()` function to save the plot as a PNG file.

Listing 7.1 displays the contents of `TrigFunctions.py` that illustrates how to render a sine wave and a cosine wave using the Python `pylab` module and saving the output to a PNG file.

LISTING 7.1 Trigfunctions.py

```
from pylab import *

linewidth = '4'

x = arange(0.0, 4.0, 0.01)
y1 = 10*sin(3*x)
plot(x, y1, linewidth)

y2 = 5*cos(5*pi*x)
plot(x, y2, linewidth)

xlabel('Radians')
ylabel('Amplitude')
title('Trigonometric Functions')
grid(True)
savefig("TrigFunctions.png")
show()
```

Listing 7.1 contains one `import` statement, followed by the variable `linewidth` that specifies the width of the curve that is rendered. The variables `x` and `y1` are used for rendering a sine wave, and the variables `x` and `y2` represent a cosine wave. The `xlabel()` and `ylabel()` functions enable you to label the horizontal and vertical axes, respectively. The `title()` function provides a title for the rendered graph. Finally, the `savefig()` function saves the rendered graph as a PNG file.

Figure 7.1 displays the result of launching Listing 7.1 from the command line on a Macbook Pro.

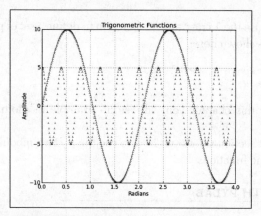

FIGURE 7.1 Trigonometric functions using `pylab`.

WORKING WITH SCIPY

`scipy` is open-source software for mathematics, science, and engineering. `SciPy` depends on `NumPy`, which provides convenient and fast N-dimensional array manipulation. `SciPy` is built to work with `NumPy` arrays, and it provides many user-friendly and efficient numerical routines, such as routines for numerical integration and optimization.

The next section shows you how to use the Python modules numpy, `pylab`, and `scipy` to render an oscillating wave pattern.

RENDERING AN OSCILLATING WAVE

The combination of the `numpy`, `pylab`, and `scipy` modules enables you to create very compact Python scripts that can create complex plots. However, these scripts are often too terse unless you have in-depth knowledge of the scientific modules for Python.

As an illustration, Listing 7.2 displays the contents of `Oscillate.py` that renders a plot of an oscillating wave that is saved as a PNG file.

LISTING 7.2 Oscillate.py

```
from scipy import special, optimize
from numpy import sin,pi,linspace
from pylab import *
```

```
func = lambda x: -exp(-(x-10)**2)
sol = optimize.minimize(func, 8.0)
x = linspace(0, 200, 5000)

plot(x, special.jv(3, x), '-', sol.x, -sol.fun, 'o')
savefig('scipy1.png')
```

The first part of Listing 7.2 contains import statements, followed by the definition of the lambda function `func`. In case you have not heard about lambda functions, they are anonymous functions (discussed briefly in Chapter 2 and also in Chapter 8). In this example, `func` is defined as an exponential function.

The next portion of Listing 7.2 defines the variable `sol` that is based on the `minimize()` function that belongs to the `scipy` module. The variable `x` is a set of values defined in terms of the `linspace()` function that we discussed earlier in this chapter.

The last two lines of code in Listing 7.2 generate and save a plot based on the variables in this code sample.

Figure 7.2 displays the result of launching Listing 7.2 from the command line on a Macbook Pro.

The next portion of this chapter discusses `TkInter` and shows you examples of rendering various GUI controls and how to render bar charts in 2D and 3D.

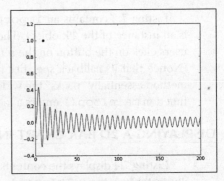

FIGURE 7.2 A damped exponential curve.

WHAT IS TKINTER?

Python supports `TkInter`, which is a toolkit for GUI development. `TkInter` provides support for various GUI controls or widgets (such as buttons, labels, and text boxes) that are used in GUI applications. `TkInter` provides widgets called `Button`, `Canvas`, `Checkbutton`, `Entry`, `Frame`, `Label`, `Listbox`, `Menubutton`, `Menu`, `Message`, `Radiobutton`, `Scale`, `Scrollbar`, `Text`, `Toplevel`, `Spinbox`, `PanedWindow`, `LabelFrame`, and `tkMessageBox`.

Some of their common attributes include `Dimensions`, `Colors`, `Fonts`, `Anchors`, `Relief` styles, `Bitmaps`, and `Cursors`.

TkInter Geometry Management

All `TkInter` widgets have access to specific geometry management methods that organize the layout of widgets. `TkInter` exposes the geometry manager classes `pack`, `grid`, and `place` that enable you to control the layout of widgets.

RENDERING A BUTTON WITH TKINTER

Listing 7.3 displays the contents of `Button1.py` that illustrates how to render a button that responds to user click events.

LISTING 7.3 Button1.py

```
from Tkinter import *

master = Tk()

def callback():
    print "You clicked the button"

btn = Button(master, text="OK", command=callback)
btn.pack()

mainloop()
```

Listing 7.3 contains an `import` statement and the variable `master` that is an instance of the `Tk` object. The function `callback()` is executed when users click on the button on the screen, which is defined via the variable `btn`. (Notice that its callback specifies the `callback()` function.) The `pack()` method essentially "packs" the widgets into a compact rectangle, and then the function `mainloop()` enters a loop and waits for user input.

DISPLAYING A 2D BAR CHART IN PYTHON AND TKINTER

Listing 7.4 displays the contents of the Python script `BarChart1.py` that illustrates how to use `TkInter` to render a bar chart.

LISTING 7.4: BarChart1.py

```
from Tkinter import *

import random

root = Tk()
width  = 600
height = 500

canvas = Canvas(root, bg='#d0d0d0', height=500, width=600)

# set-up variables
upperX        = 40
upperY        = 40
deltaX        = 10
deltaY        = 10
barCount      = 10
barWidth      = 20
barHeight     = 0
minBarHeight  = 20
maxBarHeight  = 300
lineWidth     = 3
```

```
lineColor    = "#000000"
rectColor    = ""

# main loop
# render horizontal axis
lId = canvas.create_line(upperX-deltaX,
                         upperY+maxBarHeight+deltaY,
                         upperX+2*deltaX+barCount*barWidth,
                         upperY+maxBarHeight+deltaY,
                         fill=lineColor,width=lineWidth)

# render vertical axis
lId = canvas.create_line(upperX-deltaX,
                         upperY-deltaY,
                         upperX-deltaX,
                         upperY+maxBarHeight+deltaY,
                         fill=lineColor,width=lineWidth)

# render bar elements
for b in range(0,barCount):
    if(b % 2 == 0):
      rectColor = "#" + "FF0000"
    else:
      rectColor = "#" + "FFFF00"

    upperLX = upperX+b*barWidth
    upperLY = upperY

    barHeight = random.randrange(0, maxBarHeight)
    if(barHeight < minBarHeight):
      barHeight = minBarHeight

    rId = canvas.create_rectangle(upperLX,
                                  upperLY+(maxBarHeight-barHeight),
                                  upperLX+barWidth,
                                  upperLY+maxBarHeight,
                                  fill=rectColor,width=1)

canvas.pack()
root.mainloop()
```

Listing 7.4 initializes a set of variables, followed by a code block that renders the horizontal and vertical axes. The next portion of code contains a for loop that renders a set of bar elements in a bar chart. The if/else code block uses the modulus ("%") function to alternate between red (FF0000) and blue (0000FF). Next, the upper left vertex of the current bar element is · calculated and assigned to upperLX and upperLY. The barHeight variable is assigned a random number between 0 and maxBarHeight, followed by a simple if statement that ensures that the barHeight value is at least minBarHeight.

The next portion of code in the for loop invokes the create_rectangle() method with the (x,y) coordinates of the upper left vertex of the current rectangle, its width, its height, and its fill color.

Figure 7.3 displays the result of launching the code in `BarChart1.py` in a Chrome browser on a Macbook Pro.

Now that you understand how to create a 2D bar chart, the next section shows you how to create a 3D bar chart in Python with `TkInter`.

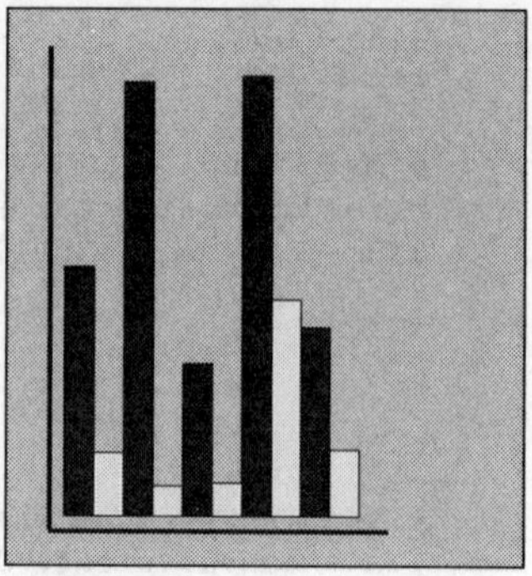

A 3D BAR CHART IN PYTHON AND TKINTER

Listing 7.5 displays the contents of the Python script `BarChart13D1.py` that illustrates how to render a 3D bar chart.

FIGURE 7.3 A bar chart in Python and `TkInter`.

LISTING 7.5: BarChart13D1.py

```
from Tkinter import *

import random

root = Tk()
width  = 600
height = 500

canvas = Canvas(root, bg='#d0d0d0',
                height=500, width=600)

# set-up variables
upperX       = 40
upperY       = 40
deltaX       = 10
deltaY       = 10
barCount     = 10
barWidth     = 40
slantX       = barWidth/2
slantY       = barWidth/4
barHeight    = 0
minBarHeight = 20
maxBarHeight = 300
lineWidth    = 3
lineColor    = "#000000"
rectColor    = ""
topColor     = "#eeeeee"
rightColor   = "#444444"
rectColors   = ["#FF0000", "#0000FF"]
points       = []
pGramWidth   = 1

# main loop
# render horizontal axis
lId = canvas.create_line(upperX-deltaX,
                  upperY+maxBarHeight+deltaY,
```

```
                           upperX+2*deltaX+barCount*barWidth,
                           upperY+maxBarHeight+deltaY,
                           fill=lineColor,width=lineWidth)

# render vertical axis
lId = canvas.create_line(upperX-deltaX,
                         upperY-deltaY,
                         upperX-deltaX,
                         upperY+maxBarHeight+deltaY,
                         fill=lineColor,width=lineWidth)

# render bar elements
for b in range(0,barCount):
    rectColor = rectColors[b % 2];

    upperLX = upperX+b*barWidth
    upperLY = upperY

    barHeight = random.randrange(0, maxBarHeight)
    if(barHeight < minBarHeight):
        barHeight = minBarHeight

    # render front face
    rId = canvas.create_rectangle(upperLX,
                                  upperLY+(maxBarHeight-barHeight),
                                  upperLX+barWidth,
                                  upperLY+maxBarHeight,
                                  fill=rectColor,width=1)

    # render top face (CCW from lower-left vertex)
    points = []
    points.append(upperLX)
    points.append(upperLY+(maxBarHeight-barHeight))

    points.append(upperLX+barWidth)
    points.append(upperLY+(maxBarHeight-barHeight))

    points.append(upperLX+barWidth+slantX)
    points.append(upperLY+(maxBarHeight-barHeight)-slantY)

    points.append(upperLX+0*barWidth+slantX)
    points.append(upperLY+(maxBarHeight-barHeight)-slantY)

    tId = canvas.create_polygon(points, outline='red',
                                fill=topColor, width=pGramWidth)

    # render right face (CCW from upper-left vertex)
    points = []
    points.append(upperLX+barWidth)
    points.append(upperLY+(maxBarHeight-barHeight))

    points.append(upperLX+barWidth)
    points.append(upperLY+(maxBarHeight-barHeight)+barHeight)

    points.append(upperLX+barWidth+slantX)
```

```
        points.append(upperLY+(maxBarHeight-barHeight)+barHeight-slantY)

        points.append(upperLX+barWidth+slantX)
        points.append(upperLY+(maxBarHeight-barHeight)-slantY)

        tId = canvas.create_polygon(points, outline='red',
                                    fill=rightColor, width=pGramWidth)

canvas.pack()
root.mainloop()
```

Listing 7.5 "generalizes" the code in Listing 7.4 in the sense that the front "face" of each bar element is calculated in the same manner. The top "face" and the right "face" are both parallelograms: each one consists of four vertices that are calculated based on the position of the current front "face" in the loop.

Figure 7.4 displays the result of launching Listing 7.5 from the command line.

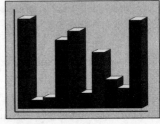

FIGURE 7.4 A 3D bar chart in Python and `TkInter`.

DISPLAYING A LINE GRAPH IN PYTHON AND **TKINTER**

Listing 7.6 displays the contents of the Python script `LineGraph1.py` that illustrates how to use `Tkinter` to render a line graph.

LISTING 7.6: LineGraph1.py
```
from Tkinter import *

import random

root = Tk()
width  = 600
height = 500

canvas = Canvas(root, bg='#d0d0d0',
                height=500, width=600)

# set-up variables
upperX        = 40
upperY        = 40
deltaX        = 10
deltaY        = 10
barCount      = 10
barWidth      = 40
barHeight     = 0
barHeights    = []
minBarHeight  = 20
maxBarHeight  = 300
lineWidth     = 3
lineColor     = "#000000"
rectColor     = ""
```

```
# main loop
# render horizontal axis
lId = canvas.create_line(upperX-deltaX,
                         upperY+maxBarHeight+deltaY,
                         upperX+2*deltaX+barCount*barWidth,
                         upperY+maxBarHeight+deltaY,
                         fill=lineColor,width=lineWidth)

# render vertical axis
lId = canvas.create_line(upperX-deltaX,
                         upperY-deltaY,
                         upperX-deltaX,
                         upperY+maxBarHeight+deltaY,
                         fill=lineColor,width=lineWidth)

for b in range(0,barCount):
    randHeight = random.randrange(0, maxBarHeight)

    if(randHeight < minBarHeight):
        randHeight = minBarHeight
    barHeights.append(randHeight)

print barHeights

# render line segments
for b in range(1,barCount-1):
    if(b % 2 == 0):
        rectColor = "#" + "FF0000"
    else:
        rectColor = "#" + "FFFF00"

    pointX1 = upperX+(b-1)*barWidth
    pointY1 = upperY+barHeights[b-1]

    pointX2 = upperX+b*barWidth
    pointY2 = upperY+barHeights[b]

    rId = canvas.create_line(pointX1, pointY1,
                             pointX2, pointY2,
                             fill=rectColor,width=lineWidth)

canvas.pack()
root.mainloop()
```

Listing 7.6 contains logic similar to that in Listing 7.5, except that Listing 7.6 renders a set of line segments instead of bar elements. Specifically, Listing 7.6 invokes the `create_line()` function with a pair of consecutive points that represent the left "edge" and the right "edge" of the bar elements that are rendered in Listing 7.5.

Figure 7.5 displays the result of launching Listing 7.6 from the command line.

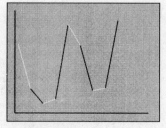

FIGURE 7.5 A line graph in Python and `TkInter`.

TRIGONOMETRIC CURVES IN PYTHON AND TKINTER

Listing 7.7 displays the contents of the Python script `TrigFunctions1.py` that illustrates how to render various trigonometric functions in Python and TkInter.

LISTING 7.7: TrigFunctions1.py

```python
from math import sin, cos
from Tkinter import *

sWidth      = 700
sHeight     = 500
Amplitude   = 150
frequency   = 1
deltaY      = 20
deltaX      = 20
basePointX  = 10
basePointY  = Amplitude+deltaY
currentX    = 0
currentY    = 0
currentY1   = 0
currentY2   = 0
rectColor   = "#ff0000"
rWidth      = 20
rHeight     = 40
maxAngle    = 720
PI          = 3.1415296
rectColors  = ["#FF0000", "#FFFF00", "#00FF00", "#0000FF"];

root = Tk()

canvas = Canvas(root, bg='#d0d0d0',
                height=sHeight, width=sWidth)

for x in range(0,maxAngle):
  # sine wave
  rectColor = rectColors[x % 2]
  currentX = basePointX + x
  currentY = basePointY + Amplitude*sin(frequency*x*PI/180)
  canvas.create_rectangle(currentX,
                          currentY,
                          currentX+rWidth,
                          currentY+rHeight,
                          fill=rectColor,width=0)

  # cosine wave
  currentX = basePointX + x
  currentY = basePointY + Amplitude*cos(2*frequency*x*PI/180)
  rectColor = rectColors[2*((x+1) % 2)]
  canvas.create_rectangle(currentX,
                          currentY,
                          currentX+rWidth,
                          currentY+rHeight,
                          fill=rectColor,width=0)
```

```
# tangent wave
currentX1 = basePointX + x
currentY1 = sin(frequency*x*PI/180)
currentY2 = cos(2*frequency*x*PI/180)

if(currentY2 != 0):
    currentY = basePointY + Amplitude*currentY1/currentY2
else:
    currentY = BasePointY + Amplitude*currentY1

rectColor = rectColors[x % 3]
# canvas.create_rectangle(currentX,
canvas.create_oval(currentX,
                            currentY,
                            currentX+rWidth,
                            currentY+rHeight,
                            fill=rectColor,width=0)
canvas.pack()
root.mainloop()
```

Listing 7.7 initializes a set of variables, followed by a `for` loop that iterates through a set of values between `0` and `maxAngle`. During each loop iteration, the position of a rectangle is calculated that is based on the value in a sine function. A second rectangle and a third rectangle are also calculated based on a cosine function and a tangent function. Thus, each loop iteration renders three rectangles, each of which "follows" a different trigonometric function.

Figure 7.6 displays the result of launching Listing 7.7 from the command line.

The next portion of this chapter shows you SVG-related Python toolkits that enable you to manage SVG documents.

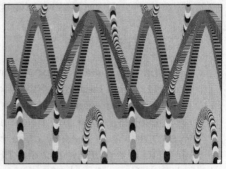

FIGURE 7.6 Various trigonometric functions in Python and `TkInter`.

THE PYSVG TOOLKIT

The `pysvg` toolkit enables you to generate SVG-based graphics, and you can download the `pysvg` toolkit here:

https://code.google.com/p/pysvg/

Install this program with this command:

```
python setup.py install
```

Listing 7.8 displays the contents of the Python script `TestSpiral.py` that illustrates how to render a set of circles that follow the path of an Archimedean spiral.

LISTING 7.8 TestSpiral.py

```python
from pysvg.structure import *
from pysvg.shape import *

import math

def testSpiral():
  mySVG = svg("a spiral")

  for i in range(1, 200):
    x = 2 * i * math.cos(2 * math.pi * i / 40.5) + 450
    y = 2 * i * math.sin(2 * math.pi * i / 40.5) + 450

    #print 'color: rgb(%s,%s,%s)' % (i, 200-i, i*(200-i)/50)
    c = circle(x, y, 0.2 * i)
    fill = 'none'
    strokewidth = 5

    stroke = 'rgb(%s,%s,%s)' % (i, 200-i, i*(200-i)/50)
    myStyle = 'fill:%s;stroke-width:%s; stroke:%s' % \
              (fill, strokewidth, stroke)

    c.set_style(myStyle)
    mySVG.addElement(c)

  mySVG.save('./testoutput/spiral.svg')

if __name__ == '__main__':
  testSpiral()
```

Listing 7.8 contains `import` statements, followed by the function `test-Spiral()` that creates an SVG document called `spiral.svg` in the `testoutput` subdirectory.

The first part of the function `testSpiral()` defines the variable `mySVG` that is an instance of an `svg` object (defined in the `pysvg` module). The next portion of Listing 7.8 contains a loop that iterates through the values between `1` and `200`. During each iteration, the loop calculates the `(x,y)` coordinates of the center of a circle, along with the stroke color and `strokewidth` (the constant 5), and then appends the current circle to the `mySVG` object.

Navigate to the `src/tests` subdirectory of the `pySVG` root directory, and launch the code in Listing 7.8 with this command:

```
python testSpiral.py
```

The preceding command creates the SVG document `spiral.svg` in the `testoutput` subdirectory. Figure 7.7 displays the result of launching `spiral.svg` in a Chrome browser on a Macbook Pro.

FIGURE 7.7 A set of circles in SVG.

THE SVGFIG TOOLKIT

The `svgfig` toolkit is another Python-based toolkit for creating SVG documents, and it is downloadable here:

https://code.google.com/p/svgfig/

Install this module with the following command:

```
python setup.py install
```

Listing 7.9 displays the contents of the Python script `Simple1.py` that illustrates how to generate a rectangle.

LISTING 7.9 Simple1.py

```
from svgfig import *
rect1 = SVG("rect", x=10, y=10, width=60, height=60, fill="red")
print rect1.xml()
```

Listing 7.9 contains an `import` statement followed by the variable `rect1` that is initialized as an SVG `<rect>` element. The print statement displays an XML-based representation of the contents of the variable `rect1`.

The output from 7.9 is here:

```
<rect y=10 width=60 fill='red' x=10 height=60 />
```

Listing 7.10 displays the contents of the Python script `Simple2.py` that illustrates how to generate the SVG document `Simple2.svg` that contains two rectangles.

LISTING 7.10 Simple2.py
```
from svgfig import *

rect1 = SVG("rect", x=10, y=10, width=60, height=60, fill="red")
rect2 = SVG("rect", x=30, y=30, width=60, height=60, fill="blue")
g = SVG("g", rect1, rect2, fill_opacity="50%")
g.save("Simple2.svg")
```

Listing 7.10 contains an import statement, followed by the definition of the variables rect1 and rect2, each of which defines a rectangle. The last code snippet in Listing 7.10 saves the two rectangles as the SVG document Simple2.svg.

Listing 7.11 displays the contents of Simple2.svg, which is the output of the Python script in Listing 7.10.

LISTING 7.11 Simple2.svg
```
<?xml version="1.0" standalone="no"?>
<!DOCTYPE svg PUBLIC "-//W3C//DTD SVG 1.1//EN"
"http://www.w3.org/Graphics/SVG/1.1/DTD/svg11.dtd">

<svg style="stroke-linejoin:round; stroke:black; stroke-
width:0.5pt; text-anchor:middle; fill:none" xmlns="http://www.
w3.org/2000/svg" font-family="Helvetica, Arial, FreeSans, Sans,
sans, sans-serif" height="400px" width="400px" version="1.1"
xmlns:xlink="http://www.w3.org/1999/xlink" viewBox="0 0 100 100">

<g fill-opacity="50%">
<rect y="10" width="60" fill="red" x="10" height="60" />
<rect y="30" width="60" fill="blue" x="30" height="60" />
</g>
</svg>
```

Listing 7.11 contains the <svg> element, whose attributes are automatically inserted for you by the svgfig module itself.

THE SVGWRITE TOOLKIT

The svgwrite module is another Python module that enables you to generate SVG documents, and you can download the svgwrite module here:

https://pypi.python.org/pypi/svgwrite/

Install this program with this command:

```
python setup.py install
```

The examples subdirectory contains various Python scripts for generating SVG documents.

Listing 7.12 displays the contents of TextFonts.py that illustrates how to render a set of text strings in SVG using various font types.

LISTING 7.12: TextFonts.py

```
import sys
import svgwrite

basename = sys.argv[0].rstrip('py')
svgname  = basename+'svg'
myText   = "This is a line of text"

def createSVG(name):
    svgWidth  = 600
    svgHeight = 300
    font_size = 20
    fontSize  = 28
    wFactor   = 2

    svgTitle = 'Text Strings and Generic Fonts'
    colors   = ('#ff0000','#ffff00','#88ff88','#0000ff')
    cCount   = len(colors)

    FFS = ('cursive','monospace','sans-serif','serif')
    dwg = svgwrite.Drawing(name, (svgWidth, svgHeight), \
                          debug=True)

    # grey background (#cccccc)
    dwg.add(dwg.rect(insert=(0, 0), \
            size=('100%', '100%'), fill='#cccccc'))

    # Add the title string
    dwg.add(dwg.text(svgTitle, insert=(0, (fontSize+5)),
       font_family="serif", font_size=fontSize, fill='black'))

    for index in range(len(FFS)):
        font = FFS[index]
        fill = colors[index % cCount]

        dwg.add(dwg.text(font+": "+myText,
            insert=(font_size, fontSize*(index*wFactor+4)),
            font_family=font, font_size=fontSize, fill=fill))

    dwg.save()

if __name__ == '__main__':
    createSVG (basename + 'svg')
```

Listing 7.12 contains some `import` statements, a set of string variables that are initialized, and then the function `createSVG()` that generates an SVG document.

The first part of `createSVG()` initializes an assortment of variables that are used as parameters in the various functions of the `svgwrite` module. The `FFS` array contains some fonts, and the `colors` array contains some colors based on their hexadecimal values.

Next, the variable `dwg` (the drawing surface) is initialized, and a grey rectangle is appended to `dwg`, as well as a title. The next portion of Listing 7.12

contains a loop, and each "pass" through the loop iterates through the array `fonts` and then prints the contents of the string `myText` with the current font and the current color. The final code snippet in the function `createSVG()` invokes the `save()` function, which creates the SVG document `TextFonts.svg` because this is the value of the variable `svgname`.

Now launch the code in Listing 7.12 from the command line and verify that you can see the SVG document `TextFonts.svg` in the same directory.

Figure 7.8 displays the contents of the SVG document `TextFonts.svg` that generates an SVG document based on the code in Listing 7.12.

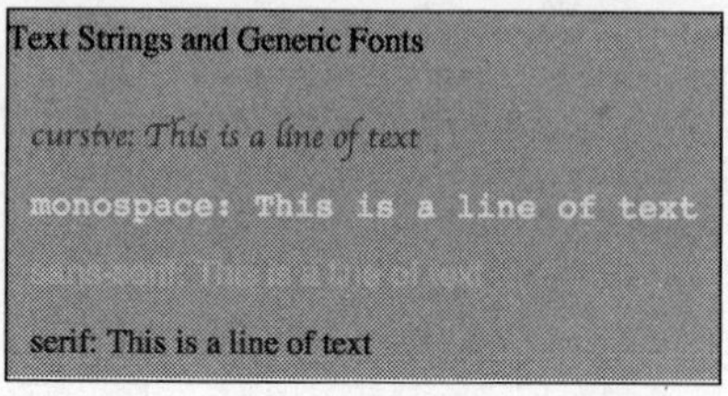

FIGURE 7.8 Generating an SVG document with the `svgwrite` module.

PARSING SVG WITH LXML

The `lxml` module is a Python module that you use in conjunction with the `etree()` function in the numpy module to parse the contents of SVG documents. If you have not already done so, install the numpy Python module on your machine.

Listing 7.13 displays the contents of the Python script `ParseSVG1.py` that illustrates how to use the `lxml` module to parse the contents of an SVG document.

LISTING 7.13 ParseSVG1.py

```
from lxml import etree

filename='Parse1.svg'
svgTree = etree.parse(open(filename,'r'))

#Array of Attribute Values
attributeValues = []

for elem in svgTree.iter():
  tagName = elem.tag.split( "}" )[0]
  print 'Element Name: ', tagName

  #check for rectangle/lines
  if tagName == 'rect':
    x = elem.get('x')
    y = elem.get('y')
    width  = elem.get('width')
    height = elem.get('height')

    attributeValues.append(x)
    attributeValues.append(y)
    attributeValues.append(width)
    attributeValues.append(height)
```

```
     print 'Detected a Rectangle'
     print

  if tagName == 'line':
    x1 = elem.get('x1')
    y1 = elem.get('y1')
    x2 = elem.get('x2')
    y2 = elem.get('y2')

    attributeValues.append(x1)
    attributeValues.append(y1)
    attributeValues.append(x2)
    attributeValues.append(y2)

    print 'Detected a Line Segment'
    print

 #if tagName == 'ellipse':
   #do something here

print 'List of Attribute Values:'
for attrValue in attributeValues:
  print attrValue
```

Listing 7.13 imports the `lxml` module to instantiate the variable `svgTree` by opening (and then parsing) the contents of the SVG document specified by the variable `filename` (which is `Parse1.svg` in this example). The main code block in Listing 7.13 is a loop that iterates through each of the elements in `svgTree`. During each loop iteration, conditional logic checks if the current SVG element is a rectangle or a line. In the case of a rectangle, the values of the attributes `x`, `y`, `width`, and `height` are appended to the array `attributeValues`. Similarly, if the current SVG element is a line, the values of the attributes `x1`, `y1`, `x2`, and `y2` are appended to the array `attributeValues`. If need be, you can also define additional code blocks for other SVG elements.

The final portion of Listing 7.13 contains a loop that iterates through the values in the array `attributeValues` and prints them.

Listing 7.14 displays the contents of the SVG document `Parse1.svg` whose contents are parsed by `ParseSVG1.py`.

LISTING 7.14 Parse1.svg

```
<?xml version="1.0" standalone="no"?>
<!DOCTYPE svg PUBLIC "-//W3C//DTD SVG 1.1//EN"
"http://www.w3.org/Graphics/SVG/1.1/DTD/svg11.dtd">

<svg>
  <g>
    <rect x="100" y="100" width="100" height="80" fill="red"  />
    <rect x="250" y="300" width="100" height="80" fill="blue" />
    <line x1="10" y1="30" x2="200" y2="350" fill="green" />
  </g>
</svg>
```

The output of Listing 7.14 is here:

```
svgTag: svg
Element Name:   svg
Element Name:   g
Element Name:   rect
Detected a Rectangle

Element Name:   rect
Detected a Rectangle

Element Name:   line
Detected a Line Segment

List of Attribute Values:
100
100
100
80
250
300
100
80
10
30
200
350
```

OTHER SVG-RELATED TOOLKITS

The D3.js open-source toolkit is a JavaScript-based layer of abstraction over SVG, and you can download the D3.js toolkit here:

http://d3js.org/

A Python-based open-source toolkit that combines Python and D3.js is here:

https://github.com/mikedewar/d3py

A bar chart with D3.js and Python is here:

http://blog.nextgenetics.net/?e=7

THE PYPROCESSING MODULE FOR GRAPHICS AND ANIMATION

The pyprocessing module is an open-source Python-based port of the Processing language, and you can download pyprocessing here:

https://code.google.com/p/pyprocessing/downloads/list

After you download and uncompress the distribution, install pyprocess-ing with this command:

```
python setup.py install
```

In case you need to install Pyglet, you can do so with this command:

```
pip install pyglet
```

Alternatively, you can use this command:

```
easy_install -U pyglet
```

If you experience errors on a Macbook, you can download the DMG file here:

http://www.pyglet.org/download.html

After uncompressing the distribution, run the following command:

```
python setup.py install
```

As a simple example, the following `pyprocessing` code renders a horizontal line segment:

```
from pyprocessing import *
size(200,200)
line(50,100,150,100)
run()
```

Navigate to the `pyprocessing` homepage for tutorials and additional code samples:

https://code.google.com/p/pyprocessing/

THE KIVY TOOLKIT

The Kivy toolkit is an open-source cross-platform toolkit for developing applications, and you can download this toolkit here:

http://kivy.org/#download

After you download and install the Kivy distribution for your platform, you can look at the samples by downloading the source code with the following command:

```
git clone http://github.com/kivy/kivy
```

Launch one of the code samples with the following commands:

```
cd $KIVYDIR/examples/demo/kivycatalog
python main.py
```

Experiment with other Kivy code samples and visit the homepage for more information about Kivy.

SUMMARY

This chapter introduced you to data visualization using Python. You learned about the Python modules `matplotlib`, `numpy`, `pylab`, and `scipy`. Next you learned how to manually create charts and graphs, along with creating some abstract visual effects using Python. You also learned about SVG-related Python modules, such as `svgwrite`, which enables you to generate SVG documents based on Python scripts.

EXERCISES

Exercise 1: Given a JSON string (refer to Chapter 6 regarding JSON) consisting of stock quotes and stock values, display a bar chart where each bar element represents the value of a stock. Make sure that you scale the bar chart so that the maximum height of any element is 200.

Exercise 2: Write a Python script that renders a multi-line graph using randomly generated values for the points on each line. (The code for the bar chart that you wrote in Exercise #1 might be helpful.)

Exercise 3: Write a Python script that renders an area graph using randomly generated values for the data. (The code for a single-line graph might be helpful.)

Exercise 4: Modify the code in `BarChart1.py` to create `SplitBar-Chart1.py`, whose bar elements are divided into two equal rectangles (one rectangle is above the other rectangle) that are rendered with different colors.

Exercise 5: Write a Python script that renders a "clustered" histogram, in which a pair of adjacent bar elements are rendered, followed by a gap, and then another pair of adjacent bar elements are rendered (and so forth). Render five pairs of adjacent bar elements separated by gaps, using the technique that you used in Exercise 4 to divide each bar element into two rectangles.

## CHAPTER 8

BUILT-IN FUNCTIONS AND CUSTOM CLASSES

This chapter introduces you to some Python built-in functions, how to create custom classes in Python, and object-oriented concepts such as inheritance and polymorphism.

The first part of this chapter discusses Python functions such as the `filter()` function, the `map()` function, and the `reduce()` function. You will also learn something about `lambda` functions, which are often used in conjunction with these Python functions.

The second part of this chapter shows you how to define custom classes and how to manage lists of objects that are instances of your custom Python classes.

The final portion of this chapter contains a basic introduction to encapsulation, single and multiple inheritance, and polymorphism in Python. There are many subtle points involving inheritance and object-oriented programming, and after you have read this chapter you can perform a "deep dive" into this topic to write object-oriented Python code.

A PYTHON MODULE VERSUS A PACKAGE

A module generally contains definitions, functions, and Python code, and it "lives" in a file with a `.py` extension. A module can also import other modules, and by convention, the `import` statements are placed at the top of the file (but this is not a strict requirement). Note that zip files and DLL files can also be modules.

However, when a module imports a directory, the presence of the file `__init__.py` is significant, because Python will then treat the directory as a package. The file `__init__.py` can contain some initialization code for the package (or, in fact, can even be empty), and such a file appears in each subdirectory that must be treated as a package by Python.

As you have seen in previous chapters, a module uses the `import` statement to import another module, and this can be accomplished in various ways. You can import a single module from a package, as shown here:

```
import myutils.xmlparse
```

The preceding code imports the `xml` submodule `myutils.xml`, and it must be fully qualified in your code, as shown here:

```
myutils.xmlparse(xmlDoc)
```

Another way to import the submodule `xmlparse` is here:

```
from myutils import xmlparse
```

Although the preceding code imports the `xml` submodule `xmlparse`, the latter is available without the package prefix, as shown here:

```
xmlparse(xmlDoc)
```

You can even import a single function from a module, as shown here:

```
from myutils.xmlparse import parseDOM
```

PYTHON FUNCTIONS VERSUS METHODS

A method is a function, but a function is not necessarily a method. A method is a function that is "attached" to an object or a class. Thus, `str.upper()` is a method, whereas `sorted()` is a function because there is no object specified for this function.

In addition, functions can be available as methods, which happens to be the case for the functions in the `re` module: `re.sub` is a function, and if you make a regex object by compiling a pattern, many of the module functions are also available as methods on the resulting object. An example is here:

```
>>> import re
>>> regex = re.compile("\d+")
>>> regex.sub # this is a method
>>> re.sub # this is a function because re is a package
```

The distinction between function and method is whether the function is defined in a class or not. Functions in a module are just functions; functions in a class are methods of the class or methods of the resulting objects.

In addition, *function* is a more general term. (All methods are functions but not all functions are methods.) Thus, the word *function* is used as a "generic term," whereas the word *method* is used specifically with regard to classes or objects (the method of the `list` type, the methods of the `str` type, and so forth).

FUNCTIONALLY ORIENTED PROGRAMMING IN PYTHON

Python supports methods (called *iterators* in Python 3), such as `fil-ter()`, `map()`, and `reduce()`, that are very useful when you need to iterate over the items in a list, create a dictionary, or extract a subset of a list. These iterators are discussed in the following subsections.

The Python `filter()` Function

The filter function enables you to extract a subset of values based on conditional logic. The following example returns a list of the odd numbers between 0 and 15 (including 0 but excluding 15) that are multiples of 3:

```
>>> range(0,15)
[0, 1, 2, 3, 4, 5, 6, 7, 8, 9, 10, 11, 12, 13, 14]
>>> def f(x): return x % 2 != 0 and x % 3 == 0
...
>>> filter(f, range(0, 15))
[3, 9]
>>>
```

The Python `map()` Function

The Python `map()` command is a built-in function that applies a function to each item in an iterable. The `map(func, seq)` calls `func(item)`, where `item` is an element in a sequence `seq`, and returns a list of the returned values.

Listing 8.1 displays the contents of `Map1.py` that illustrates how to use the `map()` function to compute the cube and the fourth power of a set of numbers.

LISTING 8.1 Map1.py

```
def cube(x): return x*x*x
def fourth(x): return x*x*x*x

x1 = map(cube,   range(1, 5))
x2 = map(fourth, range(1, 5))

print x1
print x2
```

Listing 8.1 starts with the definition of two functions, called `cube()` and `fourth()`, each of which takes a single numeric value. The `cube()` function returns the cube of its argument, and the `fourth()` function returns the fourth power of its argument.

The next portion of Listing 8.1 contains two invocations of the `map()` function. The first invocation specifies the `cube()` function as the first parameter and the integers between 1 and 4, inclusive, as the second parameter via the `range()` function. The second invocation specifies the `fourth()` function as the first parameter, along with the integers between 1 and 4, inclusive, as the second parameter.

The output from Listing 8.1 is here:

```
[1, 8, 27, 64]
[1, 16, 81, 256]
```

The Python `lambda` Operator

The `lambda` operator (or `lambda` function) enables you to define "anonymous" functions that are often used in combination with the functions `filter()`, `map()`, and `reduce()`.

An example of a `lambda` function that adds two arguments is here:

```
>>> f = lambda x,y : x + y
>>> f(2,3)
5
```

The next section shows you how to use this `lambda` function with the `reduce()` function in Python.

The Python `reduce()` Function

The `reduce(func, seq)` function returns a single value constructed by calling the binary function `func` on the first two items of the sequence `seq` to compute a result, and then applies `func` on that result and the *next* item in `seq`, and so on until a single value is returned. Thus, the `reduce()` function repeatedly performs a pair-wise reduction (hence its name) on a sequence until a single value is computed.

As an illustration, the following example defines a `lambda` function `add` and a sequence `range(1,5)` that calculates the sum of the numbers 1 through 6:

```
>>> f = lambda x,y: x+y
>>> reduce(f, range(1,6))
15
```

In case the functionality of the `reduce()` function is new to you, there are other scenarios that involve similar functionality. For example, recall that multiplication of two numbers is implemented as repeated addition (along with a `shift` operator). As a second example, NoSQL databases perform operations using map/reduce algorithms, and the reduce portion has a similar implementation.

IMPORTING CUSTOM PYTHON MODULES

In addition to importing Python Standard Library modules, you can import your custom modules into other custom modules.

Listing 8.2 and Listing 8.3 display the contents of `Double.py` and `CallDouble.py`, respectively, that illustrate this functionality.

LISTING 8.2: Double.py

```
def double(num):
    return 2*num

result = double(5)
print 'double 5 =', result
```

Listing 8.2 defines the function double() that returns 2 times its argument, followed by the variable result that is assigned the value of double(5). If you invoke Listing 8.2 from the Python interpreter or launch the program from the command line, you will see the following output:

```
double 5 = 10
```

LISTING 8.3: CallDouble.py

```
import Double
```

Listing 8.3 contains one line of code: an import statement that imports the Double module that is displayed in Listing 8.2.

Launch Listing 8.3 from the command line and the output is shown here:

```
double 5 = 10
```

The combination of Listing 8.2 and Listing 8.3 demonstrates how easy it is to import a custom Python module. However, you obviously need the flexibility of invoking imported functions with different values.

Listing 8.4 and Listing 8.5 display the contents of Triple.py and Call-Triple.py that illustrate how to achieve this flexibility.

LISTING 8.4: Triple.py

```
def triple(num):
    return 3*num
```

Listing 8.4 contains only the definition of the function triple() that returns 3 times its argument, and there are no invocations of that function or any print statements.

LISTING 8.5: CallTriple.py

```
from Triple import triple

print '3 times 4 is:', triple(4)
print '3 times 9 is:', triple(9)
```

Launch Listing 8.5 from the command line, and you will see the following output:

```
3 times 4 is: 12
3 times 9 is: 27
```

Suppose that `Triple.py` also contained a function called `quadruple()` and that you wanted to import that function. You can do so with the following variation of the `import` statement:

```
from Triple import double, quadruple
```

If you want to import *all* the functions that are defined in `Triple.py`, use this form of the `import` statement:

```
from Triple import *
```

This concludes the brief overview regarding how to import custom modules. The next section in this chapter shows you how to define your own custom classes in Python.

HOW TO CREATE CUSTOM CLASSES

The Python language supports the creation of custom classes, which is available in other programming languages, such as Java and C++. However, there is the "Python way" of creating custom classes, which you will learn about in this chapter.

As a starting point, Listing 8.6 displays the contents of `SimpleClass.py` that illustrates how to define a simple custom class called `BaseClass` in Python.

LISTING 8.6 SimpleClass.py

```python
#!/usr/bin/env python

class BaseClass:
    def __init__(self):
        self.x = 3

    def main(self):
        print 'inside main'
        print 'x:',self.x

if __name__ == '__main__':
    baseClass = BaseClass()
    baseClass.main()
```

Listing 8.6 starts with the definition of the class `BaseClass` that contains two functions. The built-in "magic" function `__init__` (explained in the next section) assigns the value 3 to the variable `x`. The `main()` function contains two `print` statements that display the string "`inside main`" and also the value of the variable `x`.

The next portion of Listing 8.6 uses conditional logic to instantiate the class `BaseClass` and assign that instance to the variable `baseClass` and then to invoke the `main()` method of `baseClass`.

The output of `SimpleClass.py` is here:

```
inside main
x: 3
```

CONSTRUCTION AND INITIALIZATION OF OBJECTS

In the previous section, you saw an example of the `__init__` function, which is one of the "magic" methods that exist in Python. Three magic methods are shown here:

```
__init__
__new__
__del__
```

In brief, the `__new__` method is invoked to create an instance of a class, which occurs when you invoke the following type of statement:

```
myObj = MyClass()
```

Next, any arguments during the creation time of an object are passed to the "initializer" method `__init__`, which specifies the behavior of an object during initialization. You can think of the `__new__` and `__init__` methods as the "constructor" of an object.

For example, consider the following snippet:

```
myObj = MyClass('pizza', 25);
```

In the preceding code snippet, the values `pizza` and `25` are passed as arguments to the `__init__` method.

Finally, when an object is deleted, the "destructor" method `__del__` is invoked, and it defines behavior during garbage collection. This method is useful when additional resources need to be deallocated. However, there is no guarantee that `__del__` will be executed, so it's better to close resources (such as database connections and sockets) when they are no longer needed.

NOTE *If you are a beginner, you rarely (if ever) need to use the* `__new__` *and* `__del__` *methods.*

There are *many* other magic methods in Python (for comparisons, numeric functions, conversions, and so forth), and an extensive list of such methods is here:

http://docs.python.org/2/reference/datamodel.html#specialnames

COMPILED MODULES

The directory that contains the module `Triple.py` will also contain the compiled version called `Triple.pyc`, which is automatically generated by

Python to improve performance. The contents of `Triple.pyc` are platform independent, and therefore machines of different architectures can share a Python module directory.

You can also invoke the Python interpreter with the `-O` flag, and Python will generate optimized code that is stored in `.pyo` files. In addition, `.pyc` files are ignored and `.py` files are compiled to optimized bytecode when the `-O` flag is used. Keep in mind that there is no difference in speed when a program is read from a `.pyc` or `.pyo` file versus from a `.py` file; the only difference is the load time.

CLASSES, FUNCTIONS, AND METHODS IN PYTHON

In high-level terms, a Python function is a block of code that:

• is called by name
• can be passed data to operate on (i.e., the parameters)
• can optionally return data (the return value)

All data that is passed to a function is explicitly passed.
On the other hand, a Python method is a block of code that:

• is called by name
• is associated with an object

A method differs from a function in two ways:

• a method is implicitly passed the object for which it was called
• a method is able to operate on data that is contained within the class

Keep in mind that that an object is always an instance of a class. If you think of a class as the "definition," then the object is an instance of that definition.

Instance variables in an object have values that are local to that object; in other words, two instances of the same class maintain distinct values for their variables. On the other hand, the value of *class variables* is the same for all the objects that are instances of the same class. In the Java world, a variable that is declared as static is a class variable, so if you change its value in one object, its new value is visible among all objects that are instances of the same class. By way of comparison, methods in C++ are called member functions, and Java contains only methods (not functions). A method can manipulate private data that is defined in a class.

One of the significant changes in Python 3.x (compared to Python 2.x) is the manner in which objects are handled. The details are not discussed in this book, but you can perform an online search to find articles that explain the differences.

ACCESSORS AND MUTATORS VERSUS @PROPERTY

Object-oriented languages, such as Java, encourage the use of accessors and mutators (often called getters and setters) rather than directly accessing a property. For example, if x is a property of a custom class, then you would have the method getX() that returned the value of x and the method setX() that set the value of x. (You would also specify an argument in the case of the setX() method.)

By contrast, Python has an @property "decorator" that lets you add getters and setters retroactively for attribute access.

Consider the following example:

```
>>> class Foo(object):
...     @property
...     def foo(self):
...         return 4
>>> obj = Foo()
>>> obj.foo
4
```

The preceding code defines a class Foo with a method called foo(). The variable obj is an instance of the class Foo, and notice how it's possible to write obj.foo to obtain the result (which is 4). This functionality is possible because of the @property decorator in Python.

Consequently, you can define your custom Python classes by "allowing" attribute access, and if it becomes necessary to add get/set methods later on, you can do so without breaking any existing code.

NOTE *Accessors and mutators are common in languages such as Java, whereas direct access is preferred in Python.*

CREATING AN EMPLOYEE CUSTOM CLASS

This section contains an example of defining a custom Python class to keep track of some employee-related information. In the object-oriented (OO) world, this type of class is called a "value object," because its only purpose is to keep track of one or more properties (such as the properties of a mailing address or a customer).

The example in this section uses accessors for accessing property values as well as accessing these values directly so that you can see how to use both techniques.

Listing 8.7 displays the contents of the custom Python class Employee. py that keeps track of an employee's first name, last name, and title.

LISTING 8.7: Employee.py
```
#!/usr/bin/env python
```

```python
class Employee(object):
    def __init__(self,fname,lname,title):
        self.fname = fname
        self.lname = lname
        self.title = title

    def firstName(self):
        return self.fname

    def lastName(self):
        return self.lname

    def theTitle(self):
        return self.title

    def main(self):
        print 'fname:',self.fname
        print 'lname:',self.lname
        print 'title:',self.title

if __name__ == '__main__':
    emp1 = Employee('John','Smith','Director')
    emp1.main()
    print 'Last Name:',(emp1.lastName())
    print

    emp2 = Employee('Jane','Edwards','VP')
    emp2.main()
    print 'Last Name:',(emp2.lastName())
    print
```

Listing 8.7 contains the definition of the Employee class, which defines the three functions firstName(), lastName(), and theTitle() that return the current employee's first name, last name, and title, respectively. In addition, the __init__ function contains initialization code that sets the values of the same three properties, and the main() function prints the values of these three properties.

The final portion of Listing 8.7 contains the standard Python idiom for distinguishing between direct execution (such as from the command line) versus simply importing a module into another Python module. In our case, this class will be launched directly, which means that the code block will instantiate emp1 and emp2, both of which are instances of the Employee class. In addition, the code initializes the properties for emp1 and emp2 and then prints the values of those properties by invoking the main() method.

In addition, you can retrieve the value of a property by invoking its associated method in much the same way that you would in other programming languages such as Java. An example of retrieving and then printing the last name of the first employee is here:

```python
print 'Last Name:',emp1.lastName()
```

As you can undoubtedly guess, you can display the first name and title of the first employee by invoking `emp1.firstName()` and `emp1.title()`, respectively.

WORKING WITH A LIST OF EMPLOYEES

In the previous section, you learned how to create the custom Python class `Employee` that keeps track of three attributes of an employee. This section shows you how to create a custom Python class called `Employees` that creates a list of `Employee` objects, where each object contains information about a single employee.

Listing 8.8 displays the contents of the Python module `Employees.py` that uses a Python list to keep track of multiple `Employee` objects, each of which represents information about a single employee.

LISTING 8.8: Employees.py

```
#!/usr/bin/env python

from Employee import *

class Employees:
    def __init__(self):
        self.list = []

    def firstEmp(self):
        return self.list[0]

    def addEmp(self,emp):
        self.list.append(emp)

    def displayAll(self):
        for i in range(0,len(self.list)):
            emp = self.list[i]
            print 'First:',emp.firstName()
            print 'Last:', emp.lastName()
            print 'Title:',emp.theTitle()
            print '--------------'

if __name__ == '__main__':
    emp1 = Employee('John','Smith','Director')
    emp2 = Employee('Jane','Edwards','VP')
    emp3 = Employee('Dave','Jones','Manager')

    allEmps = Employees()

    allEmps.addEmp(emp1)
    allEmps.addEmp(emp2)
    allEmps.addEmp(emp3)

    allEmps.displayAll()
```

Listing 8.8 starts with an `import` statement that imports the definition of the `Employee` class that was defined in the previous section.

Next, Listing 8.8 contains the definition of the `Employee` class that defines several methods. The `__init__` method simply initializes an empty list that will keep track of each `Employee` object. The `firstEmp()` method returns the first `Employee` object in the list, and the `addEmp()` method appends the current `Employee` instance to the list. The `displayAll()` method iterates through the list of employees and prints the three properties of each `Employee` object. This functionality is possible because the `Employee` object was imported, and therefore its methods are accessible in Listing 8.8.

The output of Listing 8.8 is here:

```
First: John
Last: Smith
Title: Director
--------------
First: Jane
Last: Edwards
Title: VP
--------------
First: Dave
Last: Jones
Title: Manager
--------------
```

The code sample in this section (and that in the previous section) provides an example of how you can use a collection (in the English sense of the word) of Python classes to model a real-world scenario (i.e., tracking employees in a company). Although the syntax is different, other object-oriented languages (such as Java and C#) use a similar approach.

There are several ways in which you can enhance this code sample. First, you can use a database to persist employee-related information. A database can provide various benefits, such as enforcing transaction-related integrity, and can also enable you to deploy the application to different platforms.

Second, you can provide Web services that can perform similar functionality in a Web browser instead of the command line.

A CUSTOM CLASS FOR PARSING XML WITH SAX

In Chapter 6, you learned about XML and how to write Python code that can parse XML documents. In that chapter you saw how to use a DOM-based parser, and in this section you will see a custom Python class that uses a SAX parser.

Listing 8.9 displays the contents of the Python script `PythonSAX.py` that demonstrates how to parse the XML document `testtransforms.xml`.

LISTING 8.9 PythonSAX.py.

```
import xml.sax

class SvgHandler(xml.sax.ContentHandler):
    def startElement(self, name, attrs):
```

```
        if name == "svg":
            for (k,v) in attrs.items():
                print k + " " + v

parser = xml.sax.make_parser()
parser.setContentHandler(SvgHandler())
parser.parse(open("testtransforms.xml","r"))
```

Listing 8.9 imports `sax` from the `xml` module and then defines the custom class `SvgHandler` that contains the `startElement()` function. If the `name` argument has the value `svg`, this function iterates through the name/value pairs in the `attrs` variable and prints their values.

Since Listing 8.9 processes the lone `<svg>` element and ignores the other elements in `testtransforms.xml`, only this element is displayed here (the complete file is on the CD):

```
<svg xmlns="http://www.w3.org/2000/svg" height="100%" width="100%"
version="1.1" xmlns:xlink="http://www.w3.org/1999/xlink"
viewBox="0 0 950 630"  >
```

The output of Listing 8.9 is here:

```
xmlns http://www.w3.org/2000/svg
height 100%
width 100%
version 1.1
xmlns:xlink http://www.w3.org/1999/xlink
viewBox 0 0 950 630
```

`ContentHandler` supports other methods, but the purpose of this example was to illustrate the use of the `startElement()` method. Perform an Internet search if you want to learn more about how to manage XML documents in Python.

WORKING WITH LINKED LISTS IN PYTHON

You can use Python to create other data structures that are not a part of the Python distribution. In this section, you will learn how to create a singly linked list using custom Python classes. Although they are not discussed in this book, you can create other related data structures, such as doubly linked lists and circular lists. Each node in a doubly linked list contains a reference to its predecessor and its successor, whereas each node in a singly linked list contains only a reference to its successor. A circular list can be a singly linked list or a doubly linked list; in addition, the "tail," or final node, references the "head," or root node, thereby making the list circular.

The next section contains an example of a singly linked list in Python.

CUSTOM CLASSES AND LINKED LISTS

Listing 8.10 displays the contents of `LLAndList.py` that illustrates how to create a linked list whose nodes contain the values in a Python list.

LISTING 8.10: LLAndList.py

```
class Node:
  def __init__(self):
    # contains the data
    self.data = None

    # reference to the next node
    self.next = None

# this creates a tail->head list
# instead of a head->tail list
class LinkedList:
  def __init__(self):
    self.curr_node = None

  # create and append a new node
  def add_node(self, data):
    new_node = Node()
    new_node.data = data

    # link new node to 'previous' node
    new_node.next = self.curr_node

    # current node equals the new node
    self.curr_node = new_node

  def print_items(self):
    node = self.curr_node
    while node:
        print node.data
        node = node.next

list1 = ['a', '12', 'b', '34', 'c', 'd']
myLL = LinkedList()

# add items to the linked list
for val in list1:
  myLL.add_node(val)

print 'List of Items:'
myLL.print_items()
```

Listing 8.10 contains the definition of the Node class, which creates a "value object" that will contain the value of each element in list1 via the data property. The Node class also defines the next property, whose value represents the next element in the list.

The next portion of Listing 8.10 defines the LinkedList class that performs some initialization in the __init__ method and also defines the add_node() and print_items() methods. The add_node() method adds a new node to the linked list by invoking the Node class and then updating the value of the next property appropriately.

Finally, the print_items() method displays the data value of each node in the linked list.

The output of Listing 8.10 is here:

```
List of Items:
d
c
34
b
12
a
```

CUSTOM CLASSES AND DICTIONARIES

Listing 8.11 displays the contents of LLAndDict.py that illustrates how to create a linked list in which each node references a Python dictionary.

LISTING 8.11: LLAndDict.py

```
class Node:
  def __init__(self):
    # contains the data
    self.data = None

    # reference to the next node
    self.next = None

# this creates a tail->head list
# instead of a head->tail list
class LinkedList:
  def __init__(self):
    self.curr_node = None

  # create and append a new node
  def add_node(self, data):
    new_node = Node()
    new_node.data = data

    # link new node to 'previous' node
    new_node.next = self.curr_node

    # current node equals the new node
    self.curr_node = new_node

  def print_items(self):
    node = self.curr_node
    while node:
        print node.data
        node = node.next

dict1 = {'a':'aaa', 'b':'bbb', 'c': 'ccc'}
myLL = LinkedList()

# add items to the linked list
for w in dict1:
  myLL.add_node(w+" "+dict1[w])
```

```
print 'List of Keys and Values:'
myLL.print_items()
```

Listing 8.11 contains code that is very similar to that in the previous section. The difference involves the following code block that uses a Python `dict` instead of a Python list:

```
dict1 = {'a':'aaa', 'b':'bbb', 'c': 'ccc'}
myLL = LinkedList()

# add items to the linked list
for w in dict1:
  myLL.add_node(w+" "+dict1[w])

print 'List of Keys and Values:'
myLL.print_items()
```

As you can see, the preceding code block creates a node consisting of the concatenation of the key/value pairs of each element in the variable `dict1`.

The output of Listing 8.11 is here:

```
List of Keys and Values:
b bbb
c ccc
a aaa
```

CUSTOM CLASSES AND PRIORITY QUEUES

In Chapter 3, you learned about the `Queue` data structure. In this section, you will see how to create and populate a priority queue with objects.

Listing 8.12 displays the contents of `PriorityQueue.py` that illustrates how to create a priority queue and populate the queue with instances of the custom `Task` class.

LISTING 8.12: PriorityQueue.py

```
import Queue
from random import randint

pLevel      = ''
taskCount   = 4
minPriority = 3
maxPriority = 10

q = Queue.PriorityQueue()

class Task(object):
  def __init__(self, priority, name):
      self.priority = priority
      self.name= name
      print 'Added a new task:', name
  def __cmp__(self, other):
      return cmp(self.priority, other.priority)
```

```
def displayTasks():
 ·while not q.empty():
    curr_Task = q.get()
    print 'Processing Task:', curr_Task.name

def addTasks():
  for i in range(0,taskCount):
    p = randint(minPriority, maxPriority);

    if(p < minPriority+maxPriority/4):
      pLevel = 'Low Priority'
    elif(p < minPriority+maxPriority/2):
      pLevel = 'Medium Priority'
    else:
      pLevel = 'High Priority'
    q.put(Task(p, pLevel))
  print

if __name__ == '__main__':
  addTasks()
  displayTasks()
```

Listing 8.12 starts by initializing the variable q, which is an instance of the `PriorityQueue` class in Python. Next, Listing 8.12 defines a `Task` class that performs some initialization in the `__init__` method and defines how to compare two items in the `__cmp__` method. In addition, the `displayTasks()` method displays the current set of tasks, and the `add-Tasks()` method adds a new task in the priority queue. The `addTasks()` method generates a random number for the priority of each new task and then uses conditional logic to determine whether the task has low, medium, or high priority. The final portion of Listing 8.12 invokes the `addTasks()` method, followed by the `displayTasks()` method.

The output from Listing 8.12 is here:

```
Added a new task: Low Priority
Added a new task: Medium Priority
Added a new task: Medium Priority
Added a new task: Medium Priority

Processing Task: Low Priority
Processing Task: Medium Priority
Processing Task: Medium Priority
Processing Task: Medium Priority
```

OVERLOADING OPERATORS

By way of illustration, suppose that you want to extend the add operator in Python. You can do so by overloading (that is, creating another definition for) the `__add__` method as follows:

```
class Test(object):
    def __init__(self): self.prop = 3
```

```
    def __add__(self, x):
        return self.prop + x
```

Enter the following command at the command line:

```
Test() + 4
```

You will see the following output:

```
7
```

SERIALIZING AND DESERIALIZING DATA

"Pickling" is the process whereby a Python object hierarchy is converted into a byte stream. Generally, you can pickle (serialize) any object if you can pickle every attribute of that object. Keep in mind that you cannot pickle classes, functions, and methods.

With pickle protocol v1, you cannot pickle open file objects, network connections, or database connections; however, you *can* pickle open file objects with pickle protocol v2.

Python enables you to pickle data in lists, dictionaries, and so forth, after which you can "de-pickle" (deserialize) that data.

NOTE *Pickled files can be hacked, so be careful if you receive a raw pickle file over the network, because it could contain malicious code to run arbitrary Python when you attempt to de-pickle it.*

Listing 8.13 displays the contents of `Serialize1.py` that illustrates how to serialize and then deserialize a Python object.

LISTING 8.13: Serialize1.py

```
import pickle

# Some Python object
data = [1,2,3,4,5]
print 'original data:', data

f = open('testfile', 'wb')
pickle.dump(data, f)

s = pickle.dumps(data)

# Restore from a file
f = open('testfile', 'rb')
data = pickle.load(f)

# Restore from a string
data = pickle.loads(s)

print 'restored data:', data
```

Listing 8.13 starts with an `import` statement, followed by the `data` variable that is initialized as a list containing five numbers. Next, the file `testfile` is created and the pickled contents of `data` are stored in that file. The remainder of Listing 8.13 reverses the process and prints the de-pickled contents that match the original contents of the `data` variable.

The output from Listing 8.13 is here:

```
original data: [1, 2, 3, 4, 5]
restored data: [1, 2, 3, 4, 5]
```

A minimalistic example of pickling a class is here:

```
import pickle
class MyClass:
  attribute = 'a simple attribute'

picklestring = pickle.dumps(MyClass)
```

ENCAPSULATION

One of the main reasons for public accessors and mutators is their ability to retrieve and update the values of private variables. The ability to "shield" instances of other classes from the internal implementation details of a given class is called *encapsulation*. The advantage of encapsulation is the ability to change the inner workings of a class without changing the signature of the API. As a result, instances of other classes, as well as public APIs, can continue working correctly. Thus, you don't need to worry about updating the signature of the API (provided that the method is not deprecated and replaced with a new method that has a different signature).

SINGLE INHERITANCE

There are two types of (single) inheritance that you will encounter in programming languages. "Classical" class-based inheritance that you will encounter in strongly typed languages that perform compile-time checking for variables (such as Java and C++), and the second type is prototype-based inheritance that you will encounter in functional languages such as JavaScript.

Class mechanisms in Python resemble those in C++, partly because both support multiple inheritance (discussed in the next section). On the other hand, Java supports only single-class inheritance (but a Java class can implement multiple interfaces). However, all methods in Python and Java are virtual.

Languages such as JavaScript treat functions as "first-class citizens" in the sense that they have the same "parity" as objects, whereas methods have a "subordinate" role in classical languages such as Java and C++ because methods exist only as part of a class definition. Another consideration is whether or not functions (and methods) have so-called side effects, such as modifying the value of global or static variables. In the XSLT world (briefly mentioned in Chapter 6), all variables are treated as read-only variables, which eliminates the problems associated with side effects, but at the same time, XSLT is a specialized functional programming language that is arguably more difficult to master than imperative languages such as Java and C++.

As a simple example, Listing 8.14 displays the contents of SingleInherit1.py that illustrates inheritance in Python.

LISTING 8.14: SingleInherit1.py

```
class ClassA:
    def __init__(self):
      print 'Hello from A'

    def func(self):
      print 'Hello again from A'

class ClassB(ClassA):
    def __init__(self):
      print 'Hello from B'

   #def func(self):
   #  print 'Hello again from B'

if __name__ == '__main__':
    instanceA = ClassA()
    instanceB = ClassB()

    print
    print 'instanceA:'
    instanceA.func()
    print 'instanceB:'
    instanceB.func()
```

Listing 8.14 defines ClassA with a print statement in the function __init__ as well as a print statement in function func(). Next, ClassB is defined as a subclass, or derived class, of ClassA. Notice that func() is "commented out" in ClassB and that the __init__ function also contains a print statement.

The final code block in Listing 8.14 instantiates instanceA of ClassA and instanceB of ClassB, followed by some print statements.

The output of Listing 8.14 is here:

```
Hello from A
Hello from B

instanceA:
Hello again from A
instanceB:
Hello again from A
```

INHERITANCE AND OVERRIDING METHODS

If class A is a subclass of class B, then everything in B is accessible in A. In addition, class A can define methods that:

1) are unavailable in B
2) override methods in B

If class B and class A both contain a method called func(), then func() in class B can override func() in class A. As strange as it might seem, a method of class A can call another method that is defined in class A that can invoke a method of class B that overrides it.

Python has two built-in functions that work with inheritance:

• The isinstance() method checks the type of an instance
• The issubclass() method checks class inheritance

For example, isinstance(myObj, int) evaluates to True only if myObj.__class__ is int or a subclass of int, whereas issubclass(bool, int) evaluates to True because bool is a subclass of int. On the other hand, issubclass(unicode, str) evaluates to False because unicode is not a subclass of str.

MULTIPLE INHERITANCE

The previous section showed you how to work with single inheritance, and this section briefly discusses multiple inheritance in Python. As you can probably surmise, multiple inheritance means that a class can have more than one parent class.

If you do decide to use multiple inheritance, keep the following point in mind: Suppose that ClassC is a subclass of ClassA and ClassB as follows:

```
class ClassC(ClassA, ClassB):
```

In addition, suppose that Class A and Class B *both* contain a function called func() that is not defined in ClassC. Now consider the following code snippet, where classC is an instance of ClassC:

```
classC.func()
```

Since ClassC does not contain the definition of the function func(), Python searches for func() in the parent classes. Since the search is performed in a left-to-right fashion, the preceding code snippet executes the method func() that is defined in ClassA and not the method func() in ClassB.

As another example, suppose that ClassC is a subclass (from left to right) of ClassA1, ClassA2, and ClassA3 (in this order) and that the method func() is defined only in ClassA2 and ClassA3 but not in ClassA1 or in

ClassC. Again consider the following snippet, where classC is an instance of ClassC:

```
classC.func()
```

Because of the left-to-right search rule, the preceding code snippet invokes the method func() in ClassA2 and not the function func() in ClassA3. Make sure that you remember this fact when you define classes that contain more than one parent class.

As a concrete example, Listing 8.15 displays the contents of MultipleInherit1.py that illustrates multiple inheritance in Python.

LISTING 8.15: MultipleInherit1.py

```python
class ClassA:
   def __init__(self):
     print 'Hello from A'

   def func(self):
     print 'Hello again from A'

class ClassB:
   def __init__(self):
     print 'Hello from B'

   def func(self):
     print 'Hello again from B'

class ClassC(ClassA, ClassB):
   def __init__(self):
     print 'Hello from C'

if __name__ == '__main__':
   instanceA = ClassA()
   instanceB = ClassB()
   instanceC = ClassC()

   print
   print 'instanceA:'
   instanceA.func()
   print 'instanceB:'
   instanceB.func()
   print 'instanceC:'
   instanceC.func()
```

Listing 8.15 contains code that is very similar to the code in the previous section, except that in this case ClassC is a derived class of the custom classes ClassA and ClassB. In addition, both ClassA and ClassB contain a function func() that is not defined in ClassC.

The output from Listing 8.15 is here:

```
Hello from A
Hello from B
Hello from C
```

```
instanceA:
Hello again from A
instanceB:
Hello again from B
instanceC:
Hello again from A
```

Now reverse the order of the parent classes in the definition of ClassC:

```
class ClassC(ClassA, ClassB):
```

The only difference in the output is the final print statement, as shown here:

```
instanceC:
Hello again from B
```

Although there is no reason for the following class definition, Python allows you to specify multiple occurrences of the same parent class:

```
class ClassC(ClassA, ClassB, ClassA, ClassB):
```

POLYMORPHISM

In very simplified terms, Python polymorphism allows you to define methods that "accept" instances of different classes and yet perform the intended calculations correctly.

As another concrete example, Listing 8.16 displays the contents of Polymorphism1.py that defines two custom Python classes and a method that can be invoked with instances of both custom Python classes.

LISTING 8.16: Polymorphism1.py

```
class Rect:
    def perimeter(self):
      print 'Perimeter of a rectangle'

class Square:
    def perimeter(self):
      print 'Perimeter of a square'

def calcPerimeter(obj):
    obj.perimeter()

if __name__ == '__main__':
    instanceR = Rect()
    instanceS = Square()

    print 'instanceR:'
    calcPerimeter(instanceR)
    print 'instanceS:'
    calcPerimeter(instanceS)
```

Listing 8.16 starts with the definition of the custom Python classes `Rect` and `Square`, each of which defines a `perimeter()` method. Next, the function `calcPerimeter()` is defined, which takes one argument that can be an instance of the `Rect` class or the `Square` class. The final portion of Listing 8.16 defines `instanceR` and `instanceS` that are instances of the custom classes `Rect` and `Square`, respectively. The `calcPerimeter()` method is invoked with each of these instances, and the correct method is invoked in both cases.

The output of Listing 8.16 is here:

```
instanceR:
Perimeter of a rectangle
instanceS:
Perimeter of a square
```

There are several points to keep in mind when you work with polymorphism in your custom Python code. First, other languages might require `Rect` and `Square` to be derived classes of a common class. In this example, squares and rectangles are also parallelograms, so you could define the parent class `PGram` that contains properties of a parallelogram.

Second, there is the notion of "coding to an interface," which essentially means that you specify a base class as the argument of a method so that you can pass in any derived class of the base class. In the Java world, you specify an interface as an argument to a method, and that way you can pass in any concrete class that implements the specified interface.

A third point is that polymorphic behavior in idiomatic Python relies on "duck-typing" that is described succinctly here:

https://en.wikipedia.org/wiki/Duck_typing

THE PYTHON ABC MODULE

Although Python does not provide interfaces (such as Java) or contracts, the Python abc ("Abstract Base Class," or ABC) module provides abstract base classes, a mechanism for specifying what methods must be implemented by implementation subclasses.

For example, you would expect that the semantics of a `print()` method involve printing some data, and not deleting data. The use of ABCs provides a sort of "understanding" about methods and their expected behavior. Thus, ABCs provide an intermediate solution between the free form of Python and the stricter enforcement of statically typed languages.

Although this is an advanced topic (and actually beyond the intended scope of this book), more information about the Python abc module is here:

http://docs.python.org/2/library/abc.html

SUMMARY

This chapter introduced you to some useful Python functions that can simplify your custom Python code. Next, you learned how to create your own custom Python classes in Python, and also how to work with linked lists in Python. You also learned a little bit about encapsulation, single inheritance, multiple inheritance, polymorphism, and the abc module in Python.

EXERCISES

Exercise 1: Create a set of custom Python classes that model the relationships that exist among the following 2D shapes: quadrilateral, parallelogram, rectangle, rhombus, and square.

Exercise 2: Create a set of custom Python classes that model the relationships that exist among the following entities: motorcycles, automobiles, and four-wheeled trucks.

Exercise 3: Create a Python class that defines a list of strings and then creates a linked list such that each element is inserted alphabetically into the linked list.

Exercise 4: Use the Python code for a singly linked list as a foundation for writing a custom Python class that implements a circular list with the data in Exercise 1.

Exercise 5: Use the Python code for a singly linked list as a foundation for writing a custom Python class that implements a doubly linked list with the data in Exercise 3.

## CHAPTER 9

PYTHON AND DATABASES

This chapter contains an overview of how to use Python with open-source relational databases, such as MySQL and SQLITE, as well as MongoDB, which is a NoSQL database for storing JSON-based documents. Although there are other NoSQL databases, including Riak and Redis, they are not discussed in this chapter. In case you are interested, Riak acts as an in-memory cache that can manage JSON-based documents, whereas Redis is a data store that uses key/value pairs.

The first part of this chapter contains a very brief introduction to RD-BMSes and NoSQL databases. The second part of this chapter contains Python scripts that show you how to access databases such as MySQL, SQLite, and MongoDB. Incidentally, Appendix A discusses Mongoose, which enables you to add a schema that defines the structure of documents that are stored in a MongoDB database. You will also learn a little bit about pymysql, which is easy to install and does not require a database driver for Python scripts.

The third part of this chapter briefly discusses Flask, which is a Python-based Web framework. If you have worked with systems that used route-based definitions (such as Express for NodeJS) in order to handle requests based on the contents of a URL, then Flask will be straightforward for you to learn. Conversely, you can leverage your knowledge of Flask to learn other technologies that have a similar methodology.

The final portion of this chapter is a short section that illustrates how to write simple shell scripts for extracting data from a MySQL table and then "piping" the output to a Python script to process that data.

RELATIONAL DATABASES VERSUS NOSQL DATABASES

Relational database management systems (RDBMSes) enable you to define tables that contain a specified set of columns (with different data types) in order to manage structured data. An RDBMS allows you to specify a key for a table, where a key comprises a set of columns of the table. You can also specify foreign keys, which is a way of linking a row of data in one table to a row in another table. A database schema usually consists of a collection of tables, primary keys, foreign keys, and indexes. An RDBMS models one-to-many relationships, whereby a row in one table can reference multiple rows in another table. This master-detail relationship exists for customer transactions: A purchase order (PO) is one row in a PO table, and each purchased item in the PO is a row in a PO table.

In addition, RDBMSes can easily model many-to-many relationships. For example, there is a many-to-many relationship involving a STUDENTS table and a COURSES table, because students can take multiple courses and obviously multiple students can register for the same course. The way to model this relationship in an RDBMS is to create an intermediate "join table" that contains all the columns from both tables. In addition, the primary key of the join table is the union of the columns in the primary key of the STUDENTS table and the columns in the primary key of the COURSES table.

An RDBMS also supports Structured Query Language (SQL) or some variant of SQL that enables you to execute SQL statements to retrieve the data that meets the criteria that are specified in those SQL statements. There are also six "normal forms" for a database, which is based on the type of keys in the tables. A table that is in First Normal Form has the least stringent constraints on the keys of the tables in the database, whereas a database that is in sixth normal form has the most stringent constraints.

Many applications that rely on an RDBMS as a data store have a database that is in third normal form. However, a table in an RDBMS is sometimes denormalized in order to improve performance. Another technique for improving performance involves "pinning" a table, which involves maintaining its contents in main memory. This technique can be used for tables with data that rarely (or never) changes.

On the other hand, NoSQL databases store document-based data (often involving JSON). NoSQL databases enable you to retrieve entire documents rather than providing a SQL language for retrieving "fields" in individual documents.

NoSQL databases are very well suited for managing documents containing unstructured data and semi-structured data. NoSQL databases are also a good choice for social networks that do not require a high degree of transactional support. For example, high performance (such as quickly rendering a Web page that contains images) is more important than consistency (whether different users might see a different set of images), especially if the data is constantly changing in the system.

By contrast, RDBMSes excel when there are many interdependencies among multiple tables, and also where reliable transaction support is ensured. For example, financial institutions engage in transactions involving money transfers that update multiple tables, and these transactions must be executed as an "atomic" all-or-nothing operation. In the event of some type of failure, they want to be assured that an entire transaction is "rolled back" and that tables are not in an inconsistent state.

Another way to distinguish between RDBMSes and NoSQL databases is encapsulated in the CAP theorem (also called Brewer's theorem) that deals with Consistency, Availability, and Partition tolerance. According to Wikipedia, the CAP theorem states that it is impossible for a distributed computer system to simultaneously provide support for all three of the following features:

Consistency (all nodes see the same data at the same time)

Availability (every request receives a response about whether it was successful or failed)

Partition tolerance (the system continues to operate despite arbitrary message loss or failure of part of the system)

The CAP theorem states that a distributed system can only provide two of the three features.

ODBC AND PYTHON

The Open Database Connectivity (ODBC) API standard allows transparent connections with any database that supports the interface, such as a PostgreSQL database or Microsoft Access. The strength of using this interface is that a Python script or module can be used on different databases by modifying only the connection string.

There are three ODBC modules for Python:

• PythonWin ODBC Module (limited development)
• mxODBC (commercial product)
• pyodbc (open-source Python package: *http://code.google.com/p/pyodbc*)

This chapter does not delve into ODBC-related code samples for database access, but you can perform an Internet search and you will find various articles and code samples involving ODBC.

INSTALLING MYSQL AND A PYTHON ADAPTER

You need to install MySQL as well as the Python adapter for MySQL, both of which are discussed in the following subsections.

Installing MySQL

Download and install MySQL (if you have not already done so) here:

https://dev.mysql.com/downloads/mysql/

Alternatively, you can download XAMPP (Apache, MySQL, PHP, and Perl) that is available for Windows, Linux, and OS X. The XAMPP package provides a MySQL instance, an instance of Tomcat (a servlet container), and support for file transfer protocol (FTP). You can download XAMPP here:

http://sourceforge.net/projects/xampp/

After you install XAMPP you can start and stop MySQL, Tomcat, or FTP via a pop-up "console" that provides start/stop radio buttons.

Installing the MySQLdb Adapter for MySQL

Navigate to one of the following Websites to download the MySQLdb adapter for Python:

http://sourceforge.net/projects/mysql-python/files/
http://sourceforge.net/p/mysql-python/mysqldb-2/ci/default/tree/

Download and uncompress the MySQLdb adapter, navigate to the main directory that contains the Python script `install.py`, and launch the following command:

```
python setup.py install
```

STARTING MYSQL AND LOGGING INTO MYSQL

After you have installed MySQL on your machine, open a command shell and add the directory containing the `mysql` executable to the `PATH` environment variable, an example of which is here for OS X:

```
export PATH=/usr/local/mysql/bin:$PATH
```

The following subsections explain how to start the MySQL server and also how to log into MySQL.

Launching MySQL

Launch the MySQL daemon `mysqld` by executing the following command in a command shell:

```
mysqld
```

You will see the following type of output in the command shell:

```
140126 15:08:10 [Warning] Setting lower_case_table_names=2 because
file system for /usr/local/mysql-5.1.50-osx10.6-x86/data/ is case
insensitive
140126 15:08:10 [Note] Plugin 'FEDERATED' is disabled.
140126 15:08:10  InnoDB: Started; log sequence number 0 44233
140126 15:08:11 [Note] Event Scheduler: Loaded 0 events
140126 15:08:11 [Note] mysqld: ready for connections.
Version: '5.1.50'  socket: '/tmp/mysql.sock'  port: 3306  MySQL
Community Server (GPL)
```

Logging In to MySQL

Open a second command shell, adjust the PATH variable as described in the previous section, and log into MySQL with the following command:

```
mysql -u root
```

The MySQL database will display the following type of information:

```
Welcome to the MySQL monitor. Commands end with ; or \g.
Your MySQL connection id is 1
Server version: 5.1.50 MySQL Community Server (GPL)
Copyright (c) 2000, 2010, Oracle and/or its affiliates. All rights
reserved.
This software comes with ABSOLUTELY NO WARRANTY. This is free
software,
and you are welcome to modify and redistribute it under the GPL v2
license

Type 'help;' or '\h' for help. Type '\c' to clear the current input statement.

mysql>
```

Now exit gracefully from MySQL by typing the following command:

```
Mysql> exit;
```

WORKING WITH DATABASES IN MYSQL

Log into MySQL and display the list of available databases with this command:

```
mysql> show databases;
+--------------------+
| Database           |
+--------------------+
| information_schema |
| test               |
+--------------------+
2 rows in set (0.00 sec)
```

If you are using MySQL for the first time, you will not have any databases. Create the database simpledb1 in MySQL with the following command:

```
mysql> create database simpledb1;
```

You will see the following response:

```
Query OK, 1 row affected (0.00 sec)
```

After creating the database, you can select it as the active database with the following command from the MySQL prompt:

```
mysql> use simpledb1;
```

You will see the following response:

```
Database changed
```

The next section shows you how to create and populate a table, after which you can manage the data in that table via Python scripts.

WORKING WITH TABLES IN MYSQL

This section shows you how to create a table, populate the table with data, delete a row of data, and drop a table in MySQL.

Create the table `simple1` in the database `simpledb1` as shown here:

```
mysql> create table simple1 (
    -> id int(8) default NULL auto_increment,
    -> name char(20) default NULL,
    -> userid char(20) default NULL,
    -> PRIMARY KEY (id));
Query OK, 0 rows affected (0.01 sec)
```

Next, insert three rows into the table `simple1`:

```
mysql> insert into simple1 values(1000, 'John Smith', 'jsmith');
Query OK, 1 row affected (0.02 sec)

mysql> insert into simple1 values(2000, 'Jane Edwards',
'jedwards');
Query OK, 1 row affected (0.02 sec)

mysql> insert into simple1 values(3000, 'Tom Jones', 'tjones');
Query OK, 1 row affected (0.02 sec)
```

Verify that the correct data is in the table `simple1`:

```
mysql> select * from simple1;
+------+--------------+----------+
| id   | name         | userid   |
+------+--------------+----------+
| 1000 | John Smith   | jsmith   |
| 2000 | Jane Edwards | jedwards |
| 3000 | Tom Jones    | tjones   |
+------+--------------+----------+
3 rows in set (0.05 sec)
```

You can delete a single row with this syntax:

```
mysql> delete from simple1 where id = 1000;
```

You can delete database tables in MySQL. For example, you can delete `table1` with this command:

```
mysql> drop table table1;
Query OK, 0 rows affected (0.03 sec)
```

The next section shows you a simple example of accessing a MySQL database from a Python script.

MANAGING USERS IN MYSQL

MySQL has a root user that you can use to manage users, which means that you can create, update, and delete users.

The Root User in MySQL

Log in to MySQL as the root user by typing the following command from the command line:

```
mysql -uroot -p
```

Press Enter and you will be logged into MySQL. (The root password is blank by default.)

Change the root password by typing the following command outside of MySQL:

```
mysqladmin -u root password specify-the-password-here
```

You can display the name of the currently logged-in user, along with the user's permissions, with the following command:

```
select user(), current_user();
```

Delete a user with the following command:

```
drop user ''@'localhost';
```

The next section shows you how to create a user that will be used in the Python scripts in this chapter in order to access the tables in the database simpledb1.

Creating a New User in MySQL

Log in to MySQL as the root user and create the user simple1 with the following command:

```
create user simple1;
```

You can retrieve the encrypted password for the user simple1 with this command:

```
mysql> select password('simple1');
+--------------------------------------------------+
| password('simple1')                              |
+--------------------------------------------------+
| *CCEBE4BBB649AA6CB36A61050315A9AFA24A7A87        |
+--------------------------------------------------+
1 row in set (0.04 sec)

mysql>
```

The following SQL statement displays the list of existing users:

```
select user,host from mysql.user;
```

After you invoke the preceding SQL statement, you will see the newly created user `simple1` as shown here. (Results depend on the other users that may have already been created):

```
+---------+--------------------------------+
| user    | host                           |
+---------+--------------------------------+
| simple1 | %                              |
| root    | oswald-campesatos-macbook.local |
+---------+--------------------------------+
2 rows in set (0.04 sec)
```

At this point you know how to log in to MySQL and create users in MySQL. You also know how to create databases and tables, as well as populate tables with data. The next section shows you how to access MySQL data from Python scripts.

ACCESSING MYSQL DATA FROM PYTHON

If you encounter the following error when attempting to access MySQL via the Python script in Listing 9.1, you probably have a mismatch in versions:

```
ImportError: dynamic module does not define init function (init_
mysql)
```

If you see the preceding error message, follow the steps on this Website:

https://learninglamp.wordpress.com/2010/02/21/mysqldb-python-mysql-and-os-x-a-match-made-in-satans-bum/

Listing 9.1 displays the contents of `MySQL.py` that illustrates how to retrieve the data from a table in a MySQL database from a Python script.

LISTING 9.1: MySQL.py

```
import MySQLdb

db = MySQLdb.connect("host machine","dbuser","password","dbname")
cursor = db.cursor()
query = "SELECT * FROM simple1"
lines = cursor.execute(query)
data = cursor.fetchall()
db.close()
```

Listing 9.1 starts by importing the `MySQLdb` module and then establishes a connection to the database. The variable `cursor` is initialized, and the string `query` contains the SQL statement for retrieving all the rows in the table `simple1`. The variable `lines` equals the number of lines in the table `simple1`, and the variable `data` contains the actual rows of data in the table `simple1`. The final line of code in Listing 9.1 closes the database connection.

For large tables, you can use the following:

```
row = cursor.fetchone()
```

Process the rows individually as shown in Listing 9.2, which displays the contents of MySQL2.py.

LISTING 9.2: MySQL2.py

```
import MySQLdb

db = MySQLdb.connect("host machine", "dbuser", "password",
"dbname")
cursor = db.cursor()
query = """SELECT * FROM sampletable"""
lines = cursor.execute(query)

while True:
    row = cursor.fetchone()
    if row == None: break
    #do something with this row of data
db.close()
```

The first part of Listing 9.2 is the same as Listing 9.1. However, Listing 9.2 contains a while loop that iterates through one row at a time via the fetch-one() function, whereas Listing 9.1 invokes the fetchall() function to process all the rows at the same time.

ACCESSING MYSQL DATA FROM PYTHON

Listing 9.3 displays the contents of the Python script QueryDB1.py that demonstrates how to extract data from the table simple1.

LISTING 9.3 QueryDB1.py

```
import MySQLdb

dbConn  = None
host    = "localhost"
user    = "root"
passwd  = ""
db      = "simpledb1"
query   = "SELECT * FROM simple1"

try:
  connection = MySQLdb.connect(host=host, user=user,
                               passwd=passwd, db=db)

  cursor = connection.cursor()
  cursor.execute(query)

  # generate tabular data
  for row in cursor.fetchall():
    print row[0],row[1],row[2]

  connection.close()
```

```
except:
  if connection:
    connection.close()
```

Open a command shell and type the following command:

```
python queryDB1.py
```

If everything is set up correctly you will see the following output:

```
1000 John Smith jsmith
2000 Jane Edwards jedwards
3000 Tom Jones tjones
```

If you want to generate an HTML Web page with an HTML table containing the data from the table `simple1`, you can use the following code in Listing 9.4. Notice that this code uses the "old school" style of placing data in a `table` element, whereas the modern approach is to use `div` elements.

LISTING 9.4: Table1.py

```
import MySQLdb

dbConn  = None
host    = "localhost"
user    = "root"
passwd  = ""
db      = "simpledb1"
query   = "SELECT * FROM simple1"

try:
  connection = MySQLdb.connect(host=host, user=user,
                               passwd=passwd, db=db)

  cursor = connection.cursor()
  cursor.execute(query)

  # generate tabular data
  print "<html>"
  print "<body>"
  print "<table>"

  for row in cursor.fetchall():
      print "<tr>"
      print "<td>"+str(row[0])+"</td>"
      print "<td>"+row[1]+"</td>"
      print "<td>"+row[2]+"</td>"
      print "</tr>"

  print "</table>"
  print "</body>"
  print "</html>"

  connection.close()
except:
  if connection:
    connection.close()
```

Listing 9.4 contains the `str()` function (shown in bold) in the preceding code block that converts a number into a string so that it can be concatenated with two other strings. If you do not perform this conversion, the resulting error is handled by the `except` block, which simply closes the database connection without displaying the error that occurred.

INSERTING A ROW OF DATA INTO A MYSQL TABLE

Listing 9.5 displays the contents of the Python script `InsertRow1.py` that demonstrates how to insert a row into the table `simple1`.

LISTING 9.5 InsertRow1.py

```
import MySQLdb

dbConn = None
host   = "localhost"
user   = "root"
passwd = ""
db     = "simpledb1"
insert = "INSERT INTO simple1 (id, user, userid) " + \
                "VALUES(7,'Hello Python',77777)"

connection = MySQLdb.connect(host=host, user=user,
                                passwd=passwd, db=db)

cursor = connection.cursor()
cursor.execute(insert)

connection.close()

if connection:
   connection.close()
```

If you want to use bind variables instead of hard-coded values in a string variable, you can do so in Python using the following type of code block:

```
insert = "INSERT INTO simple1 " + \
        "(id, name, userid) VALUES(%s,%s,%s)"
...
cursor.execute(insert, (4000,'Paul Smith', 'psmith'))
```

Note that it's also a good idea to use `try/except` blocks in Python code, and in database-related Python code you would use a `try` block for attempting to access a database and an `except` block for catching errors. An example is provided below:

```
try:
   connection = MySQLdb.connect(host=host, user=user,
                                passwd=passwd, db=db)

   cursor = connection.cursor()
   cursor.execute(insert)
   connection.close()
```

```
except:
  print "something went wrong"
  if connection:
    connection.close()
```

WORKING WITH THE PYMYSQL CONNECTOR

pymysql is another connector for accessing data in a MySQL database. Install pymysql by launching the following command in a command shell:

```
pip install pymyqsl
```

Listing 9.6 displays the contents of PyMySQLiteQuery1.py that demonstrates how to select data from the simple1 table that is in the simpledb1 database that you created earlier in this chapter.

LISTING 9.6: PyMySQLiteQuery1.py

```
import pymysql

conn = pymysql.connect(host='localhost', user='root', passwd='')
conn.autocommit(True)
curr = conn.cursor()

memory = '100'

curr.execute("""SELECT * FROM simpledb1.simple1""".format(memory))
for row in curr.fetchall():
  print 'Row:', row[0],row[1],row[2]

conn.close()
```

Listing 9.6 is very similar to the code in Listing 9.5 that uses the MySQLDb connector, with only minor differences. Try using this connector if you have difficulty with the MySQLDb connector. If you are able to use both connectors, you can perform benchmarks to compare them in terms of performance.

The output from Listing 9.6 is here:

```
Row: 1000 John Smith jsmith
Row: 2000 Jane Edwards jedwards
Row: 3000 Tom Jones tjones
```

The next portion of this chapter shows you how to use Python to work with a SQLITE database.

WORKING WITH A SQLITE DATABASE

Listing 9.7 displays the contents of the Python script CreateSQLiteDb. py that demonstrates how to create and populate a SQLite database with the values in the CSV file PurchaseOrder.csv that you saw in Chapter 5.

LISTING 9.7: CreateSQLiteDb.py

```
import sqlite3

mydb = sqlite3.connect('simple1.db')

c = mydb.cursor()
c.execute('create table simple1(id integer, name text, userid text)')
mydb.commit()
```

Listing 9.7 is straightforward: After importing the `sqlite3` module, it initializes the variable `mydb` as a reference to a SQLITE3 instance called `simple1.db`.

Next, the variable `c` is initialized as a cursor in order to execute a CREATE statement that creates a database table.

Creating and Populating a SQLite Table

Listing 9.8 displays the contents of `InsertSQLiteTable1.py` that illustrates how to populate a SQLite database with the values in the CSV file `PurchaseOrder.csv` that you saw in Chapter 5.

LISTING 9.8: InsertSQLiteTable1.py

```
import sqlite3

mydb = sqlite3.connect('simple1.db')

c = mydb.cursor()
employees = [
    (1000,'John Smith', 'jsmith'),
    (2000,'Jane Edwards', 'jedwards'),
    (3000,'Tom Jones', 'tjones'),
]

c.executemany('insert into simple1 values (?,?,?)', employees)
mydb.commit()
```

Listing 9.8 imports the `sqlite3` module, obtains a reference to a database called `simple1.db`, and then initializes the variable `c` as a cursor instance. The next portion of Listing 9.8 defines the variable `employees` that contains information for three employees, followed by the `executemany()` function that inserts the data into the database instance.

Listing 9.9 displays the contents of `DropSQLiteTable1.py` that illustrates how to drop a table in a SQLITE3 database.

LISTING 9.9: DropSQLiteTable1.py

```
import sqlite3

mydb = sqlite3.connect('simple1.db')

c = mydb.cursor()
c.execute('drop table simple1')
mydb.commit()
```

The first three lines in Listing 9.9 are the same as those in Listing 9.8. The new code snippet is the `execute()` statement that drops the table `simple1`.

Querying a SQLite Table

Listing 9.10 displays the contents of `ReadSQLiteTable1.py` that demonstrates how to read the contents of a SQLite table.

LISTING 9.10: ReadSQLiteTable1.py

```
import sqlite3

mydb = sqlite3.connect('simple1.db')

rowCount = 0
min_id= 100

print 'All rows in Simple1 table:'
print '--------------------------'
for row in mydb.execute('select * from simple1'):
    print('row:',row)
    rowCount = rowCount + 1
print 'Total row count:',rowCount
print

rowCount = 0
print 'Rows in Simple1 with id >= ',min_id
print '------------------------------------------'
for row in mydb.execute('select * from simple1 where id >= ?',
(2000,)):
    print('row:',row)
    rowCount = rowCount + 1
print 'Matching row count:',rowCount
print
```

Listing 9.10 starts with the usual initialization, followed by the variables `rowCount` and `min_id` that are initialized to `0` and `100`, respectively. The next portion of Listing 9.10 contains two `print` statements and a `for` loop that iterates through the set of rows that are retrieved from the table `simple1`. During each iteration, the loop prints the contents of the current row and then increments the `rowCount` variable, whose value is displayed when the `for` loop has completed.

The final portion of Listing 9.10 contains another `for` loop that iterates through the set of rows whose `id` value is at least `2000` and then displays only two rows of data.

The output from 9.10 is here:

```
All rows in Simple1 table:
--------------------------
('row:', (1000, u'John Smith', u'jsmith'))
('row:', (2000, u'Jane Edwards', u'jedwards'))
('row:', (3000, u'Tom Jones', u'tjones'))
Total row count: 3
```

```
Rows in Simple1 with id >=  2000
-------------------------------------------
('row:', (2000, u'Jane Edwards', u'jedwards'))
('row:', (3000, u'Tom Jones', u'tjones'))
Matching row count: 2
```

This concludes the portion of the chapter regarding SQLite and Python. The next portion of this chapter shows you how to work with MongoDB and Python.

WHAT IS PYMONGO?

PyMongo is a Python distribution containing tools for working with MongoDB, and it is the recommended way to work with MongoDB from Python. You can install PyMongo as follows:

```
pip install pymongo
```

Alternatively, you can use the following command:

```
easy_install pymongo
```

PyMongo documentation is here:

http://api.mongodb.org/python/current/

WHAT IS MONGODB?

MongoDB is a popular NoSQL database whose homepage is here:

http://www.mongodb.org/

Download and install MongoDB from this Website:

http://www.mongodb.org/downloads

After you install MongoDB, start MongoDB with the following command:

```
mongodb
```

You can also launch an interactive session by typing mongo in another command shell, which enables you to manage schemas and perform CRUD-like (Create, Replace, Update, and Delete) operations from the command line.

For example, the following sequence of commands shows you how to insert a new user in the users schema (which is defined in Appendix A).

```
mongo
>
> use db
switched to db db
> users = db.users
db.users
```

```
> users.find();
>
> users.insert({firstName:'a', lastName:'b'});
> users.find()
{
        "_id" : ObjectId("509425f82685d84f9c41c858"),
        "firstName" : "a",
        "lastName" : "b"
}
```

Consult the documentation for additional details about commands that you can execute in the `MongoDB` command shell.

After you have installed `MongoDB` and `PyMongo` on your machine, start `MongoDB` by opening a command shell and typing the following command:

```
mongod
```

The next section shows you how to insert a row of data into a `MongoDB` database.

A Simple Insert in MongoDB

Listing 9.11 displays the contents of `PyMongoInsert1.py` that illustrates how to create a post and insert it into a `MongoDB` instance.

LISTING 9.11: PyMongoInsert1.py
```
import pymongo
from pymongo import MongoClient
import datetime

# connect on the default host and port
client = MongoClient()

# specify the host and port explicitly:
# client = MongoClient('localhost', 27017)

# get a database instance
db = client.test_database

# get a collection
collection = db.test_collection
# create a post
post = {"author": "John Smith",
        "text": "Python and MongoDB",
        "tags": ["mongodb", "python", "pymongo"],
        "date": datetime.datetime.utcnow()}

# insert a post
posts = db.posts
post_id = posts.insert(post)
print 'post_id:',post_id
```

Listing 9.11 starts with various `import` statements, followed by the variable client that is initialized as an instance of `MongoClient`. The next portion of Listing 9.11 defines the variable db as a reference to a test database, followed by the variable collection that is an instance of a collection. The post variable defines a single post item that is inserted into the MongoDB database. The final portion of Listing 9.11 displays the id of the inserted item.

Launch the Python script in Listing 9.11 and you will see the following output:

```
post_id: 52eafe627a9b975f6dacc5e9
```

You can also insert multiple documents in one insert() statement, which is discussed in the next section.

Inserting Multiple Rows in MongoDB

Listing 9.12 displays the contents of PyMongoInsert2.py that illustrates how to create a collection of posts and insert them into a MongoDB instance.

LISTING 9.12: PyMongoInsert2.py

```python
import pymongo
from pymongo import MongoClient
import datetime

# connect on the default host and port
client = MongoClient()

# specify the host and port explicitly:
# client = MongoClient('localhost', 27017)

# get a database instance
db = client.test_database

# get a collection
collection = db.test_collection

new_posts = [{"author": "John Smith",
             "text": "Second Post",
             "tags": ["bulk", "insert"],
             "date": datetime.datetime(2014, 11, 12, 11, 14)},
            {"author": "Eliot",
             "title": "MongoDB is fun",
             "text": "Third Post",
             "date": datetime.datetime(2014, 11, 10, 10, 45)}]
posts.insert(new_posts)
```

As you can see, Listing 9.12 defines the variable new_posts that contains two items that are inserted via a single insert() statement.

The output of Listing 9.12 is here:

```
[ObjectId('...'), ObjectId('...')]
```

The `find_one()` Function

The following query uses the `find_one()` function to return a dictionary that matches the one that we inserted previously:

```
posts.find_one()
{u'date': datetime.datetime(...), u'text': u'Python and MongoDB',
u'_id': ObjectId('...'), u'author': u'John Smith', u'tags':
[u'mongodb', u'python', u'pymongo']}
```

Note that the returned document contains "`_id`", which was automatically added on insert.

The function `find_one()` also supports querying on specific elements that the resulting document must match. To limit our results to a document with author "`John Smith`", we invoke the following code snippet:

```
posts.find_one({"author": "John Smith"})
```

The preceding query returns the following result:

```
{u'date': datetime.datetime(...), u'text': u'My first blog post!',
u'_id': ObjectId('...'), u'author': u'Mike', u'tags': [u'mongodb',
u'python', u'pymongo']}
```

A query with a different author, such as `Stevens`, returns no result:

```
posts.find_one({"author": "Stevens"})
```

PYTHON AND COUCHDB

This section briefly discusses the open-source database `CouchDB` that is downloadable here:

https://couchdb.apache.org/#download

NOTE *If you encounter issues while installing* `CouchDB` *on a Macbook, this Website contains helpful information:*

http://guide.couchdb.org/draft/mac.html

After you complete the download and installation steps, launch `CouchDB` by typing the following command in a command shell:

```
couchdb
```

After a few moments you will see the following information:

```
Apache CouchDB 1.5.0 (LogLevel=info) is starting.
Apache CouchDB has started. Time to relax.
[info] [<0.31.0>] Apache CouchDB has started on http://127.0.0.1:5984/
```

PYLUCENE

PyLucene is a Python extension for accessing Lucene (an open source information retrieval library), and its homepage is here:

https://lucene.apache.org/pylucene/

You can write Python scripts that use PyLucene in order to leverage the capabilities of Lucene. PyLucene is a Python wrapper around Java Lucene that embeds a Java VM with Lucene into a Python process.
Download PyLucene here:

http://mirror.tcpdiag.net/apache/lucene/pylucene/

After you have uncompressed the PyLucene distribution, perform a "cd" into the subdirectory called jcc of the PyLucene distribution and type this command:

```
python setup.py build
```

Next, invoke the following command in a command shell:

```
sudo python setup.py install
```

A detailed list of instructions for setting up jcc (with platform-specific information) is here:

https://lucene.apache.org/pylucene/jcc/install.html

Now you need to modify the file Makefile by uncommenting the section in the file that is the closest match to your platform. Keep in mind that the settings provide a guideline, and you might need to change them for your system (as shown below).

For example, the section that is relevant to a Macbook 10.8 with Python 2.7.5 is here:

```
# Mac OS X 10.6 (MacPorts 1.8.0 64-bit Python 2.7, Java 1.6)
PREFIX_PYTHON=/opt/local
ANT=ant
#PYTHON=$(PREFIX_PYTHON)/bin/python
PYTHON=/usr/local/bin/python
JCC=$(PYTHON) -m jcc --shared --arch x86_64
NUM_FILES=8
```

After you have updated Makefile, type the following command in a command shell after you "cd" into pylucene-4.5.1-1 (the exact number depends on the version that you downloaded):

```
make
```

This concludes the database-related portion of the chapter, and the next section introduces you to Flask, which is a Python-based Web framework.

A PYTHON-BASED WEB FRAMEWORK

This section discusses `Flask`, which is a Python-based micro-Web framework. The `Flask` homepage (with a download link) is here:

http://flask.pocoo.org/

Install Flask on your machine and, after uncompressing the distribution, navigate to the top-level directory and enter this command in a command shell:

```
python setup.py install
```

The next section contains a minimal code sample that illustrates how to start Flask on its default port and also how to display a message in a browser.

A Simple Flask Example in Python

Listing 9.13 displays the contents of `HelloFlask.py` (also available on the Flask homepage) that illustrates how to start `Flask` on port `5000`, which is the default port.

LISTING 9.13: HelloFlask.py

```
from flask import Flask
app = Flask(__name__)

@app.route("/")
def hello():
    return "Hello from Flask!"

if __name__ == "__main__":
    app.run()
```

Launch Listing 9.13 via Python from the command line, and you will see the following output in the command shell:

```
* Running on http://127.0.0.1:5000/
127.0.0.1 - - [01/Feb/2014 15:39:43] "GET / HTTP/1.1" 200 -
127.0.0.1 - - [01/Feb/2014 15:39:44] "GET /favicon.ico HTTP/1.1"
404 -
```

Now launch a browser session and navigate to `localhost:5000`, and you will see the string "Hello from Flask!" on the screen.

Listing 9.13 starts by importing from the `flask` module and then initializing the `app` variable as a Flask application. The next portion of Listing 9.13 defines the route "/", which represents the default route. In other words, when users navigate to `localhost:5000`, the route "/" is matched and then the code in the `hello()` function is executed, which returns the string "Hello from Flask!".

Flask Code Samples

The Flask distribution contains a directory with the following subdirectories with Flask-based code samples:

```
blueprintexample
flaskr
jqueryexample
minitwit
persona
```

The `minitwit` code sample is a microblogging application written in Flask and SQLITE3. Here is the initial portion of `minitwit.py`:

```
# -*- coding: utf-8 -*-
"""
    MiniTwit
    ~~~~~~~~

    A microblogging application written with Flask and sqlite3.

    :copyright: (c) 2010 by Armin Ronacher.
    :license: BSD, see LICENSE for more details.
"""

import time
from sqlite3 import dbapi2 as sqlite3
from hashlib import md5
from datetime import datetime
from flask import Flask, request, session, url_for, redirect, \
    render_template, abort, g, flash, _app_ctx_stack
from werkzeug import check_password_hash, generate_password_hash


# configuration
DATABASE = '/tmp/minitwit.db'
PER_PAGE = 30
DEBUG = True
SECRET_KEY = 'development key'
```

Figure 9.1 displays a screenshot of the `minitwit` application in a Chrome browser on a Macbook Pro.

FIGURE 9.1 The `minitwit` Application in a Chrome Browser.

The `persona` sample application uses Flask, Jinja templating, and multiple routes to create an application that logs into the persona Website. This code sample is intended to give you an idea of the type of code that you would probably write for an application, but we will not discuss many of the code details.

Listing 9.14 displays the contents of the Python script `persona.py` for this application.

LISTING 9.14: persona.py

```python
from flask import Flask
from flask import Flask, render_template, session, request, json,
abort, g

import requests

app = Flask(__name__)

app.config.update(
    DEBUG=True,
    SECRET_KEY='my development key',
    PERSONA_JS='https://login.persona.org/include.js',
    PERSONA_VERIFIER='https://verifier.login.persona.org/verify',
)
app.config.from_envvar('PERSONA_SETTINGS', silent=True)

@app.before_request
def get_current_user():
    g.user = None
    email = session.get('email')
    if email is not None:
        g.user = email

@app.route('/')
def index():
    """Just a generic index page to show."""
    return render_template('index.html')

@app.route('/_auth/login', methods=['GET', 'POST'])
def login_handler():
    """This is used by the persona.js file to kick off the
    verification securely from the server side. If all is okay
    the email address is remembered on the server.
    """
    resp = requests.post(app.config['PERSONA_VERIFIER'], data={
        'assertion': request.form['assertion'],
        'audience': request.host_url,
    }, verify=True)

    if resp.ok:
        verification_data = json.loads(resp.content)
        if verification_data['status'] == 'okay':
            session['email'] = verification_data['email']
            return 'OK'
    abort(400)
```

```
@app.route('/_auth/logout', methods=['POST'])
def logout_handler():
    """This is what persona.js will call to sign the user
    out again.
    """
    session.clear()
    return 'OK'

if __name__ == '__main__':
    app.run()
```

Listing 9.14 contains routes for the default page, the login page, and the logout page, as shown here:

```
@app.route('/')
@app.route('/_auth/login', methods=['GET', 'POST'])
@app.route('/_auth/logout', methods=['POST'])
```

As you can see, there is a code block after each route that is executed when users navigate to the URL that matches the route.

Figure 9.2 displays a screenshot of the Persona Flask application in a Chrome browser on a Macbook Pro.

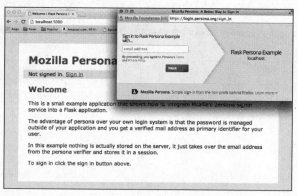

FIGURE 9.2 The Persona Application in a Chrome Browser.

Flask Templating Engine

Many templating engines are available for developing HTML Web pages, such as Jade and EJS (Embedded JavaScript, often used in NodeJS-based applications), Mustache, Handlebars, and Haml. These templating engines often use single curly braces, double curly braces, or combinations of curly braces and the "%" symbol.

If you are familiar with JSP (Java Server Pages) pages, you undoubtedly remember using "<%=" and "%>" to designate the scriptlets in those pages. The functionality in templating engines is similar, but they do have different strengths, so it's worth spending some time looking at examples of those templating engines so that you can decide which ones are most suitable for your needs.

Flask applications (including the persona sample application) use Jinja templates:

http://jinja.pocoo.org/docs/templates/

The Jinja homepage contains an extensive tutorial that illustrates how to use Jinja functionality in HTML Web pages.

Listing 9.15 displays `JinjaTemplate.html` (taken from the Jinja homepage) that contains an example of an HTML Web page with Jinja-based templating instructions.

LISTING 9.15: JinjaTemplate.html

```
<!DOCTYPE HTML PUBLIC "-//W3C//DTD HTML 4.01//EN">
<html lang="en">
<head>
  <title>My Webpage</title>
</head>
<body>
  <ul id="navigation">
  {% for item in navigation %}
     <li><a href="{{ item.href }}">{{ item.caption }}</a></li>
  {% endfor %}
  </ul>

  <h1>My Webpage</h1>
  {{ a_variable }}
</body>
</html>
```

Listing 9.15 contains a mixture of HTML markup and some templating code. For instance, the `<body>` element contains a loop that renders an unordered list, in which each item contains information that is available in the navigation object (whose contents are initialized elsewhere).

CHERRYPY

CherryPy is another Python-based and object-oriented Web framework that is downloadable here:

http://www.cherrypy.org/

CherryPy provides the following features:

- An HTTP/1.1-compliant, WSGI thread-pooled Webserver
- Support for multiple HTTP servers (n multiple ports)
- A plugin system
- Built-in tools for caching, encoding, sessions, authorization, and static content
- Swappable and customizable functionality
- Built-in profiling, coverage, and testing support

After you have installed CherryPy, navigate to the subdirectory `cherrypy/tutorial` and you will find 10 sample Python scripts that illustrate how to dynamically generate Web pages. For example, launch the first tutorial in a command line as follows:

```
python tut01_helloworld.py
```

Launch a browser and navigate to the following URL:

```
localhost:8080
```

In addition to Jinja, there are various other Python frameworks available, such as Django and web2py, which require considerably more time and effort to learn how to use them effectively. For more information about those and other frameworks, perform an Internet search and you will find many articles and tutorials for these frameworks.

SHELL SCRIPTS, SQL STATEMENTS, AND PYTHON

One of the previous sections in this chapter showed you how to invoke SQL statements inside a Python script to retrieve data from a database table. In addition, you can write shell scripts to extract data from a MySQL table and then "pipe" the output to a Python script to process the retrieved data.

As a simple example, Listing 9.16 displays the contents of the shell script `Sql1.sh` that retrieves all the rows in the table `simple1` and then uses the `pipe` command to send the rows to the Python script `Sql1.py` that is displayed in Listing 9.17.

LISTING 9.16 Sql1.sh
```
mysql simpledb1 -u root <<<"SELECT * FROM simple1"
```

Listing 9.16 invokes the `mysql` command by specifying the database `simpledb1` and the root user (which does not have a password), followed by a SQL SELECT command that selects all the rows from the table `simple1`.

LISTING 9.17 Sql1.py
```
#!/usr/bin/env python -u
import sys

while True:
  line = sys.stdin.readline()
  line = line.rstrip()

  if line:
    if (line.startswith("id")):
      print 'Comment Line:', line
    else:
```

```
      print 'Data Line:    ', line
    sys.stdout.flush()
  else:
    break
```

Listing 9.17 starts by invoking the `python` command with the "`-u`" switch, which means that the data is unbuffered. The `while` statement reads each line of input via the `readline()` function and prints the non-empty lines in the same command shell. Conditional logic is used to determine whether a given line is a comment line or a line of data.

Open a command shell and launch the following command:

```
./Sql1.sh | Sql1.py
```

The output from the preceding command is here:

```
Comment Line: id  name    userid
Data Line:    1000 John Smith jsmith
Data Line:    2000 Jane Edwards jedwards
Data Line:    3000 Tom Jones tjones
```

An alternative approach is to redirect the output from the shell script to an intermediate text file and then use the `cat` command and the `pipe` command to send the contents of the text file to the Python script, as shown here:

```
./Sql1.sh > Sql1.out
cat Sql1.out | Sql1.py
```

Compared to the first invocation, which consists of a one-line command, the preceding pair of commands might seem inefficient because of the creation of the intermediate text file that can sometimes be very large (more than 100 megabytes). However, the latter approach is advantageous when:

1) The text file is required for other Python scripts
2) The two commands are invoked at different times as "cron" jobs
3) You cannot connect directly to a database from inside a Python script
4) "Intermediate" scripts process the text file before or after the Python script
5) The text file is available for processing but the database is unavailable

The example in this section is very basic, and you can use this example as a guideline for creating shell scripts that contain much more complex SQL statements. Obviously, the associated Python scripts will be "tightly coupled," in the sense that the Python code depends on the structure of the data that has been retrieved. Moreover, the SQL commands in the shell script can join two or more tables, so you have the freedom to use whatever SQL commands you need to retrieve the data set that you need to have processed.

SUMMARY

In this chapter, you learned a little bit about RDBMSes and NoSQL databases. Next you learned how to write Python scripts for managing data in databases such as MySQL, SQLite, and MongoDB. You also learned how to use PyMongo for managing database data, along with PyLucene. In addition, you learned about shell scripts and SQL statements for processing database data. Finally, you learned about some of the features in the Flask and CherryPy micro-frameworks.

## CHAPTER 10

MISCELLANEOUS TOPICS

This chapter is primarily about more advanced Python topics, such as Networking and Threading. Keep in mind that an entire chapter could be devoted to topics in this chapter, so you will obviously get only an introductory exposure. However, you will have information that will help you decide which topics you want to explore in greater detail.

The first part of this chapter discusses Networking and starts with Python code samples that illustrate how to make HTTP requests (such as GET and POST). Next you will see how easy it is to create and launch a simple Web server in Python. In addition, this section contains Python scripts that show you how to make requests via TCP and UDP.

The second part of this chapter introduces you to Threads in Python, with an example of how to communicate between threads via queues, followed by examples of how to use pipes and the fork() command in Python. The final section in this chapter provides an eclectic mix of topics involving Python, such as Android, the Raspberry Pi, and Google Glass.

NETWORKING

Modern-day networking is interesting and sophisticated, and although we are often shielded from the underlying details, there are some situations in which knowledge of those details is helpful. Some of the common Internet protocols are HTTP, TCP, UDP, REST, and SSL.

Please keep in mind that this section provides a simplified introduction, and you can perform an Internet search to find articles with more detailed information about the topics in this section.

In simplified terms, TCP (Transmission Control Protocol) is part of the OSI (Open Systems Interconnection) model that is described in more detail here:

https://en.wikipedia.org/wiki/OSI_model

TCP is "connection oriented," which means that a connection is guaranteed between sender and receiver. By way of analogy, this is similar to a phone conversation in which you place a call and then wait until the other person responds before you start the conversation.

On the other hand, UDP (User Datagram Protocol) is connectionless, which is a "fire-and-forget" transmission mechanism, so there is no guarantee that a connection will be established. As an analogy, you send email and you do not wait to receive a confirmation. (You do receive a message if the communication failed, but this is just an analogy.)

In addition, you can send a message via unicast, which is essentially one-to-one communication: There is a single connection between a sender and a receiver. You can send a message via multicast, which is a one-to-many communication: A sender makes a connection with one or more receivers. Finally, you can send a message via a broadcast, which is a "one-to-everyone" mode of communication, where "everyone" refers to any receiver that is reachable on the current network.

Before delving into the communication mechanisms and transmission protocols between programs on different machines, let's briefly look at IP addresses.

IP ADDRESSES

An Internet Protocol address (IP address) is a label assigned to each device in a network that uses the Internet Protocol for communication. IPv4 addresses are 32-bit numbers, divided into four 8-bit numbers that are often represented in decimal form. For example, 192.168.1.104 is an IPv4 address.

In addition, there is the IPv6 protocol that involves 128-bit addresses, usually represented as eight 16-bit numbers. For example, `1823:ba4:7:4325:1:705:3:2` is an IPv6 address. Note that the IPv6 protocol was designed as an eventual replacement for IPv4.

NOTE *You can always determine your IP on a Unix system by issuing the command* `ifconfig` *from a command shell.*

Additional information about IP addresses is here:

https://en.wikipedia.org/wiki/IP_address

SPECIAL IP ADDRESSES

Several IP addresses have a special significance. These IP addresses include `localhost`, broadcast addresses, and all systems on a given subnet, as discussed in the following subsections.

Localhost

The network address "127.0.0.1" is reserved for `localhost` that also represents your machine. This IP address (often referred to as the "loopback") is intended for the machine to send messages to itself via an internal socket. Localhost is often used for testing, but it can also be used for internal messaging.

Machines with Linux, Unix, or OS X always have the file /etc/hosts that contains the definition of localhost, as well as other network-related addresses. Listing 10.1 displays the (partial) contents of an /etc/hosts file.

LISTING 10.1: /etc/hosts

```
# Host Database
# localhost is used to configure the loopback interface
# when the system is booting. Do not change this entry.
127.0.0.1       localhost
255.255.255.255 broadcasthost127.0.0.1        master
127.0.0.1       slave
```

Broadcast Addresses

A network address that ends with 255, such as 10.0.0.255, is defined as the "broadcast address." This means that if you type "ping 10.0.0.255" at the command line, every machine that is capable will respond.

All Systems on a Subnet

One important IP address is 224.0.0.1 that represents the IP address for "all systems on this subnet." In other words, all devices on a local area network (or subnet for larger networks) will listen to traffic with the destination address of 224.0.0.1.

Additional details are here:

http://www.iana.org/assignments/multicast-addresses/multicast-addresses.xhtml

LAUNCHING AN HTTP SERVER IN PYTHON

You might be surprised to discover that you can launch an HTTP server in literally one line of code from the command line, as shown here:

```
python -m SimpleHTTPServer 8000
```

Launch a browser and navigate to the following URL:

http://localhost:8000

After a few moments you will see the contents of the directory for which you launched the Python command. In fact, you can launch multiple HTTP servers by specifying different port numbers.

CREATING YOUR OWN TCP SERVER IN PYTHON

Python makes it very easy to create a TCP server, as shown in Listing 10.2 that displays the contents of MyTCPServer.py.

LISTING 10.2: MyTCPServer.py

```python
from socketserver import BaseRequestHandler, TCPServer

class EchoHandler(BaseRequestHandler):
  def handle(self):
    print('Got connection from', self.client_address)
    while True:
      msg = self.request.recv(8192)
      if not msg:
        break
      self.request.send(msg)

if __name__ == '__main__':
  serv = TCPServer(('', 20000), EchoHandler)
  serv.serve_forever()
```

Listing 10.2 contains the definition of the class `EchoHandler` that extends the base class `BaseRequestHandler`. If you are unfamiliar with defining subclasses in Python, read the appropriate section in Chapter 8. This custom class contains one function, called `handle()`, that starts by printing a message. The next portion of this function contains a loop that waits for an incoming message and then returns the same message to the sender.

The final portion of Listing 10.2 creates an instance of `TCPServer` (imported in the first line of this script) on port `20000` and also specifies the custom class `EchoHandler` as the class that will handle incoming requests.

MAKING HTTP REQUESTS

Python provides HTTP-related support that makes it very easy to retrieve the contents of an HTML Web page on the Internet.

Listing 10.3 displays the contents of `url1.py` that illustrates how to retrieve and print the contents of a Web page.

LISTING 10.3 url1.py

```python
from urllib import urlopen

name = 'http://www.google.com'
result = urlopen(name).read()
print 'result:',result
```

Listing 10.3 contains an import statement and the `name` variable that specifies the Google homepage. The variable `result` contains the contents of the homepage that is obtained by means of "method chaining": First the `urlopen()` function is invoked, and then the `read()` function is applied to the result. Method chaining is useful because it eliminates the creation of intermediate variables. In addition, you will see method chaining used in other languages (such as JavaScript, Java, and so forth). The final code snippet prints the actual contents of the Google homepage.

Listing 10.4 displays the contents of `url2.py` that illustrates how to read the contents of a Web page.

LISTING 10.4 url2.py

```
## Retrieve the contents of a URL and in the case of
## an HTML Web page, print its base url and its text
import urllib

def wget(url):
  ufile = urllib.urlopen(url)  ## get file-like object for url
  info = ufile.info()    ## meta-info about the url content

  if info.gettype() == 'text/html':
    print 'Web page Base Url:' + ufile.geturl()
    text = ufile.read()  ## read all its text
    print text
if __name__ == '__main__':
  wget('http://www.yahoo.com')
```

The code in Listing 10.4 contains a function wget() whose contents are similar to the code in Listing 10.3. The function wget() also retrieves meta data about the remote Website, and uses conditional logic to determine the type of Web page before printing its contents.

Launch the code in Listing 10.4 and after a few moments (depending on your Internet connection), you will see the entire contents of the Yahoo! homepage displayed on the screen.

MAKING HTTP GET REQUESTS

Listing 10.5 displays the contents of HttpGet1.py that illustrates how to make an HTTP GET request.

LISTING 10.5 HttpGet1.py

```
from urllib import request, parse

url = 'http://httpbin.org/get'

# Dictionary of query parameters (if any)
parms = {
 'name1' : 'value1',
 'name2' : 'value2'
}

# Encode the query string
querystring = parse.urlencode(parms)

# Make a GET request and read the response
get1 = request.urlopen(url+'?' + querystring)
resp = get1.read()
```

Listing 10.5 contains familiar code from previous examples, along with a new section of code. First there is a parms variable containing name/value pairs that will be sent to a remote Website. In your own code you would replace the name/value pairs with something else that is specific to your code. Next, the querystring variable is set to the value returned by the urlencode() method that encodes the contents of parms. The final portion of code in Listing 10.5 invokes the urlopen() function on the concatenation of the contents of the url variable and the contents of querystring. The result of invoking the urlopen() function is set to the variable get1, and then the variable resp contains the result of invoking the read() method on get1.

MAKING HTTP POST REQUESTS

Python enables you to send the query parameters in the request body using a POST method, encode them, and supply them as an optional argument to urlopen().

Listing 10.6 displays the contents of HttpPost1.py that illustrates how to make an HTTP POST request.

LISTING 10.6 HttpPost1.py

```python
from urllib import request, parse

url = 'http://httpbin.org/post'

# Dictionary of query parameters (if any)
parms = {
  'name1' : 'value1',
  'name2' : 'value2'
}

# Encode the query string
querystring = parse.urlencode(parms)

# Make a POST request and read the response
post1 = request.urlopen(url, querystring.encode('ascii'))
resp = post1.read()
```

Listing 10.6 is straightforward: The first portion of the code defines the variable url that contains post, whereas the corresponding code in Listing 10.5 contains get. The rest of the code is the same as the code in Listing 10.5, with the exception of the final two lines of code for making a POST request and then obtaining the data that is returned from that request.

WORKING WITH TCP AND UDP

Python provides support for both TCP and UDP, and the required code is surprisingly straightforward, as you will see in the following subsections.

Sending TCP Requests

The code sample in this section is from Jesse Monroy and is also available on GitHub:

https://github.com/jessemonroy650/multicast-boilerplate

Listing 10.7 displays the contents of `send_tcp.py` that illustrates how a client can make a TCP request to a server, wait for the reply, and then display the contents of the reply.

LISTING 10.7: send_tcp.py

```
#!/usr/bin/python

# Echo client program
import socket

HOST = '127.0.0.1'      # The remote host
PORT = 50000            # The same port as used by the server
s = socket.socket(socket.AF_INET, socket.SOCK_STREAM)
s.connect((HOST, PORT))
s.sendall('Hello, world')
data = s.recv(1024)
s.close()
print 'Received', repr(data)
```

Listing 10.7 imports the `socket` module and then defines the `HOST` variable as the IP equivalent of `localhost` and the `PORT` variable as `50000`. The variable `s` is instantiated as an instance of the `socket` class (via the `socket()` function). Next, a connection is established via the `connect()` method, and after the response is received, the socket is closed and the response string is displayed. Keep in mind that before you can launch the code in Listing 10.7 you must first launch the Python-based server that is discussed in the next section.

Receiving TCP Requests

The code sample in this section is from Jesse Monroy and is also available on GitHub:

https://github.com/jessemonroy650/multicast-boilerplate

Listing 10.8 displays the contents of `receive_tcp.py` that illustrates how a server can wait for TCP-based requests from one or more clients and then send a reply to each client.

LISTING 10.8: receive_tcp.py

```
#!/usr/bin/python

import socket

HOST = ''               # Symbolic name for all available interfaces
PORT = 50000            # Arbitrary non-privileged port

s = socket.socket(socket.AF_INET, socket.SOCK_STREAM)
s.bind((HOST, PORT))
s.listen(1)
conn, addr = s.accept()
print 'Connected by', addr
```

```
while 1:
    data = conn.recv(1024)
    if not data: break
    conn.sendall(data)
conn.close()
```

Listing 10.8 imports the `socket` module and then defines the `HOST` variable as an empty string and the `PORT` variable as `50000`. The variable `s` is instantiated as an instance of the `socket` class (via the `socket()` function). However, `socket` must now bind to the specified host and port number and then listen for requests from clients.

When a client initiates a request, the variables `conn` and `addr` are initialized as a socket connection and an IP address, respectively. The next portion of Listing 10.8 consists of a `while` loop whose purpose is to 1) initialize the `data` variable with data (if any) that was sent by the client and 2) return that data to the client.

After a response has been successfully made, the code exits the `while` loop and the connection is closed.

Sending UDP Requests

The code sample in this section is available here:

https://wiki.python.org/moin/UdpCommunication

The code blocks in Listing 10.9 and Listing 10.10 are the UDP-based counterparts to the TCP-based code blocks in Listing 10.7 and Listing 10.8, respectively.

LISTING 10.9: send_udp.py

```python
#!/usr/bin/env python

import socket

UDP_IP   = "127.0.0.1"
UDP_PORT = 5432
MESSAGE  = "Hello, World! udp from Rover"

print "UDP target IP:", UDP_IP
print "UDP target port:", UDP_PORT
print "message:", MESSAGE

sock = socket.socket(socket.AF_INET, # Internet
                     socket.SOCK_DGRAM) # UDP
sock.sendto(MESSAGE, (UDP_IP, UDP_PORT))

exit
```

Listing 10.9 imports the `socket` module and then defines the `HOST` variable as the UDP_IP equivalent of `localhost`, the UDP_PORT variable as `5432`, and the MESSAGE variable with a text string. The variable

sock is instantiated as an instance of the socket class (via the socket()
function). Next, the message is sent to the specified address and port using the
sendto() message.

As you can see, sending a TCP-based message (as shown in Listing 10.8)
involves the sequence "socket", "connect", and "sendall", whereas
the UDP-based counterpart (as shown in Listing 10.9) involves the sequence
"socket" and "sendto". However, before you can launch the code in Listing 10.9, you must first launch the Python script receive_udp.py, which is
a Python-based server that is discussed in the next section.

Receiving UDP Requests

The code sample in this section is available here:

https://wiki.python.org/moin/UdpCommunication

Listing 10.10 displays the contents of receive_udp.py that illustrates
how a server can wait for UDP-based requests from clients and then send a
reply to each client.

LISTING 10.10: *receive_udp.py*
```
#!/usr/bin/env python

import socket

UDP_IP = "127.0.0.1"
UDP_PORT = 5432

sock = socket.socket(socket.AF_INET, # Internet
                     socket.SOCK_DGRAM) # UDP
sock.bind((UDP_IP, UDP_PORT))

while True:
    data, addr = sock.recvfrom(1024) # buffer size is 1024 bytes
    print "received message:", data
```

Listing 10.10 imports the socket module and then defines the UDP_IP
variable as the IP-based counterpart of localhost and the UDP_PORT
variable as 5432. The variable sock is instantiated as an instance of the
socket class (via the socket() function). Next, the server binds to the
IP address and port via the bind() function and then listens for requests
from clients.

The next portion of Listing 10.10 consists of a while loop whose purpose
is to initialize the variables data and addr as a socket connection and an IP
address, respectively, after a request is received from a client.

In addition to support for TCP-based or UDP-based requests, Python provides support for unicast and/or multicast that are discussed in the following
section.

WORKING WITH THREADS IN PYTHON

The threading library can be used to execute any Python callable in its own thread. To do this, you create a `Thread` instance and supply the callable function that you wish to execute as a target. Listing 10.11 displays the contents of `SimpleThread1.py` that illustrates how to use a thread in Python.

LISTING 10.11: SimpleThread1.py

```
import time

# time measured in seconds
sleepTime = 1

def countdown(n):
  while n > 0:
    print 'Time remaining: ', n
    n -= 1
    time.sleep(sleepTime)

  # Create and launch a thread
  from threading import Thread

myThread = Thread(target=countdown, args=(10,))
myThread.start()
```

Listing 10.11 defines the function `countdown()` that contains a `while` loop that prints the value of the integers from n to 1. After printing each value, the code invokes the `sleep()` function to sleep for 1 second.

The last portion of Listing 10.11 creates an instance of the `Thread` class that invokes the `countdown()` function. Keep in mind that a thread does not start to execute until you invoke the `start()` method, which in turn invokes the `target` function with the arguments you supplied.

COMMUNICATING BETWEEN THREADS VIA QUEUES

Python provides a queue library that you can use to communicate between threads. The code sample in this section regarding queues and threads is based on the following stackoverflow entry:

http://stackoverflow.com/questions/16199793/python-3-3-simple-threading-event-example

Listing 10.12 displays the contents of `ThreadQueue1.py` that illustrates how to create a queue for communicating between two threads.

LISTING 10.12 ThreadQueue1.py

```
import threading
import Queue
import time

threadCount=3
```

```
maxCount=15
delayTime=0.4

print 'Thread Count:    ',threadCount
print 'Number of Tasks:',maxCount
print 'Task delay:      ',delayTime

# lock to serialize console output
lock = threading.Lock()

def performCalculations(item):
  # simulate lengthy calculation
  time.sleep(delayTime)

  # prevent threads from mixing output on the same line
  with lock:
    print threading.current_thread().name,item

# Each worker thread processes a queue item
def invokeWorker():
  while True:
    item = q.get()
    performCalculations(item)
    q.task_done()

# Create the queue and thread pool
q = Queue.Queue()
for i in range(threadCount):
  t = threading.Thread(target=invokeWorker)
  # thread dies when main thread (only non-daemon thread) exits
  t.daemon = True
  t.start()

startTime = time.time()

for item in range(maxCount):
    q.put(item)

# block until all tasks are completed
q.join()

# display elapsed time
now = time.time()
elapsedTime = now - startTime
print 'Elapsed time:', elapsedTime
```

Listing 10.12 defines a `performCalculations()` function that simulates some lengthy calculation. In this case, the simulation simply invokes the `sleep()` method, followed by printing the name of the thread and the item in the queue. Notice the use of the `lock` statement, which prevents the intermingling of output from different threads. The end of this section shows you the output with the `lock` statement and also the output without the `lock` statement, and the difference in the output is immediately apparent.

The next portion of Listing 10.12 defines the `invokeWorker()` function that is executed each time that a `thread` instance is launched (later in the code). As you can see, the `invokeWorker()` function retrieves the topmost element from the queue via the `get()` function and then invokes the `performCalculations()` function with that element. Since this functionality is performed inside a `while` loop, each thread will repeatedly invoke the function `performCalculations()` until the queue is empty.

The next portion of Listing 10.12 initializes the queue, followed by a loop that creates and launches the number of threads that is specified in the `threadCount` variable. Each thread `t` specifies the `invokeWorker()` function as shown here:

```
t = threading.Thread(target=invokeWorker)
```

The next portion of Listing 10.12 contains a `for` loop that populates the queue with data, and then invokes the `join()` method of the queue instance variable q to wait until all the threads have completed. The final portion of Listing 10.12 displays the elapsed time for executing the various functions in Listing 10.12.

The output from the preceding command is here:

```
Thread Count:     3
Number of Tasks: 15
Task delay:       0.4
Thread-3 2
Thread-1 1
Thread-2 0
Thread-3 3
Thread-1 4
Thread-2 5
Thread-3 6
Thread-1 7
Thread-2 8
Thread-3 9
Thread-1 10
Thread-2 11
Thread-3 12
Thread-2 14
Thread-1 13
Elapsed time: 2.00606584549
```

Compare the preceding output with the output that is generated without the `lock` statement that is here:

```
Thread Count:     3
Number of Tasks: 15
Task delay:       0.4
Thread-2 Thread-1 10Thread-3 2


Thread-2 4
Thread-1 5
```

```
Thread-3 3
Thread-2 6
Thread-1 7
Thread-3 8
Thread-2 9
Thread-1 10Thread-3 11

Thread-2 12
Thread-3 14
Thread-1 13
Elapsed time: 2.0066139698
```

CONNECTING UNIX COMMANDS WITH PYTHON SCRIPTS

In Unix it is common (and very easy) to use the output of one Unix command as the input of another Unix command. This technique relies on the Unix pipe "|" command, which can link together many commands in a single pipeline.

The Python script `Unix2Python.py` is based on the following entry:

http://stackoverflow.com/questions/11109859/pipe-output-from-shell-command-to-a-python-script

Listing 10.13 displays the contents of `Unix2Python.py` that shows you how to redirect the output of the Unix `cat` command to a Python script.

LISTING 10.13 Unix2Python.py

```
#!/usr/bin/env python
import sys

if not sys.stdin.isatty():
  input_stream = sys.stdin
else:
  try:
    input_filename = sys.argv[1]
  except IndexError:
    message = 'Specify a filename as first argument'
    raise IndexError(message)
  else:
    input_stream = open(input_filename, 'rU')

lineCount = 0
for line in input_stream:
  lineCount = lineCount + 1
  print 'Line #',lineCount,':',line
```

Listing 10.13 contains conditional logic that uses the `isatty()` function to determine whether to read from standard input (which accepts whatever you type from the command line) or to read from a file whose name you entered when you launched the Python script. In the latter case, a `try/except` block determines whether or not the file actually exists. The next portion of Listing 10.13 contains a `for` loop that either prints the text that you enter from the command line or iterates through the contents of the specified file.

Invoke the following command in a command shell, where `PurchaseOrder.csv` is the CSV file in Chapter 5:

```
cat PurchaseOrder.csv | Unix2Python.py
```

The output from the preceding command is here:

```
Line # 1 : Name,UnitPrice,Quantity,Date

Line # 2 : "Radio",54.99,2,"01/22/2013"

Line # 3 : "DVD",15.99,1,"01/25/2013"

Line # 4 : "Laptop",650.00,1,"01/24/2013"

Line # 5 : "CellPhone",150.00,1,"01/28/2013"
```

WORKING WITH PIPES IN PYTHON

You can specify various arguments for `stdin`, `stdout`, and `stderr` to simulate the variations of the Python function `os.popen()` for pipes.

Set the `stdout` value to `PIPE` and call the method `communicate()` to run a process and read all of its output, as shown here:

```
import subprocess

print '\nread:'
proc = subprocess.Popen(['echo', '"to stdout"'],
                        stdout=subprocess.PIPE,
                        )
stdout_value = proc.communicate()[0]
print '\tstdout:', repr(stdout_value)
```

The preceding code block is similar to the manner in which `popen()` works, except that the reading is managed internally by the `popen` instance. Launch the preceding code block and you will see the following output:

```
read:
    stdout: '"to stdout"\n'
```

To set up a pipe to allow the calling program to write data to it, set `stdin` to `PIPE`.

```
import subprocess

print '\nwrite:'
proc = subprocess.Popen(['cat', '-'],
                        stdin=subprocess.PIPE,
                        )
proc.communicate('\tstdin: to stdin\n')
```

More information regarding Python processes and pipes is here: ·

http://pymotw.com/2/subprocess/

THE FORK() COMMAND IN PYTHON

Python supports the `fork()` command that enables you to create a child process from an existing process.

Listing 10.14 displays the contents of `Fork1.py` that illustrates how to create a child process that can communicate with the parent process.

LISTING 10.14: Fork1.py

```
import subprocess
import os, sys

# file descriptors for reading/writing
r, w = os.pipe()

processid = os.fork()

if processid:
    print 'PARENT processid:',processid
    # This is the parent process
    # Closes file descriptor w
    os.close(w)

    r = os.fdopen(r)
    print "Parent Reading Data From the Pipe:"
    str = r.read()
    print "Parent Reading from pipe =", str
    sys.exit(0)
else:
    # This is the child process
    print 'CHILD processid:',processid
    os.close(r)
    w = os.fdopen(w, 'w')

    print "CHILD writing: Pipe Data From Child"
    w.write("Pipe Data From Child")
    w.close()
    print "Child Closing the Pipe"
    sys.exit(0)
```

Listing 10.14 starts by defining the `r` and `w` descriptions for reading and writing, respectively. In this example, the `child` process writes data to the pipe and the `parent` process reads data from the pipe. Thus, the `parent` process will close the `write` descriptor and the `child` process will close the `read` descriptor, because neither one is used in this pipe-based code sample.

Next the `os.fork()` method is invoked, which spawns a `child` process whose process id will always equal 0. We can use this fact in the `if/else` conditional logic: if the process id is nonzero, then the current process is the `parent` process; otherwise, the current process is the `child` process.

The `if` portion of the code is the parent, so the `write` descriptor is closed and the parent reads the data (when it becomes available) from the pipe with this code snippet:

```
r = os.fdopen(r)
```

Conversely, the `else` portion of the code is the child, so the `read` descriptor is closed and the child writes data to the pipe with this code snippet:

```
w.write("Pipe Data From Child")
```

In a real-world situation, the code for writing data and for reading data would probably be more complex, but this code sample contains the fundamental logic for writing to a pipe and reading from the same pipe.

NOTE
Whenever the `fork()` *function is invoked, the* `child` *process always has process id equal to zero.*

The output from Listing 10.14 is here:

```
PARENT processid: 70437
Parent Reading Data From the Pipe:
Current processid: 0
CHILD processid: 0
CHILD writing: Pipe Data From Child
Child Closing the Pipe
Parent Reading from pipe = Pipe Data From Child
```

MULTIPROCESSING IN PYTHON

Although threads are useful in Python (albeit less so than in languages such as Java), you might prefer the multiprocessing capability of Python. Threads in any language have subtle and non-obvious behavior, whereas the semantics of multiprocessing in Python might be more appealing because of the use of the `map()` function and the underlying pooling mechanism that is transparent to you.

The function `multiprocessing.Pool().map` has the following characteristics:

- The functionality is the same as the Python built-in `map()` function
- A process pool of workers is created for you
- Each input is passed to a specified function

Listing 10.15 displays the contents of `MultiProcPool.py` that illustrates multiprocessing in Python.

LISTING 10.15: MultiProcPool.py

```
from multiprocessing import Pool

def performTask(args):
  print 'job args:',args

myList = [1,2,3]
Pool().map(performTask, myList)
```

Listing 10.15 defines the function `performTask()` that simply prints the value of the `args` argument. The next portion of Listing 10.15 initializes the variable `myList` with the first three integers, then invokes the `map()` function of the `Pool` object and "binds" `performTask` to the `map()` function. The results are returned as a list after all jobs have completed.

The output from Listing 10.15 is here:

```
job args: 1
job args: 2
job args: 3
```

LOGGING IN PYTHON

Python supports the logging module, which is a port of Java-based logging functionality.

Listing 10.16 displays the contents of `Logger1.py` that illustrates how to write information to a log file.

LISTING 10.16: Logger1.py

```
import logging

LogFilename = 'myfile.log'
logging.basicConfig(filename=LogFilename,level=logging.DEBUG)
logging.debug('This message should go to the log file')
```

Listing 10.16 defines the variable `LogFilename` that specifies a log file, and then it invokes the `basicConfig()` function that writes DEBUG-level information to the log file. The last line of code in Listing 10.16 simply writes a line of text to the log file, and if you look at the contents of `myfile.log`, you will see this line of text. Each time that you invoke this Python script, a new line of text is appended to the log file, so this operation is nondestructive (which makes sense).

Listing 10.17 displays the contents of `RotatingLogger1.py` that illustrates how to rotate output through a set of log files. This Python script is based on online documentation that is here:

http://docs.activestate.com/activepython/3.1/python/library/logging.html

LISTING 10.17: RotatingLogger1.py

```
import glob
import logging
import logging.handlers

# the name of the primary log file
LogFilename = 'rotatinglogger.txt'

# define a logger and its output level
my_logger = logging.getLogger('MyLogger')
my_logger.setLevel(logging.DEBUG)

# Add the log message handler to the logger
handler = logging.handlers.RotatingFileHandler(
          LogFilename, maxBytes=20, backupCount=3)
```

```
my_logger.addHandler(handler)

# Log some messages
for i in range(10):
    my_logger.debug('i = %d' % i)

# get the list of log-related filenames
logfiles = glob.glob('%s*' % LogFilename)

# display the log filenames
for filename in logfiles:
    print(filename)
```

Listing 10.17 defines the variable `LogFilename` that specifies a log file, just as you saw in the previous section. The next portion of Listing 10.17 defines a `handler` variable that specifies the "base" logfile name and also to create 3 log files, and then adds `handler` to the current logger, as shown here:

```
handler = logging.handlers.RotatingFileHandler(
            LogFilename, maxBytes=20, backupCount=3)
my_logger.addHandler(handler)
```

The next portion of Listing 10.17 prints the integers between 0 and 9 and then displays the list of log files. The output from Listing 10.17 is here:

```
rotatinglogger.txt
rotatinglogger.txt.1
rotatinglogger.txt.2
rotatinglogger.txt.3
```

The contents of the preceding log files is here:

```
i = 9
i = 6
i = 7
i = 8
i = 3
i = 4
i = 5
i = 0
i = 1
i = 2
```

Python logging supports other useful functionality. For example, you can define multiple listeners so some logging messages go to files, other messages are sent via email, and only `ERROR-` level messages are printed to `stdout`.

PYTHON AND SERIAL PORTS

The standard Python distribution does not provide support for working with serial ports. However, the Python package `pySerial` enables you to read/write to serial ports on a machine, and its homepage is here:

http://pyserial.sourceforge.net/

Listing 10.18 displays the contents of `SerialPort1.py` (whose contents are from the `pySerial` documentation) that illustrates how to write a text string to a serial port.

LISTING 10.18: SerialPort1.py

```
import serial

# Open port 0 at "9600,8,N,1", no timeout:
# open first serial port
ser = serial.Serial(0)

# check which port was used
print ser.portstr

# write a string
ser.write("hello")

# close port
ser.close()
```

Listing 10.18 is straightforward and minimalistic. The code starts by initializing the variable `ser` as a reference to port `0` and then printing the port-specific details. The `write()` function writes the string `"hello"` to port `0`, and the `close()` function closes the port. This basic example is simply intended to show you how to write a text string to a serial port: A real-world example would send more meaningful data, but the essential logic is the same.

PYTHON, RASPBERRY PI, AND ROOMBA

The Raspberry Pi is a credit-card-sized computer, and you can attach a monitor, keyboard, or mouse via its USB ports. The Raspberry Pi homepage is here:

http://www.raspberrypi.org

The code sample in this section shows you how to control a Roomba from a Raspberry Pi. Keep in mind that this section does not provide the configuration required to set up a Raspberry Pi or a Roomba vacuum cleaner (8 million units sold as of August 2012).

The code sample in this section is available on GitHub:

https://github.com/jessemonroy650/TalkRoomba

Listing 10.19 displays the contents of `Talk2Roomba.py` that sends instructions via a serial port to cause a Roomba device to move forward.

LISTING 10.19: TalkToRoomba.py

```
import io
import select
import roomba.roomba_cmds as rc
```

```
def do_cmd(dev, cmdstring):
    f = io.open(dev, 'w+b', 0)
    for oper in (cmdstring):
        #print '%c' % oper
        f.write( '%c' % oper )
        select.select('', '',  '', 0.01) # delay
    f.close()

device   = "/dev/ttyUSB0"
cmd_strg = []

# uncomment one of the following
# play a banjo sound on the Roomba:
#cmd_strg = [0x80, 0x82, 0x88, 9]

# drive the Roomba forward:
#cmd_strg = [0x80, 0x83, 0x89, 0x01, 0x90, 0x7f, 0xff]

cmd_strg.extend(rc.roomba_safe_mode)
cmd_strg.extend(rc.roomba_drive_straight)
do_cmd(device, cmd_strg);
```

Listing 10.19 imports the modules io and select, as well as the roomba_cmds function from the Roomba module. The next portion of Listing 10.19 is the function do_cmd() that issues commands to a Roomba device that is attached to a serial port. The function do_cmd() starts by opening a device (specified by the variable dev) in binary write mode, followed by a for loop that writes each character in cmdstring to the Roomba device. After a character has been written to the serial port, the select() command specifies a delay of 0.01 seconds before the next character is written to the serial port. The final code snippet in the function do_cmd() closes the device /dev/ttyUSB0.

The main body of Listing 10.19 initializes the variable cmd_strg that contains a command sequence for playing a "banjo" or moving the Roomba forward. The final code block in Listing 10.19 contains two Roomba-specific instructions and the invocation of the function do_cmd(), as shown here:

```
cmd_strg.extend(rc.roomba_safe_mode)
cmd_strg.extend(rc.roomba_drive_straight)
do_cmd(device, cmd_strg);
```

Listing 10.20 displays the contents of PlayBanjo.py that sends instructions via a serial port to cause a Roomba device to play music.

LISTING 10.20: PlayBanjo.py

```
import io
import select

f = io.open('/dev/ttyUSB0', 'w+b', 0)

f.write( '%c' % 0x80 )
```

```
select.select('', '',  '', 0.01)

f.write( '%c' % 0x82 )
select.select('', '',  '', 0.01)

f.write( '%c' % 0x88 )
select.select('', '',  '', 0.01)

f.write( '%c' % 9)
select.select('', '',  '', 0.01)

f.close()
```

Listing 10.20 imports the `io` and `select` modules and then invokes the `open()` function to open the device called `/dev/ttyUSB0`. The variable `f` is a reference to this device, which is available for writing binary data because of the option `'w+b'` that is specified in the `open()` function.

The next portion of Listing 10.20 contains four invocations of the `write()` function and the `select()` function. Each `write()` function sends a control code (a single non-printable character) that is interpreted by the Roomba. Each `select()` function specifies the decimal value 0.01 that is the delay (in seconds) before the next command can be executed. The final code snippet in Listing 10.20 closes the device `/dev/ttyUSB0`.

PYTHON AND GOOGLE GLASS

Google Glass supports Python-based code for accessing the Glass Mirror API. The following section provides a high-level description.

The Glass Mirror API

The Google Mirror API allows you to build Glassware (mobile applications for Google Glass) that interacts with Google Glass via a cloud-based API and does not require running code on Glass. Use the Mirror API if you need:

1. platform independence
2. common infrastructure
3. built-in functionality

On the other hand, use the GDK (Glass Development Kit) if you need:

1. real-time user interaction
2. offline functionality
3. access to hardware

Another point to remember is that the Mirror API Glassware can also invoke GDK Glassware through a menu item. Thus, you can use this hybrid model to leverage existing Web properties that can launch richer applications that run on Glass.

Fortunately, there are client libraries in various languages that you can use with the Glass Mirror API. These languages include Python as well as .NET, Dart, Go, Java, JavaScript, Objective-C, and PHP. Note that some of these libraries are in alpha and others are in beta.

Jenny Murphy has created a video regarding the Glass Mirror API, which is available on the CD and also available here:

https://www.youtube.com/watch?v=w0WxkIEPJeQ

Jenny has also created a GitHub project that provides a Python-based command line interface for sending content to Google Glass using the Google Mirror API:

https://github.com/mimming/mirror-api-python-cli

Before creating Glassware via the Mirror API, you can also view the contents in the Mirror API Playground, as discussed in the next section.

The Glass Mirror API Playground

Use the Mirror API Playground to experiment with rendering content on Glass:

https://developers.google.com/glass/tools-downloads/playground

Navigate to the preceding URL, provide the project client ID for your Google API project in the text field, and click the Authorize button. After doing so, you will have authorized the Playground to send and receive data to and from your account.

If you want to see a fully deployed version of the starter project to get an idea of how it works before you start your own development, navigate to this link:

https://glass-java-starter-demo.appspot.com/

A collection of Python-based code samples is here:

https://code.google.com/p/google-api-python-client/wiki/ SampleApps#Google_Mirror_API

PYTHON AND ANDROID

The python-for-android open-source project enables you to use Python to create Android mobile applications, and you can download the code here:

https://code.google.com/p/python-for-android/downloads/list

Download and uncompress the zip file `python_scripts_r-1.zip`, after which you can look at the following code samples:

```
weather.py
take_picture.py
```

```
say_weather.py
say_time.py
notify_weather.py
hello_world.py
bluetooth_chat.py
test.py
say_chat.py
speak.py
```

The simplest example is `hello_world.py`, whose contents are here:

```
import android

droid = android.Android()
droid.makeToast('Hello, Android!')
print 'Hello world!'
```

The preceding code requires that you install the `android` module on your machine, and then you can create an instance of the `Android` class to make a toast.

The code samples in this open source project rely on `sl4a` (Scripting Layer for Android), and its homepage is here:

https://github.com/damonkohler/sl4a

The preceding link contains Python code samples, as well as code samples for other scripting languages, such as JRuby, Lua, and Perl.

You can also download the Android file `Python3ForAndroid_r6.apk` from the preceding download list and then install this `apk` on your Android device with this command:

```
adb install Python3ForAndroid_r6.apk
```

If you need to perform additional installations of this `apk`, you need to replace the existing one, so use this command:

```
adb install -r Python3ForAndroid_r6.apk
```

SUMMARY

In this chapter, you learned about networking in Python, along with general IP addresses and special addresses for your machine. Next you learned how to make HTTP-based requests in Python using `GET` and `POST`. You also learned how to work with Threads in Python. In addition, you learned how to use Python with the Raspberry Pi and Google Glass. Finally, you learned how to connect Python scripts with Unix commands, and also how to use pipes in Python.

ON THE CD-ROM

The CD contains an assortment of code samples, appendices, and figures that accompany the material in the book.

CODE SAMPLES

The CD that accompanies this book contains all the code samples to save you time and effort from the error-prone process of manually typing code into a text file. Samples are in their respective chapter folders.

APPENDICES

The CD contains appendices for the following topics:

- Appendix A: HTML 5 and JavaScript Toolkits
- Appendix B: Jython
- Appendix C: Introduction to SPA

FIGURES

All of the figures from the book, including any images or screenshots that were originally 4-color, are including in their respective chapters on the CD-ROM.

INDEX